Equity and education in cold climates

the Tufnell Press,
London,
United Kingdom

www.tufnellpress.co.uk

email contact@tufnellpress.co.uk

British Library Cataloguing-in-Publication Data
A catalogue record for this book is
available from the British Library

paperback ISBN   *1872767249*
ISBN-13   *978-1-872767-24-6*

Kindle   *978-1-872767-29-X*

Copyright © 2016 Dennis Beach and Alan Dyson

The moral rights of the authors have been asserted.
Database right the Tufnell Press (maker).

All rights reserved. No part of this publication may be reproduced, stored in a retrieval system, or transmitted in any form or by any means, electronic, mechanical, photocopying, recording or otherwise, without the prior permission of the publisher, or expressly by law, or under terms agreed with the appropriate reprographic rights organisation.

Printed in England and U.S.A. by Lightning Source

Equity and education in cold climates, in Sweden and England

edited by
Dennis Beach and Alan Dyson

Contents

Contributors ... vii

Section 1, Key themes and issues

Introduction
Equity and education in cold climates: An introduction
Dennis Beach and Alan Dyson ... 1

Chapter 1
Exploring the relationship between equality, equity and social justice in education
Kirstin Kerr and Carlo Raffo ... 13

Chapter 2
Concepts of equity in Swedish society and education: Historical perspectives
Girma Berhanu ... 27

Chapter 3
Contemporary Swedish society and education: Inequities and challenges
Girma Berhanu ... 43

Chapter 4
English society and education: Historical and contemporary inequalities and challenges
Kirstin Kerr ... 60

Chapter 5
Researching equity and inequity: The voices of marginalised people
Inger C. Berndtsson ... 80

Section 2, Developing equitable practice: case studies from England and Sweden

Chapter 6
Formation of fundamental values in the Swedish education system—a discursive analysis of policy texts
Inger Assarson, Ingela Andreasson, Lisbeth Ohlsson ... 97

Chapter 7
Using inquiry to shed light on and respond to inequities identified within a network of English high schools
Sue Goldrick ... 116

Chapter 8
Constructions of student identity in talk and text: A focus on special educational needs in Sweden and England
    Ines Alves, Ingela Andreasson, Yvonne Karlsson, and Susie Miles   137

Chapter 9
Consequences of differentiated policies and teaching practices in the Swedish school system
    Joanna Giota and Ingemar Emanuelsson   154

Chapter 10
Extending the role of the school: A case study
    Harriet Rowley   173

Chapter 11
Independent state-funded schools and system change: Addressing educational equity?
    Maija Salokangas, Christopher Chapman, Dennis Beach   193

Conclusions
    Equity and education in England and Sweden, tentative conclusions
    Dennis Beach and Alan Dyson   209

References   223

Contributors

Ines Alves is a researcher at the Institute of Education of the University of Lisbon. Her research interests are in the fields of special and inclusive education, disability and human rights. She is interested in exploring the notions of diversity and difference in a school context, and particularly in the way practitioners conceptualise and respond to pupil diversity.

Ingela Andreasson, Associate Professor at the University of Gothenburg, Sweden. Her research is within the field of special education and mainly focused on how students are assessed in their school documentation.

Inger Assarson is a senior lecturer in education Stockholm University. She had previously many years of experience as a teacher in the upper-secondary school sector. She has researched extensively on how school agents interpret policy and has had a particular interest for how schools work in relation to foundational value policies.

Dennis Beach is Professor of Education at the Department of Education and Special Education, University of Gothenburg, Sweden. His main specialisations are in the sociology and ethnography of education and education policy. He is the current Editor in Chief of the international research journal Ethnography and Education.

Girma Berhanu is Associate Professor of (special) Education at the Department of Education and Special Education, University of Gothenburg, Sweden, where he teaches research method courses and special education. He is fervently engaged in discussion of equity issues in the fields of 'race', ethnicity, special education and group-based inequalities in scholastic achievement.

Inger C. Berndtsson is a Senior Lecturer at the Department of Education and Special Education, University of Gothenburg, Sweden. She also works at the University College of Southeast Norway on a master's programme in Vision Rehabilitation. Her research interests relate to developing theory about learning to handle a new life situation pertinent to visual impairment and blindness.

Professor Chris Chapman is Director of the Robert Owen Centre for Educational Change at the University of Glasgow and Co-Director of What Works Scotland a three year ESRC/Scottish Government funded project exploring public service reform. Chris is also Senior Academic Advisor to the Scottish Government Attainment Challenge, a four year £100 million programme of work to improve outcome for disadvantaged pupils.

Alan Dyson is Professor of Education and co-director of the Centre for Equity in Education in the Manchester Institute of Education, University of Manchester. His current research interests are in the relationship between social and educational disadvantage. He has also undertaken substantial research in special needs and inclusive education.

Professor Ingemar Emanuelsson now retired, was Professor of education and special education at the Department of Education, University of Gothenburg. Specialising in differentiation effects and the development of the common compulsory school.

Joanna Giota is Professor in education at the University of Gothenburg, Sweden. She investigates factors such as special education support and teaching quality, curricula and school reforms that enhance or restrain students' growth and life chances. Most of her studies are nationally representative based on data collected within The Gothenburg Educational Longitudinal Database.

Sue Goldrick is a researcher at the Manchester Institute of Education, University of Manchester. Part of her time is spent working at the Centre for Equity in Education, where she focuses on supporting teachers to carry out their own enquiry-based activities into their practice to improve equity. She also leads a programme in Initial Teacher Education.

Yvonne Karlsson is a senior lecturer in education. Her research interest concerns children's participation and identity work in special educational activities such as remedial classes .

Kirstin Kerr is senior lecturer in education and co-director of the Centre for Equity in Education in the Manchester Institute of Education, University of Manchester. Her research interests are in the design and evaluation of complex initiatives to tackle educational disadvantage in local neighbourhoods.

Susie Miles is a senior lecturer in Inclusive Education at the Manchester Institute of Education and non-executive director of the Enabling Education Network, a unique international resource focused primarily on low and middle-income countries. Her research explores ways of documenting inclusive practice in low-income countries, and has a particular focus on the use of photography as part of participatory approaches to development and research.

Lisbeth Ohlsson is a senior lecturer in education and special education at Malmö University, Sweden. She has a research interest for complex learning situations and specifically in relation to issues of dialogue and interaction.

Carlo Raffo is Professor of Urban Education at the Manchester Institute of Education, University of Manchester. His main area of research is in the area of education and poverty and educational equity in urban contexts. He is the lead editor of the internationally distinguished book *Education and poverty in affluent countries* and author of the monograph *Improving Educational Equity in Urban Contexts*, both published by Routledge.

Harriet Rowley is a lecturer at Manchester Metropolitan University. She teaches on the BA in Education Studies and has particular expertise in policy studies. Her research interests are concerned with schools, families and communities especially those in poor urban environments.

Maija Salokangas is Assistant Professor of Educational Leadership and Management at Trinity College Dublin. Her research interests concern the interplay between education policy and practice, social justice, ethnography and comparative research.

x

Section 1, Key themes and issues

Introduction

Equity and education in cold climates: An introduction

Dennis Beach and Alan Dyson

This book is based on collaboration between two research teams. The first is the Centre for Equity in Education at the Institute of Education, University of Manchester in England. The second is the Department of Education and Special Education Equity Group at Gothenburg University in Sweden. The book has the ambition to critically address policies and practices related to education equity in the two countries. It is based mainly but not exclusively on qualitative empirical and policy research. It looks particularly at the apparent inabilities of education reform to deal with inequalities in the two countries. A number of themes are in focus:

> Educational inequality and policy interventions;
> The conceptual links between education equity and poverty;
> Identity and transition issues for young people and teachers in the past and present education economies of the two countries;
> Education and inclusion in terms of intersections of class, ethnicity, gender and disability;
> Governance issues;
> School leadership and social inclusion;
> Current priority policies.

These themes concern concepts, policies and practices of justice and equity in education. They are dealt with in the different chapters of this book, each of which tries to bring some clarity as to how and why education policy in different neighbourhoods and for different groups often results in uneven levels of educational achievement. The impact of these factors on the educational agency of young people is considered, as are the ways in which the development of education justice and equity involve processes that are enmeshed in relations that comprise education formation, contextualisation, re-contextualisation and interaction at the macro, meso and micro levels of our societies and the means by which young people are constituted as agents and subjects there. In this sense the analyses in the chapters shift the focus of education policy analysis from national policy makers to community representatives, families, teachers, managers, administrators and young people in schools and back again (Raffo and Dyson, 2007). Methodological issues are considered in relation to this shift in each separate chapter. However, there is also a specific chapter on methodology addressing one particular but valuable approach to research on marginalisation and/or disability experiences from a life-world perspective.

Thus the chapters compare education and equity in two countries, but not always and only from exactly the same comparative matrix. Rather they are in a way each a unique case that represents how the author or authors have thought through and analysed equity in their national situations. The introduction and first three chapters play an important role in framing this endeavour as they attempt to provide a framework of concepts and ideas from which the other chapters can be considered. They offer definitions of equity to these ends. In this way these opening chapters thus provide insights into concepts, theories, ideas and perspectives for thinking about, analysing and describing justice and equity policies and practices.

One question that can be asked of a book such as this one, not the least given the individually distinct characteristics of the chapters, is can such a comparison of education and equity in the two countries still be effectively constructed and why is this comparison valuable? The answer we will give, hopefully substantiated later on by the chapters themselves and their messages, is yes. The comparison is possible based on the contributions at hand and it also has some very significant points to make. For instance Sweden and England both have social democratic traditions, but of different forms and strengths. Both of the countries also have historically developed education systems that embody many different forms of justice and equity, though with a strong emphasis on re/distribution, and both have had to deal with the consequences of moving to a (partially reconstructed) post-industrial economy, with heavy inward migration. These developments have produced new challenging economic demands for the education system and changing faces of management and professionalism (Dyson et al., 2011). They are often analysed as aspects of neoliberal ideology and an influx of new public management and have included a growing internationalisation of education in terms of common policy approaches and transnational target-setting.

What can this book provide that perhaps isn't accomplished elsewhere? There is after all no shortage of books and articles that consider and in some way compare policies and practices in the education systems of England and

Sweden respectively. Sweden has had extensive international influence in early childhood education for decades but not the least in recent years this influence has extended upwards through the education system through the Swedish concept of *friskola* (independent school) in relation to the introduction and development of Academy Schools in England and Wales. Research articles have analysed and discussed these issues. Examples include Ingrid Helgoy and Anne Homme's article from 2006 on 'Policy Tools and Institutional Change: Comparing education policies in Norway, Sweden and England' in the *Journal of Public Policy* (26(2): 141-165) and several articles in a recent special issue on education inclusion edited by Martin Mills, Sheila Riddel and Eva Hjörne (2015) in the *International Journal of Inclusive Education*. Articles such as 'Children's school achievement and parental work: An analysis for Sweden', by Magdalena Norberg-Schönfeldt in the *Journal of Education Economics* (16(1):1-17) can also be considered as can 'School Size Effects on Achievement in Secondary Education Evidence from the Netherlands, Sweden and the USA' by Hans Luyten in *School Effectiveness and School Improvement* (pp. 75-99) and 'Social capital and the educational achievement of young people in Sweden' by Alireza Behtoui and Anders Neergaard in the *British Journal of Sociology of Education* (2015). All of these articles have made contributions to our relative understanding of the education systems and experiences of education inclusion and equity in the two countries.

Reading from these examples England and Sweden are we suggest counties that compared to some others are relatively well set to respond to the demands of equity in changing global circumstances. Both countries are relatively affluent, have well-resourced education systems, and have a long history of efforts to infuse concerns with equity throughout those systems. However, new challenges have emerged recently as education policies have begun to swing away from an emphasis on equity as a primary goal and toward an educational agenda informed by concerns with economic growth, the development of human capital, and marketisation (Dyson et al., 2011). This agenda poses serious challenges to traditional notions of justice and equity which this book will explore. Particular political connotations have been identified across the countries. In both countries politics of inclusion and equity have broadly been promoted mostly from the Left of the political spectrum and have been challenged historically from the traditional Right.

Disposition of the book

The book comprises two sections. Section 1, Key themes and issues, and Section 2, Developing equitable practice: case studies from England and Sweden. Their respective contents are presented below.

Section 1 Key themes and issues

Equity and education in cold climates: An introduction
Dennis Beach and Alan Dyson

Chapter 1: Exploring the relationship between equality, equity and social justice in education   Kirstin Kerr and Carlo Raffo

Chapter 2: Concepts of equity in Swedish society and education: Historical perspectives   Girma Berhanu

Chapter 3: Contemporary Swedish society and education: Inequities and challenges   Girma Berhanu

Chapter 4: English society and education: historical and contemporary inequalities and challenges   Kirstin Kerr

Chapter 5: Researching equity and inequity: The voices of marginalised people   Inger C. Berndtsson

Section 2 Developing equitable practice: case studies from England and Sweden

Chapter 6: Formation of fundamental values in the Swedish education system—a discursive analysis of policy texts.
Inger Assarson, Ingela Andreasson, and Lisbeth Ohlsson

Chapter 7: Using inquiry to shed light on and respond to inequities identified within a network of English high schools   Sue Goldrick

Chapter 8: Constructions of student identity in talk and text: A focus on special educational needs in Sweden and England
Ines Alves, Ingela Andreasson, Yvonne Karlsson, and Susie Miles

Chapter 9: Consequences of differentiated policies and teaching practices in the Swedish school system
Joana Giota and Ingemar Emanuelsson

Chapter 10: Extending the role of the school: A case study
Harriet Rowley

Chapter 11: Independent state-funded schools and system change: Addressing educational equity?
Maija Salokangas, Christopher Chapman, and Dennis Beach

Conclusions: Equity and education in cold climates: Tentative conclusions
Dennis Beach and Alan Dyson

The first chapter considers what equity can mean and how the education system might be explored in relation to these meanings, predominantly, in the recent era of neoliberal education politics. It aims to provide readers with a 'tool kit' of ideas about equity in the organisation of education systems and is followed by two chapters by Girma Berhanu that add to these conceptual discussions and give some outlines for the historical evolution of notions of equity in Swedish education and society. As the chapters make clear, in recent years, resource differences have widened among schools, among municipalities, and among pupils and these trends work against equity. They are happening at the same time as the rhetoric advocating one school for all and inclusive education has remained. The conclusions of the analysis are that although inclusion has been adopted as a policy goal, to date much of the Swedish debate has amounted to little more than the trading of abstract ideological positions with little connection to the daily realities in schools.

The next chapter is on education equity in relation to English society by Kirstin Kerr. Taking a historical and contemporary perspective on inequities and challenges, it describes the way in which distinctive notions of equity, often informed by a concern with social class, have figured in social and educational developments over the past hundred years, particularly in the second half of the twentieth century, where significant efforts were made to develop an education system that could counter the effects of—and ultimately reduce—social inequality. The chapter illustrates how these efforts have always been fragile and questioned, particularly in the last twenty to thirty years, as economic restructuring has shifted the emphasis towards a view of education for economic development rather than social equality.

Chapter 5, by Inger Berndtsson, is a methodology chapter on researching equity and inequity from a life-world perspective to more authentically capture the experiences of marginalised people. The examples given in the chapter are from people with visual impairment and blindness. It is followed by the first chapter in section 2, on the formation of fundamental values in the Swedish education system as seen through a discursive analysis of policy texts. This chapter, by Inger Assarson, Ingela Andreasson and Lisbeth Ohlsson, concerns a distinctive feature of the Swedish education system that seeks to operate on the basis of *värdegrund*—an explicit set of fundamental, equity-oriented values. The chapter explores the reality of the concept based on a research project financed by the Swedish National Agency of Education.

Chapter 7, 'English schools tackling marginalisation', by Sue Goldrick, is linked to the chapter by Assarsson et al. but also reports on a somewhat different attempt to embed values of equity into schools. It is based on work by researchers at the University of Manchester with networks of schools in a collaborative process of inquiry aimed at understanding equity-related issues. Teams of school staff, supported by university researchers, have identified issues relating to equity in their schools. They have then explored those issues and taken action to address them. An attempt is made to develop a framework which might help schools to consider and work more effectively on inequities. The framework represents a way of conceptualising and responding to diversity in schools, which is also the theme of the chapter immediately following it.

Chapter 8, by Ines Alves, Ingela Andreasson, Yvonne Karlsson and Susie Miles, is about the increased diversification of classrooms in recent years and how this has placed additional demands upon teachers who strive to facilitate the learning and participation of all pupils. It reports from a range of research into processes of identifying, categorising and responding to the perceived individual differences of learners. Relatively sophisticated means of responding to individuals are described, but so too are processes of categorisation that are shaped by institutional and policy demands that have little to do with enabling individuals to flourish. The chapter concludes by considering whether mass education systems such as those in England and Sweden can ever hope to respond effectively to individual differences.

How systems have worked in these respects in one of these countries (i.e. Sweden) is looked at next, in the chapter by Ingemar Emanuelsson and Joana Giota. This chapter explores some of the consequences of inequality in special education practices. It has been developed from two longitudinal and nationally representative studies on the extent and forms of integrated as compared to segregated special education support offered to students in the Swedish comprehensive school over a period of twenty-nine years. The relations between support, background variables, and goal attainment in Grade 9 are presented. The analysis is based on data from 35,000 students born in 1972, 1977, 1982 and 1987 and from head teachers for older (n=683) and younger (n=250) students in the Swedish compulsory school. The results suggest that school problems are still seen as caused by student characteristics rather than shortcomings of school and teaching. Equal opportunities for learning and growing in school are not supplied and pupils with SEN are still at serious risk of being marginalised.

Chapter 10 by Harriet Rowley is based on a case study of a community-oriented school in England confronted by the challenge of the poor educational outcomes of many learners there from economically poor families. The chapter differs from the former in terms of its case study approach and by specifically focussing on the perceptions of students and their families rather than on the views of professionals. It concludes by considering whether it is realistic to expect schools to intervene in non-educational issues and, insofar as this is possible, what kinds of conditions are necessary for such interventions to stand a chance of success.

In chapter 11, by Maija Salokangas, Christopher Chapman and Dennis Beach, specific challenges offered toward education equity are examined in relation to the recently emerging phenomena of independent and state funded school chains (ISFS) vis-à-vis Academies in England and so-called Free Schools (*Friskolor*) in Sweden. The development of federations or chains of schools is given particular attention. Empirical studies in England (Chapman 2013, 2014) are presented identifying the impact of 'performance federations' and 'academy chains' on student outcomes and in Sweden the relationship between education and profit is analysed.

The final chapter in the book is the conclusions chapter by Alan Dyson and Dennis Beach. This chapter opens by returning to the equity framework proposed in chapter 1 and considering the extent to which England and Sweden can be regarded as having equitable education systems. Some deep-seated commitments to equity are found. However, achievements are also undermined by countervailing tendencies towards elitist and human capital views of education embedded within neoliberal approaches to social and economic development. The differences between Sweden and England, and the successes—however limited—of policy makers and practitioners, suggest that alternative approaches to education justice and equity are possible, even if they are frequently limited.

(Re)conceptualising education justice and equity policy aims and possibilities

There are many questions that could be posed in relation to education justice and equity based on the chapters in the book and the conclusions we have drawn from them. These questions can be formed both in policy terms, in relation to outcomes and achievements, and as an ambition to initiate yet further discussions relating to how concepts of education justice may be framed and what consequences this framing can have. They are about the possibility of justice and equity in education in the two countries.

When considering these issues of the possibility of justice and equity in education and society, and the viability of an educational politics for justice and equity, the suggestions of this book often revolve around the need to take head of complexity. Sharon Gerwitz's mapping of the field of education justice and equity in 1998 (Gerwirtz, 1998) and her presentation of Marion Young's (1990) notion of relational justice is important to consider here, we feel, as is Terri Seddon's critique of Gewirtz (Seddon, 2003), and Nancy Fraser's (1997) perspective on distributional and representational justice upon which Seddon's critique of Gewirtz's analysis was primarily based. Carlo Raffo's (2014) book on educational justice and equity with respect to family, community, the geographies of space and place, gender and ethnicity, is also of value here.

These different works each belong to a tradition of justice research that is concerned with autonomy and agency in education politics and/or society, and how they impact on important identity processes and practices, in ways that can directly marginalise, psychologically constrain, and/or socially, politically and economically discriminate against particular groups. As do several of the chapters in the present book, they ask questions like why educational inequalities and injustices exist, how do they impact on the experiences and opportunities of young people, and what educational policy and practice responses have been implemented to deal with them. These questions help form a relational perspective on education justice and equity that accompanies at least two other approaches that are in a sense fused in the conclusions we have drawn: specifically 'rights based reasoning' about justice and a human capital approach that may currently be hegemonic.

We are in a sense then at least partially and cautiously optimistic about the possibilities of at least some limited advances in terms of justice and equity in our two countries. Some other perspectives question this kind of optimism however and strongly critique the very limited concept of justice and equity that is possible in societies such as ours (e.g. Cole, 2003). Our cautious optimism likens that of Gewirtz (1998) when she refers to Iris Young's Five Faces of Oppression as a starting point for thinking in these terms. These faces are: the Exploitation of the wealth that workers create through their labour power; the Marginalisation of those who are unable to keep steady employment because of for instance disabilities, education levels, age, discrimination and poverty;

the presence of Powerlessness and Cultural Dominance through one group's experiences, cultural expressions and history being defined as superior to others; and finally the use of Violence to keep a group 'in its place': this can be symbolic or repressive State-sanctioned violence, to enforce for instance racial segregation, break up strikes, or 'contain' crime within neighbourhoods that have been 'written off' by law enforcement. It may, according to Young, also include the relative social tolerance of public violence toward certain stigmatised groups based on race and sexuality. Reflecting on and acting in relation to these five faces of oppression for the 'participation and inclusion of everyone in educational and social life' will help us to better attend to the particular 'affiliations, feelings, commitments and desires of marginalised groups'.

This is a message that is also operating throughout the present book. It requires us to address the complex nature of justice and equity from both distributive and relational positions, without ignoring the historical, political, economic and cultural (including legal) legacies—i.e. structures—that inform, inhibit, and or extend, the heterogeneous agency of individuals in different ways (Dyson et al., 2011). It involves valuing the autonomy of individuals in all its diversity and difference whilst also recognising that autonomy is part of a broader civic context of material history that constrains individualistic cultural relativism and 'pure' notions of autonomy and choice. As Raffo (2014) notes, agency depends on both individual circumstances, the relations people have and/or are able to form with others, their capabilities to recognise agentic possibilities and mobilise their agency in their own interests, and the social, cultural and economic conditions and contexts within which potential obligations, options and freedoms can and should be achieved. And this is a problem. Justice and rights to equity may still be subjected to bourgeois limitations and bourgeois notions of just deserves, and these are extremely class and racially biased as well as strongly shaped by a hegemony of difference and able-ness that diminishes the educational opportunities of people with physical and or mental disabilities.

Thus, according to the chapters in this book the measure of justice and equity in education should not only be made in terms of equal access to distributed resources. It should also be about history, structural relations, political decisions, attitudes, hegemony, and the availability of pedagogy and a curriculum that will build onto the experiences and understandings of all young people, without marginalisation, by providing possibilities to develop and engage fully in their learning. Researching justice and equity in these circumstances involves studying, describing and theorising about how learning contexts, both inside and outside school, may or may not challenge recognisable faces of oppression. It involves researching how education systems and practices differentially generate constrained sets of educational expectations and constrained sets of educational possibilities and trajectories (Dyson et al., 2011; Raffo, 2014).

Researching educational justice and equity should perhaps therefore involve examining not only redistribution but also how agentic developments and rights are mediated and restrained by material, cultural, social and psychological experiences within school, beyond school, and by the relationships of the Law and place and space that link the two together in the media, common sense, social conventions and limitations. This implies researching the ways in which the particular concerns of groups or individuals on curriculum content or forms of assessment and management are negotiated. It concerns the possibilities and restraints of an *enlivened and agentic justice from above and below*, that aligns with a policy emphasis on process, autonomy and aspiration, of a kind that can enhance a range of real agentic alternatives and commitments for expanding and developing the diverse educational capabilities that can provide all young people regardless of class background, gender, race, ethnicity or definitions of able-ness with the right to core intellectual engagement in/through advanced schooling. Just giving equal shares of time or money will not compensate for the unfairness of existing social and educational arrangements. Redistributions are a compromise, and they always have been. Changes to the social order and currently alienated social relations in education and culture might make a difference. But this kind of 'revolution' is probably not economically feasible or socially possible today. Research on and for education justice and equity may well be research that analyses if and how a revolution of/in learning can occur, what might characterise its preconditions, and what the forms of its main logically necessary and unnecessary contradictions may be.

Chapter conclusion

In concluding the introduction we have to say that the class divisions in England and Sweden have remained very powerful, despite decades of policies for so-called democratic and inclusive education, and many groups are not only at risk of increasing social exclusion, but also of increasing economic exclusion. Moreover, our education systems seem to be becoming more polarised today at the same time as they also seem to be fracturing horizontally into schools that confer systematically differing amounts of cultural and social capital to their clientele. As Kerr suggests in this volume, differences in assessment related to family income, father's occupation and mother's education widen at each stage of the education system and children with a higher social class background who start with a low assessment of relative cognitive ability when young eventually overtake those with a lower social class background who were initially assessed as having high ability. Poor educational outcomes are also typically concentrated in areas where other forms of disadvantage are concentrated, with this leading to pupil populations with high levels of disadvantage (Raffo and Dyson, 2007). Rather than offering a route to social mobility our education systems are still reproducing inequality. They disadvantage learners with less immediate access to the conventional forms of social and cultural capital.

12

Chapter 1

Exploring the relationship between equality, equity and social justice in education

Kirstin Kerr and Carlo Raffo

Introduction

This chapter has two main purposes. The first is to explore what the terms equality, equity, and social justice might mean in relation to education, and how those terms relate to one another. This is complex because often they are used interchangeably without perhaps fully appreciating both their differences and their connectedness. The second is to consider how the education system might be explored in relation to notions of equality, equity and social justice. Such ideas have influenced different aspects of the education systems in England and Sweden and elsewhere, for example: structural arrangements, in terms of how education systems are organised and how learners gain access to those systems; the educational processes learners experience; and what are seen to be the most important outcomes of education, such as examination results, personal development and well-being, and employability.

In addressing these issues, this chapter aims to provide readers with a range of ideas about equality, equity and social justice which they can use to critically explore their own thinking, particularly in relation to how such issues might be embedded in wider school and societal contexts. As UK-based researchers, our examples are drawn largely from England and the literature we draw upon is English-language literature. However, as other chapters in this book demonstrate, there are similar issues in Sweden and the framework we offer is, we suggest, widely applicable. On the other hand, the chapter does not seek to engage fully in the complex philosophical debates surrounding notions of equality, equity and social justice (for a more extensive discussion see Raffo, 2014). Rather it aims to present readers with some of the main ideas put forward by key thinkers, and then to explore how these ideas—albeit presented here at their most basic—can be used to help unravel educational debates and dilemmas. For example, is creating a socially just education system about providing all learners with the same education insofar as possible, and so emphasising equality? Is it about encouraging diversity so that learners can have different experiences which reflect their particular backgrounds? While this may be unequal, could it also be fairer or more equitable, in offering all learners an education tailored to their needs and interests?

Both arguments have their merits and drawbacks. How they might be balanced raises numerous dilemmas. As this chapter argues, there are no clear cut answers as to what an equitable and socially just education system would look like. Nonetheless, the ideas it introduces can inform readers' understandings of the issues raised throughout this book.

Equality, Equity, and Social Justice: a related set of concepts

In setting out to explore ideas about equality, equity and social justice, it is necessary, firstly, to make a distinction between these terms. While closely linked, they are not the same, and the distinction between them is particularly important for our purposes. At its most basic, equality can be thought about in terms of the extent to which a situation is the same, or similar, across groups of people with different characteristics. This may be in relation to outcomes, or engagement in particular opportunities and processes, access to resources, or in the treatment people receive (Ainscow et al., 2012). Inequality, conversely, can be thought about in terms of differences between the situations of groups of people.

When there are notable differences, or inequalities, between the situations of different groups, the notion of equity can then be used to invite some consideration of how these differences are distributed. Are they found to be equally distributed across different population groups (so for instance, are the same range of examination outcomes seen across all children, even when comparisons are made in relation to gender, or ethnicity, or socio-economic background), or are they distributed systematically in ways which indicate that some groups are faring worse (so, for instance, do children living in poverty systematically attain least well in examinations)? Where there are systematic differences, the situation can be considered inequitable if it indicates that particular groups are being disadvantaged by the ways in which society works, and the social, cultural, economic and political processes that help to lead to particular outcomes (Braveman, 2003, Braveman and Gruskin, 2003).

In making this case, it is important to note that not all inequalities invite the judgement that society is working in ways which are unfair and inequitable. For instance, mortality rates may be unequally distributed, with older people having systematically higher mortality levels than younger people—a pattern which could be expected regardless of other social and economic differences within the population. But if the economically poorest groups in society are, for instance, found to have a systematically lower life expectancy, this could be considered unfair and inequitable. Thinking about issues of equity and inequity—rather than just equality or inequality—therefore invites judgements about whether the differences observed are fair or not. A social justice dimension then comes into play. From a social justice perspective, inequities are morally unacceptable because they suggest that society is operating in ways which perpetuate the marginalisation and disadvantage experienced by particular groups (Fraser, 1996). To create a more socially just society, ways have to be found to intervene in the processes that help to create and perpetuate inequities.

These ways of thinking about equality, equity and social justice, can all be applied to education. For instance, the identification of systematic differences in outcomes for different groups of children has been used an important means of highlighting educational inequalities—which in turn are indicative of inequities and of social injustice. The practice of measuring children's educational attainments and comparing different groups of children is, for instance, central to the OECD's reporting on education and the rankings it gives to the performance of different countries' education systems. Different national education systems have also given high priority to measuring and comparing children's outcomes. In England, for example, this has been facilitated by a system of standardised national testing which in turn has revealed a number of inequalities, most pressingly, a close association between socio-economic status and educational attainment. As an analysis by Perry and Francis concluded:

> Social class remains the strongest predictor of educational achievement in the UK, where the social class gap for educational achievement is one of the most significant in the developed world
> (Perry and Francis, 2010, p. 2)

National testing has also revealed systematic educational inequalities in relation to children's ethnic backgrounds. For instance, Cassen and Kingdon (2007) have documented how nearly half of all low achieving learners are white British males; and that Chinese—and Indian-heritage learners are most successful in avoiding low attainment, while Caribbean learners are least successful. A strong spatial dimension to educational inequalities has also been revealed with poor attainment being concentrated in low income neighbourhoods which are often characterised by other markers of disadvantage including, for example, significant levels of sub-standard housing, ill health, and unemployment (Dorling et al., 2007).

On the basis of such analyses, there is a case for action which will improve attainments for those learners who appear to be losing out within current educational arrangements, and which will narrow any systematic gaps in outcomes between the most and least advantaged. This stance, in itself, appears reasonably straightforward and defensible; if some groups have poor educational attainments, then doing something to improve their attainment will create a more equitable situation (Kerr and West, 2010). But examined more closely, this situation is not quite as straightforward as it may at first appear. While inequalities can be identified by comparing outcomes, this does not actually explain why different groups achieve different outcomes, and what might, therefore, need to be done to change this situation. For example, although poor attainments are concentrated in low income communities, attainment data does not explain why and how poor outcomes arise and are perpetuated in these communities, nor does it suggest what actually needs to be done to counter the social injustices experienced by learners (Ainscow et al., 2008).

It is therefore also necessary to look beneath the patterns revealed by measuring outcomes, and to illuminate the dynamic processes which generate inequitable life experiences, and which are likely to lead to poor outcomes for particular groups of children (Kerr et al., 2014). In considering why, for instance, social class is such a strong predictor of educational outcomes in England, the existing research literature points to a number of important interrelated factors. Amongst other things, the availability of economic resources can have dramatic impacts on how young people access, experience and achieve in the education system (Power et al., 2003). Despite the introduction of universal free and compulsory schooling, financial resources still give an advantage in pursuing educational attainment. Parents with greater financial resources are more likely to be able to secure access higher attaining schools for their children, by buying either private schooling or housing in a good catchment area (Bell, 2007, Ireson, 2004). Educational resources such as a computer, a room of one's own for study, and so on, are also costly. In addition, financial resources can have indirect impacts on children's educational experiences and outcomes. For example, poverty can lead to stress and depression, which in turn can affect parenting (Duncan and Brooks-Gunn 1997; Mortimore and Whitty 2000; Whitty 2002). Living in poor or overcrowded housing is also linked to poor health and lower attainment (Bartley et al. 1994; Douglas 1964), and school moves due to residential mobility can have a very negative impact on attainment (Strand and Demie 2006).

More generally, the social, cultural and personal consequences of economic hardships for children's educational experiences and outcomes are wide ranging (Bartley, 2006). These may range from family strife and conflict emanating from not being able to cope financially, to a lack of self-respect and dignity about living in poverty in a society that apparently has so much to offer and which the media glamorises as being open to all sorts of possibilities. In addition, the concentration of poverty in certain communities can also have the effect of fragmenting relationships and networks of support, distancing people ever more from potential developments in their localities, and stigmatising those areas, and people in those areas (Wacquant, 2008). Such processes (and the ones outlined here are just indicative of a much wider range of factors at work in children's lives) can influence the way in children engage with education and what they might achieve (Walker, 2006).

It is, furthermore, not just factors outside school that are implicated in creating inequities in education. Within school systems, there are also examples of educational processes that are inequitable and unjust (Reay, 2006). These can include: a lack of appropriate educational resources to support particular groups of learners to engage fully with education (Teese and Polesel, 2003); teaching and learning in schools which may do little to engage with children's experiences outside school (Riddell, 2007); and a lack of representation of children and their families in the processes of education (Dean et al., 2007). These inequities come about as of result of the operation of power, discrimination and/or disadvantaging processes in schools and educational systems.

Understanding such processes can help to challenge the simplistic—and often deficit—discourses that tend to be used by policy makers in an effort to explain educational inequities and to justify particular policy decisions. For instance, there is a strong policy rhetoric in England which suggests that learners from disadvantaged backgrounds lack aspiration, and that their attainments are low because they *choose* not to buy in to the opportunities the education system offers them—and persist in this even when steps are taken to ensure they have increased access to the resources they might need to succeed (Gove, 2013). But, as the discussion so far has indicated, such a stance fails to recognise and engage in the complex and socially unjust processes which have helped to lead to these outcomes. The choices children make in relation to education, and the opportunities that are accessible to them, may well be constrained by a complex set of circumstances and issues, rather than being a matter of free choice (Walker 2006).

This discussion, while necessarily brief, is indicative of a wide ranging and complex set of issues which are integral to creating a more equitable and socially just education system. It has suggested that creating such a system is not simply about changing the distribution of educational outcomes, but also about intervening in the underlying processes which systematically disadvantage some groups of children—relating to individual, family and community circumstances, and to the workings of schools and education systems, and to the interrelationships between these. However, there is another fundamental issue which the discussion has yet to address and to which we will now turn—namely, what should a socially just education system, which is fair for all learners, actually be seeking to achieve?

Different forms of equity and social justice

With considerable emphasis being put on educational attainment by national and international monitoring systems, discussions about equity and social justice can often be dominated, as the English case illustrates, by a concern to narrow attainment gaps. The danger with this is that the questions of what a more socially just education system would actually look like, and whether narrowing gaps in attainment should actually be its primary goal, may be overlooked. Although not widely discussed in the education literature, a broad ranging review of the literature in the fields of health, politics and social policy, suggests a number of ways in which fairness or social justice could be defined when seeking to redress identifiable inequities, and these can help with thinking more broadly about what a more equitable education might look like. To this end, four broad definitions are outlined below, each with strong philosophical precedents. These can be used as lenses for looking at education systems and bringing different concerns about social justice into focus. They are as follows:

1. Justice as equality of rights—This implies that fairness will be achieved if everyone has the same rights to be treated in the same way. This principle underlies legally enshrined conventions to protect inalienable human rights, which assert that all humans should have equal rights to fair treatment (see the UN declaration of human rights (www.un.org/en/documents/udhr/). However, depending on its application, such a definition can promote equity

in some instances, while condoning inequity in others. For example, Marshall (cited Heater, 1999) makes the case that to be equal as citizens, people must have the same legal status, and that this is more important than equalising socio-economic disparities. He argues:

> Equalisation is not so much between classes as between individuals within a population which is now treated for this purpose as though it were one class. Equality of status is more important than equality of income. (p. 5)

This then begs questions about whether, even if people are equal in status with the same legal rights, they are equally able to act on these.

This notion of justice as equal rights can be applied to the education system in various ways. One clear example of this principle at work is that, following the Education Reform Act of 1988, England has had a national curriculum which prescribes common content for most learners. This content may, of course, be viewed as more or less suited to different groups of learners, but there is, nonetheless, equality in terms of all learners have equal rights to access the same subject knowledge. Contrastingly, notions of social justice as equal rights have also been used to promote differentiation. One example of this is where parents have acted on their equal right, as set out in law, to have access to a 'good' or 'appropriate' education for their child, and have used this to argue that their child requires differentiated provision.

2. Justice as equality of outcomes across social groups—This means reducing and ultimately eliminating the gaps between the outcomes achieved by the most advantaged and least advantaged social groups. An important qualifier here is that any gaps should be reduced by improving the achievements of the less advantaged, not by lowering the achievements of the most advantaged (Sen 2002). Again to give an illustration from within English education, since the late 1990s there have been a number of policy initiatives intended to reduce gaps in attainment by introducing standardised formats for teaching literacy and numeracy. Although introduced nationally, these were intended to be of greatest benefit in the lowest achieving schools, by raising their quality of teaching.

3. Justice as equality of achieving a minimum common standard—This requires the setting of minimum levels or standards that all groups are expected to achieve. For example, Adam Smith, in the 1818 version of his work *An Inquiry*

Into the Nature and Causes of the Wealth of Nations spoke about justice in terms of ensuring all people were entitled to the 'necessaries' for leading a civilised life:

> By necessaries I understand not only the commodities which are indispensably necessary for the support of life, but what ever the custom of the country renders it indecent for creditable people, even of the lowest order, to be without. (Smith, 1818)

Within all sectors of society, this notion of minimum entitlements, and ensuring that people have, at minimum, the ability to act on their social, civil and political rights, has become a powerful force in policy reform. English governments have, for example, set a number of targets for educational attainment, some of which have been developed to ensure a basic level of literacy and numeracy skills across the population, so that, insofar as possible, everyone has the skills needed to participate actively in civic life.

4. Justice as equitable processes in meeting the needs of diverse individuals— This suggests that fairness requires differential treatment in order to take account of diversity. For example, Kymlicka (1995) has argued that, as a general principle, minority groups who are most disadvantaged within society require additional rights and resources to allow their needs to be met equitably alongside those of majority groups. So, learners and their families who first language is not the language used in school, may require additional teaching and learning resources, support in developing home-school relations, special allowances for assessments, and so on.

Inherent in each of the definitions of justice set out above, are sets of underlying ideals which refer both to how people should be treated, and to what they can be expected to achieve. In turn, these definitions suggest different ways of judging to what extent a situation may be deemed equitable, and of thinking about how policies might be developed to support the creation of a more socially just education system. In recognition of this, Sen (2002) argues that the development of greater equity and social justice is, philosophically at least, a matter of 'weighting—and perhaps even a compromise—between divergent considerations' (p. 660).

Rawls (1971) similarly proposes that social justice may require different forms of equity in different situations. He suggests that in some instances social justice requires equality (for example, access to equal basic liberties), while in others, it requires that resources are distributed in such a way as to have most benefit for the least advantaged (with this helping them to achieve a certain standard, and/or bringing their achievements closer to those of the most advantaged, and/or have equal access to particular opportunities). In addition, it is also important to recognise that different forms of social justice are not necessarily exclusive. For instance, to meet a common standard could also mean minimising divergence between social groups. Thus, in some instances, alternative definitions of social justice could be simultaneously and harmoniously pursued—while in others they may demonstrate a conflict of interests.

Significant as these different ways of thinking about equity and social justice are, it is also important to bring a human dimension into the discussion, and to recognise people's role as social actors—their 'agency'—as a further important dynamic. This suggests that achieving greater justice or fairness is not simply a case of distributing resources so that people can achieve particular ends (with the net result of equalising their attainments gap, or meeting individual needs or other goals), but also of actually responding to what people want to achieve, and their own values and aims.

Fraser (1996), for example, makes a distinction between policies which redirect resources to support marginalised groups, but in doing so mark them out as 'different and lesser' (p. 46), and those which actually seek to value and build on the resources held by marginalised groups. In doing so, she refers to 'redistribution' and 'recognition'. Redistribution is about how are resources distributed and who has access to these. In education, for instance, the case might be made for distributing resources in an unequal way in order to enable all learners, regardless of their backgrounds, to access high status knowledge and cultural resources. Recognition, by contrast, is about acknowledging that different groups of learners may have different priorities and anticipate different life trajectories, to those presented by an education system's emphasis on academic learning and progression to further and higher education. This suggests that a fairer education system would be one which not only redistributed resources in a socially just way, but which supported and gave equal status to a wide range of educational goals and trajectories, and the acquisition of different types of skills and knowledge. Such issues, relating to the recognition of learners' own values, goals and ambitions, are also often captured in the literature through the notion of capability. The Overseas Development Institute defines capability as: The ability of a person to achieve the … various combinations of valuable beings and doings that are within a person's reach, reflecting the opportunity of freedom to choose a life that a person values. (2001, p. 2)

A number of commentators have explored how taking a capability-led approach to developing social justice in education could assist in broadening thinking about what a fair educational system should be seeking to achieve. Alongside attainment-oriented outcomes, this would bring into focus young people's decisions and choices about education, the values and freedoms they have to make these choices, and their wider well-being. For example, Walker (2006, p. 180) proposes an eight point 'capability list'—a brief flavour of which is provided below—which suggests that an equitable education system would be one which helps all learners to develop the following capabilities:

1. Autonomy—being able to have information on which to make choices and to plan for life after school.
2. Knowledge—developing knowledge of school subjects that are intrinsically interesting or instrumentally useful for post-school choices, access to powerful analytical knowledge … knowledge for critical thinking, for debating complex moral and social issues, for active enquiry, and fair assessment of the knowledge gained.
3. Social relations—the capacity to participate in a group for friendship and learning and being able to work with others to solve problems.
4. Respect and recognition—developing self-confidence and self-esteem, respect for and from others, empathy and skills for dialogue and debate, valuing difference.
5. Aspiration—developing the motivation to learn and succeed and to have a better life.
6. Voice—developing the skills for participation in learning, for speaking out and not being silenced or excluded through pedagogy, or power relations, or harassment.
7. Bodily integrity and bodily health—learning how to be safe, and to make choices about lifestyle and sexual relationships.
8. Emotional integrity—developing emotions and imagination for understanding, empathy, awareness and discernment.

As well as broadening thinking about the nature and content of education, notions of capability can also help to bring issues of power in education to the fore. Fraser's (1996) argument that the way in which supporting marginalised groups may actually further marginalise them is a case in point.

In introducing the ideas of capability, and of redistribution and recognition, and in starting to use them to think about education, the different 'lenses' for thinking about equality, equity and social justice presented at the start of this section, still retain their value. Socially just ways still need to be found to meet the diverse needs of individuals, and to ensure that recognition does not reinforce marginalisation. A focus on equalising by reducing gaps is still required—even if the focus is on issues relating to gaps in voice or integrity rather than examination results. The principle of equal rights remains important, as does ensuring that all learners achieve the basic skills needed to actively participate in their communities and society more broadly.

Exploring the education system

Having started to consider the nature and purposes of a more equitable and socially just education system, and particularly so in relation to capability, we now also need to start to think about how best to understand and monitor the education system in ways which can better support equity and social justice. In doing so, it is necessary to revisit some of the issues discussed throughout the chapter about the extent to which debates about equity and social justice in education should be framed around measured attainment, as opposed to other comparable outcomes and experiences.

For Sen (2002), debates about equity and social justice begin to take on 'real' meaning when they are applied to concrete contexts. He argues that:

> [equity] as an abstract idea does not have much cutting power, and the real work begins with the specification of what it is that is to be equalised. The central step, then, is the specification of the space in which equality is to be sought, and … [this involves] such questions as 'equality of what?' (2002, p. 660)

One way of exploring the education system, and addressing the question 'equality of what?' is to consider the system as made up of different 'spaces' within which fairness or social justice issues arise. To date, the heavy reliance on examination-based data as a means of identifying inequalities has tended to focus attention specifically on the 'space' of educational outcomes, and within this broad context, on measurable, cognitive attainment. However, if issues of capability are also to be brought into the discussion, it is necessary to develop a more extensive 'map' of educational spaces in which different processes can be considered.

In simple terms, such a map must focus attention on four main contexts:

1. The context of the system itself

In relation to this, questions can be asked about whether access to the system is just or fair, how fairly resources are distributed within the system, and whether practices and processes within the system are inherently equitable. Resources cover a wide range of factors including, for example: 'professional resources'—e.g. skilled teachers; 'material resources'—e.g. access to equipment and other facilities; and 'intellectual resources'—e.g. access to wide ranging curricula.

2. The context of outcomes from the system

Fairness or social justice issues to be considered in this context include how far achievements are equally distributed across learners, and whether the system impacts on learners' life-chances in equal ways. Achievements can be broadly conceptualised in terms of:

1. outputs—this refers to measurable cognitive attainment (generally in the form of standardised test results)
2. personal outcomes—referring to personal values, attitudes, aspirations, and other 'affective' social characteristics
3. opportunities—referring to individuals' capacities to use their experience, knowledge and qualifications effectively to engage in society.

In addition, the education system can have social outcomes beyond the sum of outcomes achieved by individual learners. This is to draw attention to the socially transformative potential of education for families, communities, and society more broadly.

3. The dynamics of the social context in which the education system is located

The point to be made here is that education does not take place in a social vacuum. Learners enter the system from very different social backgrounds and exit into very different social situations. If these contexts are marked by disadvantage, inequality and inequity, this will inevitably impact on the education system and its outcomes. There are questions to ask, therefore, about equality, equity and social justice in social contexts and about the education system's interactions with those contexts. For instance, are all learners valued equally within the system?

4. The context of learners' capabilities

This raises questions not only about learners' abilities to pursue particular outcomes (with this relating to their access to resources—both within the system and from within their communities), but also about whether learners want, and feel able, to pursue the outcomes presented within the system. To what extent are learners' choices freely made, or constrained by circumstances? How far are they able to make autonomous and informed decisions about their learning and future trajectories? When considering these issues, it will be important to explore issues including:

1. what learners bring to the education system
2. how learners respond to the system and the values inherent in this
3. how the system responds to learners and the backgrounds they bring to the education system

To determine the state of equality, equity and social justice in education, a series of questions could be asked which relate to these broad contexts. These could include, for example:

Learners' capabilities and equitable educational processes

1. How do learners respond to the education system and the aims and values inherent in this?
2. How does this relate to learners' social characteristics—e.g. the knowledge, skills and attitudes they bring into contact with the system?
3. How does the system respond to different learners and the backgrounds they bring to the education system?
4. How is access to the resources held by the education system distributed?
5. What are the processes by which the system makes use of resources?

Equality of Educational Outcomes (Individual)

6. How are the outcomes of education distributed?
7. How do outcomes relate to access to resources?
8. How do outcomes relate to life chances?

Equality of Educational Outcomes (More broadly)

9. What are the social consequences of education?
10. Is society more equitable as a result of education?

By asking these questions of the education system (or of particular educational spaces) it should be possible to assess the state of equality, equity, and social justice, both in a systematic way and at a variety of levels—ranging from individual classrooms to national policy documents—and to use this to inform policy and practice debates.

Concluding comments

This chapter has introduced a number of key debates and concepts relating to equality, equity and social justice. These embody four broad principles which can usefully guide discussions in educational contexts, namely:

1. Issues of inequity and social justice can be said to arise where there are systematic differences in processes and outcomes relating to markers of social advantage. In relation to this, it is necessary to consider issues of agency, and whether the choices people make are 'free' or 'constrained'.
2. Questions about equality, equity and social justice are necessarily multiple in their nature—how are differences distributed across population groups? Are these differences inequitable? If so, what are the processes which create these inequities? What would need to happen to address these inequities? What forms of social justice would need to be pursued?
3. Different ideas about equity and social justice can help to illuminate some of the complex issues with which policy makers and practitioners must engage. In effect, they can be used as 'lenses' through which to interrogate different situations, or to explore a single situation from various perspectives. This is valuable in demonstrating conflicts of interest, and/or ways of accommodating different interests and agendas.
4. There are a number of educational spaces which must be explored in discussion about equality, equity and social justice in education. These refer to learners themselves, the processes of the education system and resources it holds, the outcomes of education—broadly conceived—and the wider social dynamics in which these are embedded.

These principles must inform discussions about the directions in which policy and practice must develop if they are to support the development of more socially just and equitable education systems.

Chapter 2

Concepts of equity in Swedish society and education: Historical perspectives

Girma Berhanu

Introduction

The chapter outlines the historical evolvement of the concepts of equity in Swedish society and education through the prism of *comparative* lens. The concept of equity is problematic in cross-border comparative studies. One precondition to conducting a cross-border study of equity in education and society is a conceptual discussion of the concept itself, as this has considerable influence on theory, methodology, and practice. There may not be huge differences in the conception of equity between for instance Sweden and England. However, even modest differences and similarities help us investigate taken-for-granted assumptions and develop a deeper understanding of our own value systems and practices, thereby navigating into new perspectives in order to reveal alterative options. It is obvious that the two countries have made efforts toward equitable education. However, the ways these are played out in practice are conditioned by the histories of the countries, current situations, and specific notions of social justice. My assumption is that, despite some differences in educational histories and in political and social development, including cultural identities, similarities could be traced in the conceptual approach. One aim in this chapter is to explicate the historical and cultural embededness of the concepts, understandings and interpretations of equity in society, and education in the context of Sweden.

The chapter explores the different understanding of equity, the conceptual framework as well as the constrains these impose on enacting equity, in particular in education, in the context of Sweden through the prism of a cultural historical, linguistic, and political lens. The chapter sheds light on the multidimensional nature of equity, the tension between these dimensions in being sensitive to the mediated nature of equity practices, as well as differences in the context and levels within which education is enacted (Gewirtz, 2004; Moreno Herrera, Jones, and Rantala, 2006).

I hope, therefore, to highlight culturally embedded understandings of equity across national contexts. I believe this knowledge will contribute to a better understanding of theories and practices in a comparative research framework. The literature is replete with findings that, in both Sweden and England, education is given an enormous burden to carry in balancing increasingly liberated market driven economies with the requirements of a socially just society. Although this chapter focuses on the Swedish experience, the recent reforms in both countries are couched in the rhetoric of diversity, choice, and difference—which often turn out to be reproducing inequities in society as well as in education. This historical process will be highlighted, as it has had an effect on the traditional conception of equity (e.g., Beach and Dovemark, 2007; Beach and Sernhede, 2011; Harling, 2014).

Equity in the Swedish educational system

The General Context

Sweden is a wealthy, highly educated, and healthy society with one of the highest standard of living in the world. In comparison to even many well-developed countries, Sweden is one of the leading countries at successfully combining equity and social inclusion with high economic efficiency. The tradition of universalism and comprehensiveness with minimisation of streaming and tracking has been the hallmark of the Swedish education system. Redistribution policies underpinned by high levels of taxation and public spending still appear to have strong social consensus. Sweden has, at the same time, undergone a dramatic transformation within the past two decades. The changes are framed within neoliberal philosophies that place greater emphasis on devolution, marketisation (driven by principles of cost containment and efficiency), competition, standardisation, individual choices and rights, development of new profiles within particular school units, and other factors that potentially work *against* the values of diversity, equity and inclusion.

In 1842, a policy termed *allmän folkskola* (folk school) came into force. Before that education was reserved only for middle—and upper-class society. The policy was primarily meant to provide schooling for all citizens, although in practice two parallel school systems evolved: one for the poor and disadvantaged, and the other for stronger elements of society. Even so, the policy's intention was noble, and we can still trace Sweden's long tradition of comprehensive, compulsory, and equivalent education from this time. It is also from this time that special needs education established its roots as a two-track system (i.e., special education and regular education settings crystallised). In the special education track the so-called problem-child was categorised using different nomenclature such as idiot, poor, feeble-minded, imbecile, and dullard. As we entered into the mid twentieth century, these categories changed into intellectually disabled, learning disabled, and mentally retarded. During the last two decades the general category became pupils with special needs but with a new culture of diagnosis based on neuropsychiatric methods, such as ADHD, DAMP,[1] autism, or Aspergers syndrome, are on the rise. This indicates how classification and categorisation has been an activity 'as old as schools themselves' (Hjörne, 2004; Mehan, 1993, p. 243; Skolverket, 2005).

Since then a number of school reforms have taken place that aim at a school system combining quality and equality. Education can be described as one of the cornerstones of the modern welfare state. This has been manifested heavily in Sweden, which was dominated by a social democratic model. Strong Labour parties were able to secure broad support for their policies during the inter-war period and after the Second World War, with solidarity, community and equality as the keywords. There were high hopes that uniform, free-of-charge education for children from all social strata would contribute to equality and justice, and promote social cohesion. Although the belief in the potential of education in this respect may have faded, education is still regarded as one of the major methods of preventing unemployment, social exclusion, and ill health (Arnesen and Lundahl, 2006). 'Hence, contemporary policy for equity is very much a latter day echo of the social democrats' age-old concept of the 'peoples' home" (OECD, 2005b).

Most of the modern history of Sweden is characterised by collective action spearheaded by a social democratic welfare state and is a prominent example of social democratic welfare state favouring full employment and a focus on minimising differences, social alienation and exclusion as opposed to individual responsibility and market solutions (Arnesen and Lundahl, 2006; OECD,1999a, 1999b, 2005a; Wildt-Persson and Rosengren, 2001). This political and cultural background has been instrumental in creating an early and fertile platform from which to criticise the traditional special educational and exclusionary approach and to formulate concepts such as normalisation, integration and mainstreaming (Nirje, 1992; Wolfensberger, 1972). This background has fostered awareness and

1. ADHD—Attention deficit hyperactivity disorder;
   DAMP—Deficits in attention, motor control, and perception.

cultural messages of the significance of social inclusiveness and has resulted in organisation changes such as closing large institutions for intellectually disabled persons and building community-based residential, learning, and working environments. This was a remarkable achievement by any standard. The social motives of education that are citizenship, social integration, social equality and democracy had as much importance as economic motivations, not only in Sweden but also in Scandinavia as a whole. However, in the last decade's welfare and education policies have been increasingly influenced by market logic, and economic motives have been given more weight. The neoliberal wave in the 1980s and 1990s also had an impact in the Scandinavian countries. Several researchers question whether it is still reasonable to speak of a distinct Nordic welfare model any longer. However, Kautto, Fritzell, Hvinden, Kvist, and Uusitalo (2001) and Vogel, Svallfors, Theorell, Noll, and Christoph (2003) come to the conclusion that the Nordic countries still stand out from other European and OECD nations, and there is reason to speak about a Nordic welfare model. The question of whether this is also true for education is, however, seldom or never addressed. (Arnesen and Lundahl, 2006, p. 286)

The slogan 'A school for all' (*En skola för alla*) embellished most of the policy documents and government-commissioned reports and propositions in the 1960s, 70s, and through until the late 1980s as a component of the inclusive and caring welfare state. In 1962 (LGR 62), a nine-year unified compulsory school program for all children ages seven to sixteen was introduced. This compulsory curriculum emphasised that pupils come at the centre of the learning process and that they should be helped to achieve multi-sided development within the framework of a school for all or a common frame of reference.

Current Swedish educational policy documents recognise that students are different. That has important implications in how schooling is organised and therefore the learning process and the avenues to reach goals. The curriculum states clearly that consideration should be taken of the different abilities and needs of the students. There are different ways to reach the goal. 'Hence teaching cannot be designed in the same way for everyone' (LPO, 1994; Skolverket, 2011). At the time of writing this paper, Sweden has gone through a range of policy reforms. The changes were triggered partly by Swedish children's disappointing performance or lower levels of knowledge in international studies such as PISA (Programme for International Student Assessment) and *TIMSS* (*Trends in International Mathematics and Science Study*). To help combat this trend, the country has introduced several changes to its school system, such as a new education act, new curricula, introduction of teacher certification, and new grading system. These policy changes and reforms have yet to be thoroughly evaluated (e.g., Skollag, 2010:800; LGR 11, SKOLFS 2010:37).

While Swedish education policies have a solid history and culture of solidarity, community, and social responsibility, Sweden also has deep cultural values and historical heritage that support self-realisation, individual productivity, competition, and social competence. However, recent trends show that there seems to be a conjunction in a direction of 'business oriented management styles' characterised by an overemphasis on efficiency, standardisation, consumerism, individual choices and rights and a de-emphasis on collectivism and solidarity. Reports evidence not only fragmentation of educational policy-making but also contradictory messages related to conception of knowledge, social justice, equity, and equality issues (e.g., Beach and Dovemark, 2007; Korp. 2006, 2011). This has also had an impact on student achievement profiles and marginalised a large segment of the student population from ordinary educational settings.

The Swedish public education system is composed of compulsory and non-compulsory schooling. Compulsory education includes regular compulsory school, Sami[2] school, special school, and programs for pupils with learning disabilities. Non-compulsory education includes the 'preschool class,' upper secondary school, upper secondary school for pupils with learning disabilities, municipal adult education, and adult education for adults with learning disabilities. The nine-year compulsory school program is for all children between ages seven and sixteen. All education throughout the public school system is free. There is usually no charge to students or their parents for teaching materials, school meals, health services, or transport. The education system has focused on providing equality of opportunities and equivalence of outcomes (www.skolverket.se, OECD, 2005b). However, the system has undergone a number of important reforms in the past twenty or so years that have a strong bearing on equity. We will address this issue in the next section.

Equity, equivalence and equality

The concept of equity does not render itself easily for interpretation as it is also entangled with the concept of equality and equivalence. The specific purpose of this chapter is not to address the complexity surrounding clarity of the concept. It is important, however, to outline the concepts evolution in its social and historical

2. Sami is an ethnic group with ill-defined genetic origins, living in the northern areas of the Scandinavian Peninsula and Russia.

context. It is also imperative to relate the concept with other studies beyond the countries being treated here. This conceptual discussion in its historical context is a prerequisite for a cross national and comparative studies. As elsewhere, the semantic problems between equity, equality, and equivalence must be discerned even in the Swedish discourses.

Since the early nineteenth century, when elementary school was regarded as a basic school for all, equity has been and is still a central element in the Swedish educational policies, ordinances and directives. 'Equity is a general term indicating 'fairness;' for example, that principles of justice have been used in the assessment of a phenomenon' (Wildt-Persson and Rosengren, 2001, p. 307). Equity in the school is guaranteed by both the previous and the latest Swedish Education Act. All children and young people shall, regardless of gender, geographical residence, and social or economic situation, have equal access to education in the public school system for children and young people. The Act stipulates that consideration must also be afforded to pupils with special needs. The school has a special responsibility for those pupils who, for different reasons, experience difficulties in attaining the established educational goals. The links between education and the rest of society are widely recognised, and one task of the school system is to foster in children a spirit of equality and democratic values (Skollag, 2010:800; also LGR 11, SKOLFS 2010:37; LPO, 1994).

Swedish efforts in the past to promote equity through a variety of educational policies have been fascinating. Those early educational policies including the macro-political agenda focused on a social welfare model that have helped diminish the effects of differential social, cultural and economic backgrounds on outcomes. 'Studies have also shown that inequalities in Swedish society have diminished over the last century in the sense that the influence of a number of background factors important for educational attainment — parents' class or social position, cultural capital, type of community and gender— have been reduced'(Wildt-Persson and Rosengren, 2001, p. 299). This may be described mainly as the result of a combination of educational policies and welfare policies that have been the central features of the cultural, historical, and political heritage in Nordic societies.

The main question is how this critical equity issue can be addressed in a decentralised educational system that was introduced about eighteen years ago. How can we guarantee those values without an effective system of indicators to measure and monitor equity? What does follow–up and evaluation look like? I do not claim to provide a complete description of this complex research area. I do, however, provide some examples that bear on inclusive practices both negatively and positively.

The Swedish constitution recognises equal human worth and respect for the freedom and dignity of the individuals. The principles laid down there are sources for the curriculum's goals and objectives. In that respect:

> An important principle in achieving equity has been and still is the compensatory principle, i.e., that the state should not remain neutral in issues relating to equal opportunity. Differences among geographical regions, social or economic groups must not be attributable to any form of discrimination that would indicate that the principle of equality has been neglected. (Wildt-Persson and Rosengren, 2001, p. 301)

Other than the comprehensiveness of the Swedish school system, the adult education is another crucial aspect of equity because it affords training and education for under-educated and unmotivated young people. It provides them with a chance to rejoin school as well as carry on with their working lives (OECD, 2005b). Equity carries a particular significance for children with special educational needs. The majority of these children are integrated into regular child-care activities, compulsory schools and upper-secondary schools. There are, however, eight special schools for pupils with hearing/vision and physical disabilities, as well as some schools for mentally handicapped pupils. A total of one percent of all pupils in the compulsory and upper-secondary school levels are in such segregated settings (Skolverket, 2005; Statistics Sweden, 2009; Vislie, 2003; Wildt-Persson and Rosengren, 2001). This is minimal by international comparison (OECD, 1999a; 2000a, 2000b). Nonetheless, since early 1990s the situation has deteriorated.

The number of pupils placed in educational programmes for learning disabled children has increased dramatically. In general, the number of children defined as 'special needs' has shown a steady increase. In addition, there has been a dramatic increase in the number of private schools. Variances between schools and municipalities and student achievement, including segregation and persistence socioeconomic differences among the school populations, have been the post-decentralisation policy phenomenon. All the indicators of the National Agency for Education compiled through evaluations, case studies, and supervision, testify to this fact. This situation seems to have gotten worse since the Conservative party took power in 2006. One may question whether decentralisation and equity are contradictory or incompatible? One might also argue that, isn't it the Conservative party that are against equity and for differentiation, as always, rather than something connected to decentralisation? Decentralisation is part of a policy package that increases differences in internal and external performances but it does not cause them (see Wernersson and Gerrbo, 2013, for extensive analysis of this issue and numerous references therein).

While the influence of a number of background factors significant to educational attainment, such as parental social position, cultural capital, type of community and gender, may have diminished over the last century (Jonsson, 1993; Wildt-Persson and Rosengren, 2001), there is a cause for concern for how long such declines will persist and caution is needed if the traditional model is to survive. While there are signs that inclusive education as envisaged in the Salamanca declaration (UNESCO,1994) is being exercised at different levels, gaps in research and follow-ups are most noticeable in this area. Moreover, an over representation of minority pupils in special educational placements (Berhanu, 2008) and significant gender differences in specific disability categories (Skolverket, 2005), as well as in general learning outcomes and methods of testing and assessment, are areas of grave concern requiring further research.

For instance, as regards average achievement, a number of studies have demonstrated that average test achievement has risen since the reform. According to Björklund et al., (2004), the achievement gain is stronger in private schools. But it is unclear whether this is attributable to the quality of the teaching or to the increased classification by ability taking place in these schools. Further, Björklund et al. use an interaction term with social background and find that, unfortunately, immigrants and low-socioeconomic status pupils have not gained from the overall quality improvement—not even in absolute terms (OECD, 2005:20; Korp. 2011; also Wernersson and Gerrbo, 2013).

Evaluating equivalence

Although the concepts of equity, equality, and equivalence are inextricably intertwined, they do not convey exactly the same meaning. As I understand the concept, 'equivalence' represents or encompasses the other two in Swedish discourses, although this is a bold statement. Englund (2005) notes that the concept has undergone significant changes and has been given different authoritative interpretations:

> Viewed from a longer-term perspective, the concept has undergone a displacement whereby its substantial meaning and the contextual criteria involved in it have changed from consisting of types of goals such as unity, common frames of reference, and equal value of continued studies, to a situation where supplementary goals have been added; these are often vague and in total opposition to the original objectives. These new goals can accept difference and individuality independently of shared frames of reference. They have also become equivalence's link to freedom of choice and parents' rights. (Englund, 2005, p. 42)

Equivalence is used, to mean 'of equal worth' (Wildt-Persson and Rosengren, 2001 p. 308) and does not imply a strict criterion for comparing two objects, but does assume comparability. Educational paths, for example, can be equivalent, but do not necessarily have to contain identical courses and subjects to have the same value. In line with this, the idea of one school with a common curriculum for all can be problematic if not totally questionable. Lindensjö notes that the

> reforms in Sweden have led to the insight that it is difficult to attain true equality without promoting uniformity, which in turn is seen as negative. Therefore, the term equivalence has become central in the Swedish Education Act and has thus come to replace equality as the adjective describing the principles of equity
> (in Wildt-Persson and Rosengren, 2001, p. 308).

The principle of fair education as embedded in the concept equivalence has been operationalised in the Education Act. The Education Act stipulates that the education provided within each type of school should be of equivalent value, irrespective of where in the country it is provided. The curriculum (Lp. 94)[3] written under a conservative government (1991–1994), states:

> National goals specify the norms for equivalence. However, equivalent education does not mean that education should be the same everywhere or that the resources of a school should be allocated equally. Accounts should also be taken of the varying circumstances and needs of pupils

---

3. Both the new curriculum (Lgr 11: 2011) and the new Education Act (Skollag, 2010) have similar messages and content as in the previous curriculum (LPO 94) and the Education Act (1985) although the wordings vary to some extent.

as well as the fact that there are a variety of ways of attaining these goals. Furthermore the school has a special responsibility for those pupils who for different reasons experience difficulties in attaining the goals that have been set for the education. (Lp. 94p. 4)

Further, it states that education shall be adapted to each pupil's circumstances and needs. However, that does not mean that results should be equal. The term 'quality' is also a crucial term used inseparably with the other three central terms in government reports because the quality of services at all levels of the educational system can have serious implications for equivalent education.

However, the performative displacement of the concept of equivalence (Englund, 2005) is significant vis-à-vis the previous curriculum (LGR 80) where in equivalent education was considered in terms of equal access to education and the possibility of creating a common frame of reference for all pupils. That is, 'By applying an obligatory syllabus, which encompasses the same subjects and materials in all schools, society presents a common frame of reference as well as an equivalent education to all citizens'. (Lgr 80, p. 15). As the new policies incorporate supplementary goals such as increased individualisation, freedom of choice, parents' rights, etc., achieving the goals of inclusive education become difficult. This underlines the fine balance between autonomy and communitarianism in playing out in policy discourses (cf. Englund, 2005).

A conceptual model of equivalence has been developed by the National Agency for Education to enable it monitor equivalence and it is currently being applied (Table 1[4]). This elegant model encompasses three critical areas: equal access, equivalent education and the equal value of education. These can also be described as equal opportunity strategies, equal treatment strategies and equal outcome strategies. These critical areas are structured within three general areas: prerequisites, process and results.

4. Adapted from Wildt-Persson and Rosengren, 2001, p. 310.

Table 1

Equivalence in Schools

Prerequisites	Process	Results
Equal access to education	Equivalent education	The equal value of an education
Regardless of:		With respect to:
Gender Geographical location Social circumstances Economic circumstances	Within every type of school Wherever in the country a school is run	Further study Society Working life

Equal Access

Equal access includes factors such as educational options, information regarding current options, admissions and the selection process, gender, and social circumstances.

Equivalent Education

Other central factors for ensuring equivalence in education include the following (Wildt-Persson and Rosengren, 2001, p. 311-312), Education offered; teaching carried out in accordance with the relevant curriculum program, program targets and syllabi; sufficient time for learning; trained staff; an effective school principal; support for students; pupils evaluation on an equal basis. The last four are central conditions to enhance inclusiveness and participation in the daily life of school.

Equal Value

The following are central to the equal value of educational programmes: further study; society; working life. It is through this indicator system that the participation and learning progress of pupils with special educational needs, and culturally and socially disadvantaged segments of the school population, can be monitored. A summary of the general trends according to these indicators includes the following points: growing inequalities and varied results between schools and pupils; an increase in special educational placements; and an increase in labelling of 'special needs' (for instance, dysphasia, autism, ADHD, socio-emotional problems). However, there is still a huge information gap on equity with respect to pupils with special needs education. It is critical to include specific categories within the indicator system in order to gather information on inclusive and exclusionary processes and on the participants, in particular within the regular education system.

To sum up, the two notions (i.e., equality and equity) were in some way understood/ interpreted (in the Swedish context) in the same way as Herbert J. Gans (1973) holds that

> Equity requires some degree of equality, for inequality is unfair. Conversely, more equality would itself bring about greater equity, and once major inequalities were removed, individual cases that might require some new inequalities in the name of equity could then be dealt with more easily. (Gans, 1973, p. 77)

The discourses related to equity, equivalence, and equality in Swedish educational policy and practice are linked to the international discourses as presented in, for instance, OECD (2001), Demeuse, Crahay, and Monseur (2001), and Hutmacher, Cochrane, and Bottani (2001). Four basic interpretations of equity can be discerned in these international literatures:[5] Equity of access or equality of opportunity; Equity in terms of learning environment or equality of means; Equity in production or equality of achievement (or results); Equity in using the results of education. Table 1 can be matched to the above interpretation of equity/equivalence.

5. *Equity of access or equality of opportunity:* Do all individuals (or groups of individuals) have the same chance of progressing to a particular level in the education system? *Equity in terms of learning environment or equality of means:* Do all individuals enjoy equivalent learning conditions? This question is generally taken to mean: Do disadvantaged individuals or groups benefit from a learning environment equivalent to advantaged individuals or groups in terms of the level of training of their teachers and other staff, and the quantity and quality of teaching resources and approaches? *Equity in production or equality of achievement (or results):* Do students all master, with the same degree of expertise, skills or knowledge designated as goals of the education system? Most particularly, do individuals from different backgrounds achieve, over the period of education or training, equivalent outcomes? Do all individuals have the same chance of earning the same qualifications when they leave, and can they do so, independent of their circumstances of origin? This concern about equality in achievement is founded on an ideal of corrective justice and is inevitably accompanied by a desire to narrow the gap between high and low performers from the start to the end of their programme of education *Equity in using the results of education:* Once they have left the education system, do individuals or groups of individuals have the same chances of using their acquired knowledge and skills in employment and wider community life? (See Wernersson and Gerrbo, 2013, for empirical based analysis of these terms and line of reasoning compiled by a large number of Swedish researchers).

Evaluation and assessment: Learning outcomes

The new grading system[6] that came into force in 1994 has also been a source of debate about equity in Sweden (Wildt-Persson and Rosengren, 2001). According to this system,

> grades are to be given according to nationally formulated criteria denoting certain qualities of knowledge and skills corresponding to the syllabus for a given subject. The possible grades are: 'pass', 'pass with distinction' and 'pass with special distinction.' When a student in compulsory school fails to meet the criteria of the syllabus, no grade is given; in upper secondary school, the grade 'fail' is given. The criteria, however, are to be based on curricula and syllabi, without reference to the accomplishments of a pupil's peers. This system of grading is referred to as absolute in comparison with its predecessor, a relative system, in which grades were awarded on a Gauss curve denoting the normal performance for a given age group of pupils. The possible grades had been 1,2,3,4 and 5, with 5 denoting the best performance.
> (Wildt-Persson and Rosengren, 2001 p. 303)

Issues of accountability as described above (and coordinated by the National Agency for Education) are exerting some pressures on schools to document not only equal access and equivalent education, but also effectiveness in terms of outcomes. This emphasis on accountability represents a significant shift from issues of access and quality of services. Systems of assessment, monitoring, evaluation, and documentation of effectiveness in terms of learning outcomes and equity remain lacking and need attention (see Peters, 2003, for similar observations on the experiences of the counties of the North).

Sweden has very few examinations, grades, or certificates in comparison with many other countries in Europe. Until recently no grades were awarded for subjects before 8th or 9th grade in the compulsory school. At the end of comprehensive education, tests are mandatory in Swedish, English, and mathematics. However, at upper secondary levels, tests are compulsory in the first course of study in core subjects. Generally, teacher assessments are viewed as having higher validity values than tests (OECD, 2005). This limited use of testing and grading is commendable. However, the culture of testing

---

6. At the time of writing this chapter the grading system was under revision.

has entered the school system and the new government is pushing for more nationally administered tests even at lower grades such as third grade. Currently the assessment system has reached a crossroad concerning whether or not formative-summative assessment should be or could be combined. The tension is fresh at the time of writing this paper. The impact of this decision on inclusive practices is obvious.

The state changed its role from steering by rules to steering by goals and results. This 'Goal-directed management reform' which replaced the '*Regel* (rule) system' confines the state's role to formulating general 'goals' to be achieved by each local government, and local governments have sole responsibility for carrying out the activities. That gives local governments a free hand to achieve the goals through different means, strategies, and 'cultures,' such as consensus, political compromises, and pragmatic solutions embedded in obscure messages. This would appear to usher us into not only variant educational processes, outcomes and procedural/ institutional cultures in variant municipalities, but also into confusion and an erosion in terms of educational visions such as equity and equality of educational opportunities including specific philosophies such as inclusive education, mainstreaming, and 'a school for all.'

Conclusion

While Swedish education policies have a solid history and culture of solidarity, community, and social responsibility, Sweden also has deep cultural values and historical heritage that support self-realisation, individual productivity, competition, and social competence. Democratic values and participation in school and society are essential elements in the Swedish social fabric. Democracy is a cornerstone and founding value of the Swedish curricula and educational legislation. Fostering democracy and raising democratic citisens are principal functions of schools. Equity is also an essential element. Since the early nineteenth century, when elementary school was regarded as a basic school for all, equity has been and is still a central element in the Swedish educational policies, ordinances, and directives.

Equity in the school is guaranteed by the Swedish Education Act. This Act stipulates that consideration must also be afforded to pupils with special needs. Each school has a special responsibility for those pupils who, for different reasons, experience difficulties in attaining the established educational goals (Skollag, 1985:1100; Skollag, 2010:800).

Within the past decades, however, Sweden has undergone a dramatic transformation. The changes are framed within neoliberal philosophies such as devolution (devolvement of responsibilities to local authorities), market solutions, competition, 'effectivity', and standardisation, coupled with a proliferation of individual/parent choices for independent schools, all of which potentially work against the valuing of diversity, equity, and inclusion. Marginalisation and segregation of socially disadvantaged and ethnic minority groups have increased. Result and resource differences have widened among schools and municipalities and among pupils. Swedish efforts in the past to promote equity through a variety of educational policies have been fascinating. Those early educational policies, including the macropolitical agenda focused on the social welfare model, have helped to diminish the effects of differential social, cultural, and economic background on outcomes, and on the development of special educational services as well as inclusive learning settings. This has come under threat. There is still some hope, however, of mitigating the situation through varied social and educational measures combined with an effective monitoring system and a stronger partnership and transparent working relationship between the central and local government systems. Research and follow-up are crucial in this process.

On the positive side, there are still commendable activities and policies in Sweden that promote special education and social inclusion. Acclaiming Sweden's past achievements with regard to special education, inclusion, and equity as well as social justice, an OECD report has stated that 'the tools to achieve equity in Sweden have not been added as corrections to the education system—they are at the heart of the Swedish model.' That model includes:

> A strong, popular, and successful preschool combining care, nurture, and education
> A well-designed, broad and attractive comprehensive curriculum
> An encouraging and non-threatening learning culture for all
> Opportunities for bridges and second chance provision at all levels
> Absence of dead ends
> Equivalence of qualifications
> A long-standing tradition of democratic adult education
> (OECD, 2005, p. 48-49).

There is a cause for concern for how long Sweden's positive reputation, particularly in the areas of integration. 'A school for all,' equity, and social welfare will persist given the drastic changes that have taken place within a short span. Caution is needed if the traditional model that favoured the development of special education and inclusive education in Sweden is to survive.

Author Note

Some sections of this Chapter have been adapted from the author's own texts (Berhanu, 2008, 2009, 2010, 2011, Berhanu and Dyson, 2012; Berhanu, Dyson, and Luciak, 2013).

Chapter 3

Contemporary Swedish society and education: Inequities and challenges

Girma Berhanu

A number of educational reforms have been devised and implemented in Sweden in the 1990s, the consequences of which have yet to be mapped out and evaluated. The reforms revolve around the political management of schools, including a decentralisation of school management that empowers municipalities to be in charge of school affairs within their jurisdiction. Marginalisation and segregation of socially disadvantaged and ethnic minority groups has increased. Resultant resource differences have widened among schools and municipalities and among pupils. The paradox is that all these trends that work against inequity are happening while, at the same time, the rhetoric advocating a school for all and inclusive education have become policy catchwords. As Skidmore (2004) observed, based on his experiences in the U.K., inclusion has become a buzzword in educational discourse. Although inclusion has been adopted as a policy goal, to date much of the Swedish debate has amounted to little more than the trading of abstract ideological positions, which has little connection with the daily realities in schools. In practice, the trend may be described as *excluding the included* (Berhanu, 2010; Harling, 2014).

How are we going to deal with the common frame of reference which has been and is still Sweden's fundamental value, a cornerstone of social justice, in the face of a strong trend towards difference, individuality, competition, and freedom of choice spearheaded by the neoliberal political agenda? What do equity, equivalence, and equality mean in educational practice in the face of shifting political discourse and rhetoric?

In a recent article, Helena Korp (2011) succinctly captured the history, latest trends, and practice of the Swedish education system in particular with regard to tracks for vocational and academic education:

> The Swedish education system has been identified as a model unitary system: one in which students from different social backgrounds and

with different results and interests study together up to the age of 16, and with an upper secondary school catering for all. This unitary system was the result of successive integrative reforms during the course of the twentieth century, which were guided by a strong general commitment to equalising educational opportunity through delaying educational choice and differentiation, and to raising the general level of education in the population. (Lundgren, 1979; Erikson and Jonsson, 1993)

The latest step in this integrative policy was taken in 1994, when vocational upper secondary programs were extended to be the same length as the academic programs (three years) in order to provide all students with a common set of general skills and knowledge as well as basic entrance qualifications for higher studies. The idea was to even out status differences between vocational and academic programs and to promote non-traditional educational choice and lifelong learning (Government proposition 1990/91: 85). However, these intentions have not been realised as it was hoped; differences in educational results between students in vocational and academic programs are still significant as are the transition rates to higher education. Programs that recruit students with predominantly working-class background (especially male students from the working class) lag far behind. The proportion of students that drop out or leave school with incomplete grades is also significant.

The current, recently re-elected, right-wing coalition government blames the unitary model for these problems. In 2008, they proposed a reform that represents a major step away from the unitary upper secondary school system with separate tracks for vocational and academic education (Proposition, 2008/09: 199). The reform, which includes lower entrance demands for vocational programs and only academic programs qualifying for university studies, will be implemented in 2011.
(Korp. 2011, pp. 21/22)

Education as a vehicle for advancing social justice had given way to ideals based upon personal choice and competition and its role was more or less that of a commodity to be traded in the market place. The language was that of the market (e.g., price labels on pupils, effectiveness, target fulfilment) rather than that of the social inclusion of difference and diversity. The education for all movement was transformed to a structure of capitalism in the 1990s and the rhetoric of inclusion became a metaphor for the dominance of human capital, manifested in personal choice, over social justice. Citizenship was replaced by human rights stressing the individualisation of rights and promotion of dominant social interests (Arnesen and Lundahl, 2006; Dahlstedt, 2007; Englund, 2005; Persson and Berhanu, 2005; Wernersson and Gerrbo, 2013 and references therein). In his recent book, Bauman (2004) maintains the view that we have moved away from the social state, which was committed to inclusion, to an exclusionary state committed to criminal justice and penal or crime control following the considerations of criminalising the poor.

Education is a basic right for all citizens. School communities must be inclusive of all children regardless of disability, socioeconomic background, creed, gender, or ethnicity. Schools should also recognise the unique contributions that children with special needs make to community life. With this basic tenet in mind, Sweden has adopted inclusive education as a guiding principle to guarantee equality of access in education to all and also as part of a human rights approach to social relations. The values involved relate to a vision of a whole society, of which education is a part. Issues of social justice, equity, and choice are central to the demands for inclusive education. This vision is concerned with the well-being of all pupils and with making schools welcoming institutions (Skollag, 1985:1100; Skollag, 2010:800)

Research has demonstrated that on a number of levels inclusive education is preferable to segregation. Recent studies have shown that special needs pupils in inclusive settings have made greater academic progress. It is not only that students make good progress in an inclusive setting but also that inclusive education compared with segregated settings results in more positive social relationships. These provide all students with enhanced opportunities to learn from each other's contributions. Studies also demonstrate that inclusive educational arrangements are beneficial for students without disability. There is a strong argument in research literature and policy documents that pupils with special needs should be taught in mainstream settings alongside children of their own age, so far as possible. (see Artiles, Kozleski, Dorn, and Christensen, 2006, for some of the research literature on this topic). However, the situation in Sweden leaves much to be desired. It is particularly worrisome that more and more pupils with special needs, socially disadvantaged students, and pupils with immigrant backgrounds are increasingly marginalised from mainstream settings (e.g., Gustafsson, 2006; Wernersson and Gerrbo, 2013 and numerous references therein).

A number of government financed national-level studies have recently been conducted to assess the nature, intensity, and level of school participation of children and youth with disabilities. The studies are also intended to address societal or organisational issues as well as a relatively neglected research area, individual participation in the classroom. Other studies have aimed at identifying favourable factors and good examples at different educational levels that contribute to participation and equality (Berhanu, 2006, 2011 and references therein).

Unfortunately, there are too few comprehensive studies that map out the level of participation and the extent of inclusiveness of disabled children in the ordinary school system in Sweden. There are too few studies that document educational inclusion in terms of comparing pupils' development in special and regular education. However, the indication (in terms of children's social and cognitive development) is in line with the international studies that show special-needs students educated in regular classes do better academically and socially than students in non-inclusive settings (Baker, Wang, and Walberg, 1995; Peetsma, Vergeer, and Karsten, 2001). Some Swedish studies have shown that inclusion has a positive effect on pupils' self-concept (e.g., Emanuelsson, 2003; Westling Allodi, 2000, 2002). This is in line with international research findings (Baker et al., 1995; Lipsky and Gartner, 1996).

Many of the social and educational changes made in the early 1990s were dramatic. Observers might ask why there occurred such a huge shift from the traditional inclusive, collective frame of reference and social justice towards individual rights, parental choice, and market oriented policies. Signs of such changes could be observed already in late 1980s. But the landmark was the accession to power of the right wing party in 1991 (coalition government headed by conservative Carl Bildt during 1991-94). The country was in deep recession and employment rates fell, followed by a sharp decrease in social expenditures and a move towards further socioeconomic inequalities. The situation abated in the mid-1990s. In consequence of this political change, however, education was increasingly regarded as a private rather than a public good. Rationales for educational attainment changed from emphasis on collective values and social community to a focus on individual rights, academic progress, and choice. A new financial system was introduced that essentially moved resource allocation from the national to the local level, combined with a new type of steering and control mechanism (Arnesen and Lundahl, 2006; Englund, 2005; OECD, 2005; Wildt-Persson and Rosengren, 2001). This was not an accidental phenomenon. It is part and parcel of global phenomena in our late modernity (Bauman, 1992), high modernity (Giddens, 1990), and late capitalism, phenomena that are deeply entrenched with values of effectiveness, competition, standardisation, freedom of choice, and increasingly individualist and elitist culture (also Dahlstedt, 2007).

In particular, the impact of the decentralised educational policy on equity is pervasive. Two studies confirm that:

> educational expenditure per student (measured in terms of money or teacher density) has fallen rather dramatically during the 1990s— followed by a slight increase after the turn of the millennium. According to Björklund et al. (2004), the teacher/student ratio has decreased by 18.7% during the 1990s. Whether this can be directly attributed to the decentralisation or to the impact of the economic downturn of the 1990s remains an open question.
> ([Björklund, Edin, Frederiksson, and Krueger, 2004; Ahlin and Mörk, 2005] as cited in OECD, 2005b, p. 17)

Paradoxically, in the footsteps of the introduction of inclusive education, the number of pupils labelled as having special needs increased dramatically. Teachers found themselves incapable of dealing with pupil diversity in the classroom and meeting individual student needs. This has often been regarded as schools' failure to meet the diverse needs of pupils, manifesting itself in resignation and distress among teachers and pupils not achieving set targets. It is clear that there are differences between municipalities and large differences in the type of provision they have made. Most of the reports on inclusion and equity practices indicate that inclusion is happening. However, up-to-date and reliable time series data and data on the number of pupils who are included in the ordinary classroom or on the occurrence of exclusionary special units (classes) are lacking. Even the definition or construction of special needs is shifting and is fluid. There seems to be no effective mechanism installed to monitor inclusive/exclusionary processes at regional and national levels (see, e.g., Heimdahl Mattsson, 2006; Nilholm, 2006a), which makes it difficult to document equity in education (Persson and Persson, 2012).

On the positive side, there are still commendable activities and policies in Sweden that promote social inclusion. For instance, the system offers a possibility for youngsters who fail at some stage to move on into further education via individual or tailored programs. A generous school system guarantees free education (including free books, meals, and transportation to the nearest school) for all in compulsory education. Free access is also guaranteed in state-run higher education and in municipal adult education (www.skolverket.se). There is, however, a cause for concern for how long Sweden's positive reputation will persist given the drastic changes that have taken place within a short span. Caution is needed if the traditional model is to survive (Berhanu, in press; Lindblad and Lundahl, 2014; OECD, 2005b).

Differentiation, Ex-(in)clusion and categorisation

As mentioned earlier, the post-war Swedish educational policy measures are characterised by comprehensiveness, equity, and *inclusion* as coined in the slogan 'A school for all.' That did not stop differentiation, classification, and categorisation of children or segregated educational placements. In fact, paradoxically, the amount of special education, as Emanuelsson, Haug, and Perrson (2005) noted, has increased steadily. Vast differences have been observed in how pupils with special needs are actually defined and registered in different municipalities. This is, of course, partly the consequence of a decentralised education system that manifests itself in divergent local practices (Göransson, Nilholm, and Karlsson, 2011).

There are different interpretations of the importance of levels, categories, and differentiation, particularly in relation to receiving support or eligibility for special schools or special programmes. Göransson et al. (2011), who conducted a series of studies in this problematic area, concluded:

> Regarding the importance of categories in obtaining support, policy documents do not clearly state that a medical diagnosis is necessary for receiving extra support in regular compulsory schools. Instead, these documents mention educational categories. But medically based categorisations are needed for: (1) determining the eligibility for special schools and special programmes, and (2) receiving support from the National Agency of Special Needs Education and Schools. So, one conclusion of the present analysis is that *national policies and practices leave a lot of room for interpretation at municipal and school levels, which generates vast differences.* Regarding support in municipalities, we can first conclude that there is a need for additional overarching data. But clearly,

there are vast differences between the municipalities. This applies to: (1) issues related to values and goals; (2) the organisation and placement of pupils; and (3) the importance of categorisation. For example, more than 60% of the municipalities indicated that medical diagnosis was of little or no relevance for receiving special support, whereas other municipalities indicated that such a diagnosis was relevant.

(Göransson et al., 2011, p. 550)

The categorical model described in several Swedish reports is the one referred to in the international research (see Mitchell, 2005, 2010) as the within-child model, the medical model, the psych-medical model, the discourse of deviance, the defect model, and the pathological model. In this paradigm, school failure is ascribed to some defect, pathology, or inadequacy located within the student. The relational model is variously referred to as the social model, the socio-political model, the socio-political paradigm, and the deficient system model. In line with this, the term students with difficulties was challenged and began to be replaced by students in difficulties (Emanuelsson, Persson, and Rosenqvist, 2001). Fierce criticism against the traditional and categorical special pedagogical perspective has brought about a paradigmatic shift and a policy deeply ingrained with a relational perspective (which is more environment oriented) as a guiding principle. However, the categorical perspective, which is associated with traditional, segregative, and exclusionary approaches, has not given way to the relational perspective. In fact, the categorical perspective made an upsurge in the 1990s and has since then dominated both special education research and praxis in Sweden. The recent growth in categorisation, identification, and classification within the framework of 'redesigning regular education support' in the ordinary school system in an effort to facilitate inclusion has been criticised by one prominent Swedish professor of special education:

> Once children are identified as 'different' ... they become problematic to mainstream schools and teachers. From within the categorical perspective the process of labelling children as 'having difficulties' has the effect of investing the source of any difficulty or problem within the child. Once this process is complete, then it becomes easier to transfer the responsibility to 'specialists' trained to deal with the 'problems' exhibited by the child.
>
> (Emanuelsson, 2001, p. 135)

One in five compulsory school pupils in Sweden is judged to be in need of special needs education (Asp-Onsjö, 2006). This means that approximately 200,000 pupils in Sweden receive some kind of special educational support during the school year. At the same time, the number of pupils enrolled in special schools for the intellectually disabled (*särskolan*) has increased from .9% to 1.4% during the last 5 to 6 years (Skolverket, 2002a). 'From 1992 to 2001 the number of students registered in schools and classrooms for students with severe learning disabilities ... has increased by 67%.' (Rosenqvist, 2007, p. 67)

In the beginning of the 1990s, a Special Educator Programme was launched that would have significant impact on the praxis of special/inclusive education in Sweden. The programme was in line with a relational or system-based perspective on educational difficulties. In addition to carrying out teaching tasks, Special Educators are expected to supervise, consult, and counsel regular teachers on how to meet the needs of all pupils. In line with this, all teacher trainees study special needs education within the so-called General Field of Education and may also study this field of knowledge within an eligible field of study or in specialisation courses. The programme was well under way until five years ago. Then, a new conservative government came into power and 'discredited' it. In 2008, the government reinstituted a special teacher programme in which trainees will be expected upon completion to work directly with individual pupils. (The programmes are: Postgraduate Diploma in Special Needs Training with specialisation in Intellectual Disabilities; Postgraduate Diploma in Special Needs Training with specialisation in the Development of Language, Writing, and Reading; Postgraduate Diploma in Special Needs Training with specialisation in Mathematical Development). The focus will therefore be the student, not the system, a dramatic shift from the previous perspective. Currently both programmes exist side-by-side, are offered at an advanced level, comprise 90 credits, 1-½ years of full-time study, and qualify graduates for specialist tasks in schools. The new Special Education Teachers should be able to analyse school difficulties at the individual level in different learning environments and be able to *personalise* the school activities (SFS [Swedish Code of Statutes], 2008:132). The vision from the government's side is now that equivalence is strengthened through early identification/detection and interventions for students in need of special education and individualised support measures. From school authorities, the importance of special education expertise of all categories of teachers is strongly emphasised. The tricky question is whether this trend enhances or hinders the inclusive school agenda that the government itself set as a goal. All these changes have implications on the process of differentiation, individualisation, segregation, and categorisation.

In a recent large scale study conducted by Giota and Emanuelsson (2011a, 2011b) on head teachers' judgments of school difficulty, the traditional conception of school difficulties emerged that 'social background and context as well as schoolwork content and teaching habits are judged as key factors behind the students' difficulties and need for special education support. In general, however, school problems and students' difficulties seem still to mainly be seen as caused by student characteristics and disabilities rather than as shortcomings of school and teaching' (see also, Persson, 2008; Giota, et al. 2009).

A similar study conducted by Isaksson, Lindqvist, and Bergström, (2010) with a title *Pupils with special educational needs: A study of the assessments and categorising processes regarding pupils' school difficulties in Sweden* indicated that there were three different patterns or models for identifying and supporting pupils with special educational needs: a pedagogical, a social, or a medical model. Various professionals were involved in different ways in each model. Another finding was that school personnel did not find it easy to sort out and assess 'special educational needs' and that the identification of such needs was conditioned upon resources available for the schools.

> Until the early 1990s, resources to the schools, including resources for special education, were strictly regulated and distributed based on the total number of pupils in the school. Currently, the municipalities distribute economic resources to the schools in terms of unspecified block grants. This system encourages schools to identify as many pupils with special educational needs as possible, since they may then generate additional economic resources for the school (Jóhanneson, Lindblad, and Simola 2002). To the extent that individual shortcomings take center stage at the expense of social and environmental aspects of teaching, a built-in conflict regarding the demand for individual adjustment on the one hand and inclusion within the social group on the other becomes apparent (Telhaug, Mediås, and Aasen 2004; Egelund, Haug, and Persson 2006). (Isaksson et al., 2010, p. 134)

Integration and inclusion have been used interchangeably in Swedish educational discourses. Most people are familiar with the term *integration*. The term *inclusion* has been difficult to translate into Swedish. That has left many with considerable ambiguities about the use of the term. As in many other countries, there is confusion and controversy over the semantics of inclusion. This demonstrates the problematic nature of terms when they cross over into use in other cultures. Many have questioned whether the new terminology means only a linguistic shift or a new agenda. In the first translations into Swedish of UNESCO's Salamanca Statement and Framework for Action, *inclusion* was translated as *integration*.

Although there is still a conceptual problem of clarity, the difference between integration and inclusion has been sorted out and technically defined by the experts (see, e.g., Nilholm, 2006a, 2006b). The message of inclusive education as outlined in the Salamanca statement has now begun to permeate the Swedish language, at least in official documents. The social model of disability and the relational nature of disablement have been officially accepted, which implies that schooling as such 'is more or less disabling or enabling' (Corbett and Slee, 2000, p. 143). This in turn requires schools to restructure and adjust their learning environments, pedagogical methods, and organisational arrangements. Despite or, rather, because of the inflated discourses of inclusion and revamping of inclusion policies, the practice is often short of advocacies. Unless a whole range of activities, including branding activities and attitudes, are brought under control, legislation alone will not bring about the desired results.

Finally a couple of factors that challenge inclusive education and/or the concept of inclusive education in Sweden appear to be, according to Göransson et al. (2011):

> (I) Parents and children increasingly select the schools. (II) Work within the schools is of an increasingly individualised character; it emphasises individuality at the expense of other values such as fellowship, solidarity and equal opportunity. However, the authors concluded that comparing inclusiveness with standards of what inclusive education should be is one thing. Comparing inclusiveness of various education systems is something else. So, we are content that *in an international comparison, Swedish classrooms are largely democratic; most pupils enjoy participating in school activities and influencing them.* (Göransson et al., 2011 p. 551)

Similarly, Tideman (2007) wrote 'although the overall picture in some respects is complicated and problematic, Sweden might still be considered in the vanguard of special education development in inclusive education, thus making the further development of policy and practice intriguing and worthy of attention' (p. 1947).

Ethnic Minority and Socially Disadvantaged Pupils

Sweden explicitly adopts multiculturalism and cultural diversity in an atmosphere of mutual tolerance (LPO 94 [Curriculum for the Compulsory School System, the Preschool Class and the Leisure-Time Centre]); however, terms such as ethnicity, colour, and race remain obscure in official taxonomies, educational policies, and school practices. The complex relationships that exist between ethnicity, socioeconomic factors, special needs education, gender, and so forth have recently become a subject of research interest (Berhanu, 2008; Fridlund, 2011; Rosenqvist, 2007).

A recent report by Gustafsson (2006, p. 93) concludes that during 1992-2000 a consistent and linear increase occurred in school segregation in relation to immigration background, educational background, and grades. A national tracking system enables observation of variable achievement among groups of students. Students with foreign backgrounds receive lower average grades than do their peers, fewer qualify for higher education, and they have a higher dropout rate from upper-secondary education. Some recent Swedish studies indicate over-representation of immigrant students and socially disadvantaged students out of all proportion to their numbers in special schools and classes (Bel Habib, 2001; Hahne Lundström, 2001; Skolverket, 2000). These students were categorised in diffused, vague, symptom-based and pedagogical-related terms such as *concentration and behavioural problems, speech and language difficulties, unspecified 'poor talent,'* or *developmental retardation*. However, extensive and longitudinal studies have yet to be carried out in this specific problem area (see Rosenqvist, 2007) and there is a need for a coherent cumulative body of disproportionality research.

A recent literature review (Berhanu, 2008; Berhanu and Dyson, 2012), demonstrates that the problem is related to, among other reasons, unreliable assessment procedures and criteria for referral and placement; lack of culturally sensitive diagnostic tools; the static nature of tests, including embedded cultural bias; sociocultural problems, family factors, and language problems; lack of parental participation in decision-making; power differentials between parents and school authorities; institutional intransigence and prejudices; and large resource inequalities that run along lines of ethnicity and class.

Disproportionality is a significant phenomenon in all of the education systems for which good evidence is available. This is the case regardless of the demographics of the school population or the structures and procedures of the special education system. Disproportionality is not confined to countries (such as the German-speaking ones) that have historically had high levels of segregation. On the contrary, education systems (such as those in Scandinavian countries) that are relatively inclusive place a high value on equitable provision and outcomes, and are located in relatively equal societies, also display disproportionality. So too do special education systems (such as those of the UK) that offer additional provision to children on the basis of educational 'need' without requiring a diagnosis of disability (Berhanu and Dyson, 2012; see also Dyson and Gallannaugh, 2008).

Disproportionality is most marked in those categories of special education that lack precise diagnostic criteria. In practice, this means those that relate to general learning or social difficulties rather than to physical, sensory, or intellectual impairment. One interpretation of this is that the prejudices of teachers and administrators operate unchecked by objective criteria during the identification and assessment process; this then results in negative interpretations of over-represented groups' characteristics and behaviours. However, it is notable that these groups also tend to do poorly in regular education systems and experience the greatest socioeconomic disadvantages. It is equally plausible, therefore, that over-representation reflects accurately the actual difficulties these groups experience in education systems. These difficulties may in turn be attributable to the marginalised social status of these groups, which education systems fail to address, but for which they are by no means entirely to blame. Overall, there is no one group that is particularly at risk of over-representation in special education (or exclusion from access to its resources), and there is no single explanation for disproportionality. However, although multiple explanations are needed in order to cover the multiple forms of disproportionality in Europe in general and in Sweden in particular, a common theme is that those groups that are most at risk of wider social and educational marginalisation tend also to be most at risk of disproportional representation (usually, over-representation) in special education. Disproportionality can therefore be regarded as a product of social marginality rather than as a product of the structures and procedures of special education systems (Berhanu, Dyson and Luciak, 2013).

It is obvious that the education system has come under serious pressure during the past two decades due to massive migration. This exogenous shock has changed the ethnic landscape and composition dramatically and has ushered Sweden into an era of multiculturalism and globalisation. On the negative side, this rapid demographic change has also brought with it ethnic segregation and inequalities, particularly in large cities, on top of already existing inequalities between municipalities and social groups due to decentralisation and competition. That presents a major challenge to policymakers in terms of social integration generally, and educational inclusion specifically unless *targeted positive discriminatory* measures are put in place. Such measures, however, are anathema to Swedish policy principles (OECD, 2005).

A report by Gustafsson (2006, p. 93) concludes that during 1992-2000 a consistent and linear increase occurred in school segregation in relation to immigration background, educational background, and grades. A national tracking system enables observation of variable achievement among groups of students. Students with foreign backgrounds receive lower average grades than do their peers, fewer qualify for higher education, and they have a higher dropout rate from upper-secondary education. There are also differences in achievement between girls and boys. Girls receive higher average grades in the majority of all subjects in compulsory and upper-secondary school (OECD, 2005, cited in Wildt-Persson and Rosengren, 2001, p. 306). Results from national examinations in compulsory and upper-secondary schools demonstrate this difference in the subjects of Swedish and, to some extent, English, but show no difference in results in mathematics (ibid).

It is presumed, on the basis of a large number of indicators, that over the next decade Swedish society will become increasingly multi-ethnic and multilingual, and the number of disadvantaged children will substantially increase. An estimated twenty per cent of the Swedish population has an immigrant background. It is expected that the demographic landscape in the year 2020 is that thirty per cent of all working age individuals in Sweden will have had their roots outside of Sweden (Leijon and Omanovic, 2001; Statistics Sweden, 2009). Many students are at greater risk of needing special education services when they are poor or of a minority race or language. The need for addressing and reviewing scientific and methodological problems explaining over-representation and educational outcome differences related to race, ethnicity, and socioeconomic status becomes imperative.

While there is no conclusive evidence to suggest that over-representation of minority pupils or pupils with immigrant background or socially disadvantaged groups of students in special educational placements is nationwide, the phenomenon can be identified in large cities where there are concentrations of immigrants. The over-representation is not a new phenomenon. What is new is that new forms of exclusionary measures are taking place while the force of rhetoric toward inclusive measures is gaining substantial momentum in the pedagogical discourse. This Swedish experience is exactly similar to the practices in England, as captured in the words of Florian and Rouse (2001):

> Whilst the government calls for more inclusion and a greater recognition of diversity, it continues to promote social and educational policies that are not supportive of the development of inclusive schools. Indeed, many of the existing market place reforms ignore diversity and stress priorities that make it hard for schools to accept children who will not help them to meet their academic targets.   (Florian and Rouse, 2001, p. 400)

The analysis both from England and Sweden (in this book) indicates how the structure of schools as organisations creates special educational needs rather than differences or diversity between individual pupils. The lack of holistic, contextual, and ecological perspectives is visible because the measures used to send these children to special schools emerge from being entirely concerned only with pupils' cognitive, emotional, and pathological problems. To rectify this misguided practice, we need to, as Artiles (2003) correctly argued, transcend the traditional individualistic perspective and infuse a social justice dimension so that the improvement of educational experiences and life opportunities for historically marginalised students is of central importance (pp. 194-95). Future studies in Sweden should systematically evaluate the following area of problem or research questions (see Losen and Orfield, 2002):

> What is the chain of events that sets certain students, from various backgrounds, in certain school districts, on the road to special education placement or special schools?
> Is there one or many patterns?
> By what criteria do those responsible for special education placements evaluate students for these programs? (Rosenqvist, 2007)
> How is this cycle initiated and how can it be stopped?

What are the students actually like?
What are the criteria for referral and special educational placements?
What is the parental role or role of culture in this process, and how do parents perceive their responsibility?
To what extent do social factors override (special) educational efforts intended to rectify school failures?

There are some signs that at least the school authorities are aware of the problem. The public media and several researchers have dealt with the phenomenon of disproportionality, and that has led to increased awareness of the problem. Data from a recent study do not support the existence of disproportionality at a national level, although it does appear to be concentrated in large cities. The distribution of disproportionality suggests the dubious nature of the diagnostic procedure and the assessment culture (Berhanu et al. 2013; Rosenqvist, 2007).

The road forward

The fragmentation of educational policymaking that we have witnessed in the past two decades has negatively affected in particular already vulnerable groups such as the disabled, ethnic minority students, and socially disadvantaged segments of the population. On the basis of a large number of indicators, we can presume that over the next decade Swedish society will become increasingly multi-ethnic and multilingual, and the number of disadvantaged children will increase substantially. An estimated twenty per cent of the Swedish population comes from an immigrant background. As stated earlier, it is predicted that in the demographic landscape in the year 2020 some thirty per cent of all working age individuals in Sweden will have had their roots outside of Sweden. (Leijon and Omanovic, 2001; Statistics Sweden, 2004).

The challenge in Sweden is to meet these changes and still guarantee equivalence in the education system. Sweden has developed a broad follow-up system and quality indicators in order to monitor changes within the system. However, the indicator systems do not specifically show the nature, extent, and processes of inclusive and exclusionary processes within the regular system. Since a return to the former centralised management system is unlikely, constant flow of monitoring, evaluation, and inspection, and a stronger partnership between the central system and the local level, and even parents and schools, as well as between municipalities, must be established in order to mitigate variance and inequalities. Stronger central government authority over educational priority funding will be critical for at-risk groups, either in the form of targeted central budgets, or in terms of regulatory power over municipal education outlays (OECD, 2005).

Responses and challenges to inclusive education in general and the quality and extent of special education services are varied and complex. Sweden's cultural and political heritage could have been ideal to fully implement inclusive education as envisaged in *The Salamanca statement and framework for action* (UNESCO, 1994). However, the new political movements and policies that dominate the Swedish educational system have created contradictory and conflicting realities that work not only against fundamental equity issues but also against the long Swedish tradition of universalism, comprehensiveness and egalitarianism (e.g., Beach and Dovemark, 2007; Beach and Sernhede, 2011; Korp. 2006, 2011).

Apart from the obvious policy shifts that brought about contradictions in the education system, the very nature of our humanity and social activities also are filled with some dilemmas and contradictions. However, policies and practices can either strengthen or weaken the complexities emanating from this. The dilemmas revolve around individually and collectively based ideas of democracy and categorisation (social stigmatisation/segmentation) versus individuality, utility and culture, the public and personal domains, economy and welfare, individual agency versus collective action, autonomy, and communitarianism. This has definitely shaped the policy and services for special needs pupils and the general structure of special education.

A number of government funded studies have been conducted recently to investigate the participation and inclusion of disabled pupils at different levels of the education system, particularly at individual, classroom, and school levels, and conferences are being held linked to these studies. There is therefore some hope that the studies will reveal micro—and meso-level activities that hinder or enhance full participation of students with special needs and *problematise* further real-world dilemmas, including the growing culture of diagnosis. Significant factors that may facilitate physical, social, and curricular inclusion have been identified: competent personnel, differentiation in the curriculum, favourable assessment methods, collaboration between the teaching staff, class size, involvement by school leadership, continuous and intensive in-service staff training, partnership with parents, and economic factors. Moreover, the concept of participation has to be further *problematised*. It is one of the least empirically defined core concepts and is broadly misconceived. It is complex, multidimensional, subjective, and context-bound.

Author Note:

Some sections of this chapter have been adapted from the author's own texts (Berhanu, 2008, 2009, 2011; 2012; Berhanu, Dyson, and Luciak, 2013; Berhanu, in press).

Chapter 4

English society and education: Historical and contemporary inequalities and challenges

Kirstin Kerr

The purpose of this chapter is to provide an overview of historical and contemporary inequalities in England and the challenges these present. It discusses how English society has been—and continues to be—shaped by patterns of socio-economic inequality. It will also consider the somewhat contradictory position the English education system occupies in relation to these patterns, simultaneously serving to replicate inequalities while also acting as a policy vehicle for intervening in these. Throughout the chapter, it will be argued that this situation can perhaps best be understood in terms of the English education system's continual efforts to reconcile three ongoing and oftentimes competing priorities. The first of these is to ensure the education system develops the skills and knowledge needed to support economic growth—or in other words, to meet the human capital needs of the economy. A second is to ensure that in doing so, the education system is of high quality—an aim often referred to as creating an 'excellent' education system. A third is to ensure that in meeting these aims, the education system's processes and outcomes do not systemically advantage some groups over others, leading to the replication of wider inequalities. A challenge at the core of the English education system is to find ways of both realising and balancing these priorities. This challenge is made more difficult still by the lack of a consistent, overarching view about the wider societal purposes of education. As the chapter will demonstrate, there has been remarkably little public- or policy-oriented debate about what the English education system should ultimately be seeking to achieve.

In discussing these issues, the chapter focuses on developments since the 1940s, as this decade marks an important juncture in English society. During the 1940s, the foundations of the modern English welfare state were laid, and through the 1944 Education Act, the basis for the current national education system was created. This established free secondary education from ages 11-15 (raised to 16 in 1972) and set out to cater equally for all children across age, aptitude and ability. Since 1944, as successive governments have sought to balance competing priorities, the English education system has also been characterised by continual and sometimes rapid reforms. For example, since free secondary education was introduced, this has been organised in many different ways. In the 1950s, a selective system dominated which sorted pupils into different types of schools (grammar, technical and secondary modern) intended to cater for pupils of different aptitudes and abilities. The 1960s saw a shift to a largely non-selective 'comprehensive' system of secondary education, and since the 1980s, there have been many efforts to diversify 'comprehensive' schools, for instance, by allowing schools to pursue different subject specialisms.

These educational reforms must also be considered in the light of the UK's changing economic situation. In the early 1950s, low-skilled manual labour in manufacturing and heavy industry made up about forty per cent of total employment, with this falling to approximately eight per cent by 2012 (Philpott, 2012). This decline has been matched by a growth in service industries, and since the 1980s in particular, there has been 'a rise in skilled employment for people performing managerial, professional and technical jobs—so-called knowledge workers ... and a rise in essentially low-skilled employment performed by a group classified as 'personal services' and 'sales and customer services' workers' (Philpott, 2012, p. 3). As this suggests, the kinds of human capital required of young people entering the labour market have changed considerably since free secondary schooling was introduced.

Although the picture presented above is highly simplified, it nonetheless indicates the shifting nature of England's socio-economic context, and the continual rebalancing of competing priorities within its education system, both of which are central to the story of inequalities in English society and education. But there are also two constant factors which underpin this story and which must be surfaced in addition. One is the highly unequal nature of English society. For instance, recent analyses from the OECD reportedly place the UK—of which England is the largest constituent country—as having the fourth highest level of inequality in the OECD after Mexico, the US and Israel (Hargreaves, 2013), and as being well above OECD norms in terms of the gap between rich and poor, earnings inequality, income poverty, and the lack of social mobility. Further to this, Dorling suggests that in recent years inequalities in the UK have actually increased, and in one interview he argued that: 'in countries like Britain, people last lived lives as unequal as today, as measured by wage inequality, in 1854, when Charles Dickens was writing Hard Times' (O'Hara, 2010).

The other constant, as touched on earlier, is the political belief that educational reforms can be used to create a more equitable society. For instance, Michael Gove, Secretary of State for Education from 2010-2014, argued that 'schools should be engines of social mobility, helping children to overcome the accidents of birth and background to achieve much more than they may ever have imagined' (Gove, 2011). Ever since the post of minister for education was created by the 1944 Education Act, it is essentially this same sentiment which ministers have used to justify their proposed reforms, even when these have differed markedly. For example, in the foreword to the report *Half our future* (Central Advisory Council for Education [England], 1963) which was influential in the shift towards comprehensive secondary schooling, the then Secretary of State for Education argued it was essential for all children to have the opportunity to achieve to their full potential—a stance all subsequent Secretaries of State would doubtless endorse.

Drawing the discussion together in a simple summary, the English context is highly unequal and the English education system is seen as one means of addressing inequality. To do so, it must find ways to create a system which is at once excellent, equitable, and able to service the economy, interpreting these priorities within the socio-economic context of the time. The rest of this chapter is therefore devoted to exploring these issues in greater depth, and will be divided into three sections as follows. Firstly, it will provide a detailed assessment of patterns of inequality in English society, and specifically in relation to educational attainment. Secondly, it will outline the history of education reforms in England, and the ways in which these have sought to balance concerns about excellence, equity and human capital. Thirdly, it will briefly consider contemporary developments and challenges in the English education system.

Historical and contemporary inequalities in England

Societal inequalities

Historically, England has been a deeply unequal society and in many respects remains so today. As the Equalities and Human Rights Commission's (EHRC) report, titled *How fair is Britain?* states:

> all too many of us remain trapped by the accident of our births, our destinies far too likely to be determined by our sex or race ... far too many

of us are still born into families without the material or social capital to give us the right start in life ... we are not yet a fair society.

(EHRC, 2011, p. 7)

The EHRC analysed inequalities in Britain in relation to age, disability, gender, race and ethnicity, religion or belief, and sexual orientation, across the following domains: life, legal security, physical security, health, education, employment, standard of living, care and support, power and voice. While noting areas in which progress has been made over time—for instance, in terms of real-term life expectancy, income levels, educational attainment, women's employment rates, and equalities legislation—it found less evidence to suggest any pronounced narrowing of the gap in outcomes between more and less advantaged groups. Highlighting the unequal nature of contemporary Britain, it found that:

> Educational outcomes differ markedly by gender, socio-economic group, ethnicity and disability.
> 'Income poverty remains persistent for some groups such as women with children, ethnic minority groups and families with disabled members' (EHRC, 2011, p. 651).
> 'The experience of poverty is closely related to poorer outcomes in terms of living conditions, overcrowding, crime in the neighbourhood and destitution—leading to poor health and low life expectancy' (EHRC, 2011, p. 652).

A particularly striking feature of the report's analysis is that across all the population groups and domains it examines, poverty, as well as being a root cause of inequalities in itself, is extremely powerful in exacerbating other forms of disadvantage. This interaction creates two particularly influential dynamics within English society. The first is longitudinal, relating to disadvantage as it is experienced across the life course. As Hills et al. (2010) note, differences between more and less advantaged groups tend to:

> cumulate across the life cycle, especially those related to people's socio-economic background. We see this before children enter school, through the school years, through entry into the labour market, and on to retirement, wealth and resources for retirement, and mortality rates in later life. Economic advantage and disadvantage reinforce themselves across the life cycle, and often on to the next generation.

(Hills et al., 2010, p. 1)

The second is spatial, drawing attention to the fact that multiple disadvantages tend to be found together in geographical concentrations, creating neighbourhoods which can, themselves, be considered 'disadvantaged'. Such neighbourhoods are often characterised overall by poor outcomes, including, for instance, high levels of unemployment, ill health, and teenage pregnancy. It also 'seems likely that the concentration of disadvantage in particular places deepens the effects of the problems that people living in these areas face' (Dyson et al., 2011, p. 74). Such neighbourhoods are a particularly noticeable characteristic of urban contexts, where the processes of industrialisation—and more recently, de-industrialisation—have created concentrations of sustained disadvantage.

How to tackle such complex and sustained patterns of inequality has long been a concern of local and national policy makers. During World War II, a high degree of social and political consensus emerged around the state's responsibility to mitigate unacceptably high levels of disadvantage in the general population. In 1942, in a landmark report, William Beveridge, a senior civil servant, set out what he saw as the five 'giant evils' that plagued society and the inequalities of which they were indicative. These were: Disease—indicating the need for equal access to health care; Want—the need for equal access to a basic income; Ignorance—the need for equal access to educational opportunity; Squalor—the need for equal access to adequate housing; and Idleness—the need for equal access to gainful employment. This report, known as the Beveridge Report, (Beveridge, 1942), was rapidly followed by legislation introducing free access to education and health care, state pensions, and housing, unemployment and sickness benefits. Such measures were intended both to create a minimum floor beneath which no-one should fall, while also creating a platform from which people could better themselves if they had the ability to do so—or to use a more contemporary term, to achieve social mobility.

This universally progressive approach, of making greatest provision for those most in need, has since become a central tenet of many of the UK government's efforts to address inequalities. For instance, between 2010-2014, the Conservative-Liberal Democrat Coalition government introduced a national framework for promoting social justice for families experiencing multiple disadvantages and a national strategy for reducing child poverty with the aim of ending child poverty in the UK by 2020 (DWP and DfE 2014). Indeed, David Cameron, Prime Minister since 2010, has committed himself to creating a 'classless society' in which 'it should make 'no difference' to people's life chances whether 'you are from the north or in the south, whether you're black or you're white, a man or a woman, the school you went to, the background you have, who your parents were' (cited Barnes, 2013).

It is notable that, Cameron, like many before him, has equated the creation of a more equitable society with the creation of a 'classless society'; as Simon (1991, p. 35) notes, the landmark welfare reforms of the 1940s were an explicit attempt to move away from the 'stagnant, class-ridden depressing society of the 1930s'. Although the notion of social class is often less explicitly acknowledged in contemporary English society, it is still important in exploring inequalities, as it links inequalities relating to economic circumstances to a much wider set of social factors. For instance, in the Great British Class Survey (GBCS), Savage (2013) defines social class as not only inextricably associated with income, but also with 'social capital (the number, and also the status of people one knows), and cultural capital (the extent and nature of cultural interests and activities)'. The GBCS also found that the idea of social class is still highly pertinent to contemporary British society, with Savage concluding that:

> the British class system is becoming more polarised between a prosperous elite and a poor 'precariat' ['precarious proletariat'], and also that what used to be termed the middle and working classes seem to be splintering into social classes with systematically differing amounts of cultural and social capital. The British class system is hence fracturing horizontally, at the same time that social divisions are becoming more entrenched. This is a sobering picture which demonstrates that class divisions remain very powerful—even if they have changed in their nature.   (Savage, 2013)

Notably, this 'splintering' is also taking place in a society where the shift from a manufacturing to a service economy means that traditional forms of 'working class' employment are typically no longer available. This suggests that the poor 'precariat' are not only at risk of increasing social exclusion, but also of increasing economic exclusion. It also has significant implications for the education system. It suggests the need for a system which can not only develop the human capitals to connect the 'precariat' to current and future employment opportunities, but which also ensures that they are, to use Fraser's term (as discussed in Chapter 2) 'recognised' within the system.

Educational inequalities

Patterns of inequality in the English education system do much to mirror those seen within English society more broadly; as Perry and Francis (2010, p. 2) note 'social class remains the strongest predictor of educational achievement in the UK, where the social class gap for educational achievement is one of the most significant in the developed world'. Many analyses have used receipt of Free School Meals (FSM)—state-funded meals for pupils from low income families—as the best available indicator of a child's socio-economic background, and therefore as a means of identifying educational inequalities relating to class background. For instance, data published by the Department for Education (DfE, 2014a) reports GCSE (General Certificate of Secondary Education) examination results for FSM pupils compared to all other pupils. It shows that although gaps in attainment between these groups have narrowed by small amounts in recent years, in the 2012-2013 academic year only 38.7 per cent of FSM pupils achieved five or more higher GCSE grades (A*-C), compared to 65.3 per cent of all other pupils. Furthermore, as seen in the previous section, economic disadvantage again interacts strongly with a range of other variables. For example, when combining gender, ethnicity and FSM, Hills et al. (2010) found that:

> By age 16 ... White British, Black Caribbean and mixed White and Black Caribbean boys receiving Free School Meals have the lowest average assessment of any group identified by gender, ethnicity and Free School Meals status, apart from Gypsy and Traveller children
>
> (Hills et al., 2010, p. 23)

It is also worth citing at some length Hills et al.'s analyses of patterns of educational inequality over the course of children's school careers:

> ... social background really matters. There are significant differences in 'school readiness' before and when children reach school by parental income and mother's education ... every extra £100 per month in income when children were small was associated with a difference equivalent to a month's development. Rather than being fixed at birth, these differences widen through childhood. For recently born children a similar process seems at work to that already observed in the 1970s. Children with a higher social class background who start with a low assessment of

relative cognitive ability when young eventually overtake those with a lower social class background who were initially assessed as having high ability. Looking from age 3 to age 14, differences in assessment related to family income, father's occupation and mother's education widen at each stage (although they then narrow slightly between 14 and 16), in contrast to differences related to ethnicity, which narrow or even reverse during childhood. (Hills et al., 2010, 22)

Patterns of educational inequality also reflect wider spatial patterns of inequality. Poor educational outcomes are typically concentrated in those places where other forms of disadvantage are concentrated. Schools in such areas are, in turn, likely to attract pupil populations with high levels of disadvantage, which may, in turn, act to depress institutional and individual levels of attainment. It seems highly likely that poor educational outcomes in these places are strongly related to children's family, community and social backgrounds—for instance, in the ways in which their families engage (or fail to engage) with learning (Desforges and Abouchaar, 2003), or in the attitudes and expectations that are typical for their parents and peers (Goodman and Gregg, 2010), or in the physical and psychological constraints that are created by where they live (Green and White, 2007; Kintrea et al., 2008), and in the access children and families have to the sorts of cultural and social capital which could support their schooling (Teese and Polesel, 2003). The danger is that, rather than offering a route to social mobility, the education system reproduces inequality, particularly for learners with less access to the forms of social and cultural capital favoured by the system (Reay, 2006).

Education policy makers have, therefore, understandably been preoccupied with finding ways to intervene effectively in the relationship between education and disadvantage and the challenges this presents. The following section considers how some of the most significant reforms in English education since the 1944 Education Reform Act have sought to achieve this.

An overview of education reforms in England

Given the English education system's near constant process of reform, it is possible only to present a brief and somewhat selective overview in this chapter. As such, a chronological account is offered which takes the 1944 Education Act as its starting point and focuses on secondary education, where efforts to balance quality, equity, and human capital needs have been of particular concern.

As noted in the chapter's introduction, the 1944 Education Act was important in its intention to create an education system which would cater equally for children of all ages, abilities and aptitudes. However, it said little about what the education system needed to achieve this should look like, either in terms of curricula and pedagogy, or the organisation and management of schools, seeing these as matters for Local Education Authorities (LEAs) and schools to determine. At secondary level, the arrangement which emerged nationally took the form of a tripartite system. This consisted of grammar schools—intended to cater for those most suited to academic study; technical schools—intended to cater for those with an aptitude for sciences, engineering, and related fields; and secondary modern schools—intended to cater for pupils with a more vocational orientation. This arrangement was premised partly on a belief that whether children were academically-, technically-, or practically-minded could be identified using intelligence tests administered in the last year of primary schooling. It also, to some extent, mirrored the economy of the time, creating pathways to higher education and professional employment through grammar schooling, to skilled work in industry through technical education, and to a wide range of lower-skilled positions in industry and manufacturing in particular, through secondary modern education.

Supporters of the tripartite system saw this as a means of giving all pupils equal opportunities to develop their particular talents and to access employment, assuming parity of esteem between different types of school. More specifically, they also saw it as creating an opportunity for social mobility by allowing working class pupils to access grammar (and to a lesser extent, technical) schools. However, as it became embedded, this system also became more controversial from an equity perspective. Only small numbers of technical schools were actually established, catering for about four per cent of pupils, while grammar schools catered for around twenty per cent, and secondary modern schools for around seventy-five per cent (Tomlinson, 1991). There was, moreover, strong evidence of social stratification across school types; as Dale and Ozga (cited Tomlinson, 1991, p. 105) argue, 'for all the talk of 'parity of esteem' [the tripartite system] reflected divisions of class and subject status'. For instance, working class children were found to be under represented in grammar schools, even though the most academically able pupils in secondary modern schools were found to be equal to their grammar school counterparts (Central Advisory Council for Education [England], 1963).

Reflecting a growing feeling that the tripartite system was not only failing to provide equality of opportunity, but was disadvantaging the majority of pupils, a government report—known as the Newsom Report—was commissioned 'to consider the education between the ages of 13 and 16 of pupils of average or less than average ability' (Central Advisory Council for Education [England], 1963). Notably, while supporters of the tripartite system had assumed that children from all social backgrounds would be equally able to access all types of schools, the Newsom Report acknowledged that children enter the school system from very unequal contexts and made the link between poor education outcomes and social background. For instance, it stated that 'linguistic inadequacy [and] disadvantages in social and physical background ... may ... partly account for the undue proportion of children from working-class backgrounds who appear as below-average' (Central Advisory Council for Education [England], 1963, pp. 15-16). In its recommendations, the Report emphasised the need for high quality teaching and for a suitably broad and challenging curriculum which also had vocational relevance and links to employment. In addition, it recommended that: 'a programme of research in teaching techniques designed, particularly, to help pupils whose abilities are artificially depressed by environmental and linguistic handicaps should be instituted by the Ministry' and that 'an interdepartmental working party should be set up to deal with the general social problems, including education, in slum areas' (Central Advisory Council for Education [England], 1963, p. xvi).

The Newsom Report was also associated with a growing movement to restructure the education system and to create non-selective, comprehensive secondary schools which would cater equally for all pupils (DfES, 1965)—though when asked by government to draw up plans for moving to a comprehensive system, a small number of LEAs chose to retain grammar schools. Those in favour of comprehensive reform argued that it would remove the structural inequalities created by the tripartite system by establishing a system where all learners, regardless of their social backgrounds, would have the same type of schooling. In short, there would, in principle, be equality of opportunity within the system.

As comprehensive education became established, its promise of equality of opportunity encountered considerable challenges. A central difficulty arose from the fact that although, by restructuring the system, comprehensive schools removed the social hierarchy of school types, the neighbourhoods they served were still highly unequal, with schools in disadvantaged urban areas in particular struggling to achieve good outcomes. Thus, even if not formally selective, the system nonetheless remained socially stratified, reflecting the spatial distribution of wider disadvantages.

The significance of the challenge this posed is succinctly captured by Jackson (2007) in his commentary on Anthony Crosland, Secretary of State for Education from 1965-1967:

> [Crosland] argued that if the aspiration of 'equality of opportunity' was to be taken seriously, as the ambition to neutralise the impact of the individual's social class background upon their life chances, then it would in fact require a significant reduction in inequality of condition. As long as privileged individuals were capable of greatly advantaging their children in terms of education, financial assets and cultural resources, equality of opportunity would remain a sham. (Jackson, 2007, p. 219)

Some small scale efforts were put in place to mediate the inequalities children from disadvantaged backgrounds experienced outside school, which originated in their family and community contexts. These included Educational Priority Areas (EPAs) which provided small amounts of funding for local action research projects in disadvantaged areas—but which proved both an ineffective and insufficient mechanism to interrupt the link between education, disadvantage and place (Smith, 1987). Furthermore, marked disparities were found in the educational provision made by different LEAs, and at school-level, in the curricula and teaching approaches adopted. This variation meant that there were still stark inequalities in learners' experiences of education, as well as in their education outcomes. In short, the structural reform of the system, coupled with small-scale interventions like EPAs, was found not to be enough to overcome the systematic disadvantages experienced by the least advantaged pupils.

By the mid-1970s, this situation—coupled with the pressures created by rapid industrial decline—had resulted in sustained attacks on the comprehensive ideal. These focused on concerns about declining educational standards, poor teaching, irrelevant curricula and poor preparation for employment (see Cox and Boyson, 1975, 1977). In his 1976 Ruskin College speech, the then Prime Minister James Callaghan, explicitly engaged with these issues. He argued that it was unacceptable that 'for many years the accent was simply on fitting a so-called inferior group of children with just enough learning to earn their living in the factory', and set out a series of priorities for educational reform. He stated:

The goals of our education ... are clear enough. They are to equip children to the best of their ability for a lively, constructive, place in society, and also to fit them to do a job of work ... There is no virtue in producing socially well-adjusted members of society who are unemployed because they do not have the skills ... ... This means requiring certain basic knowledge and skills and reasoning ability. It means developing lively inquiring minds and an appetite for further knowledge ... It means mitigating as far as possible the disadvantages that may be suffered through poor home conditions or physical or mental handicap.   (Callaghan, 1976)

This marked the beginnings of a shift to establish central control over the English education system, with this being seen as a means to: bring about national curriculum reform and ensure access to a core curriculum for all; monitor standards of performance and the use of resources nationally; ensure the quality of teaching; and develop the human capital needed to strengthen the economy.

This gradual shift in power—from LEAs and schools, to central government—laid the foundations for the 1988 Education Reform Act (ERA), (HM Government, 1988), which, in a marked departure from previous arrangements, sought explicitly to apply market place principles to the English education system. Central to this was the introduction of a government-prescribed National Curriculum, with a linked system of Standard Attainment Tests to be administered nationally at ages 7, 11 and 14, with GCSEs (General Certificate of Secondary Education) being introduced at age 16. As Barber (1994, p. 356) argues, 'through the National Curriculum and Assessment [the ERA] provided for accountability: they would provide a standard measure against which competing schools could be compared.' Following this, a national system for inspecting schools was established in 1992 through the creation of the Office for Standards in Education (Ofsted). As a quasi-government body, Ofsted was positioned to ensure that schools were implementing centrally-determined reforms and achieving centrally-determined standards, and to apply punitive sanctions when this was not the case.

A further important shift was the introduction of open school enrolment. This effectively removed the previous system of school catchment areas which allocated children a place at their local school, and instead enabled parents to choose (high attaining) schools for their children. It also changed the way in which funding was distributed to schools, with funds being allocated per pupil and then managed by schools. For children in disadvantaged areas, open enrolment was seen as a mechanism to enable them to 'escape' from poor attaining local schools and to attend higher attaining schools in other areas. At a system level, by placing schools in active competition for pupils, policy makers also assumed that open enrolment would drive up standards across the system, supporting the creation of an education system which was excellent overall. To ensure that LEA arrangements did not prevent schools from competing effectively for pupils, schools were also given the option to opt-out of LEA management and to become 'grant maintained', with this allowing them greater freedoms with regard to their financial and staffing arrangements. Some limited efforts were also made to introduce greater diversity into the market through the creation of a small number of City Technology Colleges—schools specialising either in technology or modern languages.

Since the ERA, this explicit application of market place principles to the state education system has cast efforts to balance the competing demands of excellence, equity, and human capital in stark relief. A good illustration of this is provided by the multi-stranded policy approach pursued by the successive Labour governments which held office from 1997-2010. Firstly, throughout their time in office, these Labour governments fostered a culture of 'performativity' (Broadfoot, 2001), in which schools were held individually, directly, and publicly to account for their attainment. Among the accountability measures introduced was the publication of school league tables, intended to support parents to choose higher attaining schools for their children. Further to this, and particularly in their early period in office, Labour governments also sought to identify generalised models of 'good practice' which could benefit all schools' performances, and targeted interventions which would improve the performance of particular underachieving groups. For instance, national models for teaching literacy and numeracy in primary schools were introduced in an effort to ensure that all schools—regardless of the neighbourhoods they served—would provide the same quality of teaching and learning in these subjects. Effectively, this allowed central government to intervene directly, not just at school level, but also at classroom level, and to ensure that nationally-determined criteria for excellent teaching and learning, and leadership and management practices, were being met.

These Labour governments also introduced further measures to allow schools greater formal freedoms from local management arrangements, again so that they could pursue their self-improvement. For example, schools were able to apply for 'foundation status' which allowed them to become their own admissions authority and to take ownership of their own land and assets. During the 2000s, the first academies were also established in disadvantaged areas—these being schools which, freed from local authority control and managed by sponsoring bodies, were expected to be able to develop 'innovative responses' to 'historic under-performance' (NRU, 2003).

To a large extent this first strand of policy, with its emphasis on school improvement, attributed the poor educational outcomes experienced by many of those living in disadvantaged neighbourhoods primarily to failings in the schools which served them. It assumed that, through internal reforms, schools should be largely able to compensate for the disadvantages experienced by their pupils, and that schools in disadvantaged areas would simply have to work harder than their more advantaged counterparts to achieve the same standards (Ofsted, 2000). Over Labour's time in office, this stance did become more tempered, with, for example, a growing recognition that national models of good practice may need to be locally tailored for schools serving challenging neighbourhood contexts, and indeed, that these schools might need to pursue different strategies in order to raise attainment (Thrupp and Lupton, 2006). Nevertheless, the emphasis remained squarely on school reform and on market place competition as central to raising standards.

By contrast, Labour's second strand of policy, pursued in tandem, explicitly set out to intervene in inequalities which originated outside schools, in family and neighbourhood contexts. Labour governments therefore introduced a range of family- and neighbourhood-focused interventions which aimed to offset these wider disadvantages—some of which focused on outcomes in specific domains (for instance, education, health, and employment), while others took a more holistic approach to neighbourhood renewal. Within education, a particularly notable example was the introduction of national initiatives, firstly for extended schooling and then for extended services. These cast schools as catalysts for addressing wider disadvantages by 'offer[ing] services to families who might otherwise be hard to reach, and ... build[ing] relationships with adults who might not trust other public services' (Dyson and Raffo, 2007, p. 299). For instance, the national framework for extended services set out the expectation that schools would provide a 'core offer' of: high quality child care from eight a.m. to six p.m., a varied menu of extra-curricular activities, parenting support, swift and easy access to a range of specialist support services, and community access to learning opportunities (DfES, 2005). An equally wide range of positive outcomes were anticipated as a result, including improved employment, health and attainment outcomes, and reductions in crime and anti-social behaviour.

A third strand which is worthy of note, even if it largely failed to come to fruition, was Labour's commitment to exploring how the education system might be 'personalised' to better meet the needs of all learners individually and the human capital needs of employers. For instance, a working group was established to make recommendations for the reform of the curriculum and qualifications for 14-19 year-olds (Working Group on 14-19 Reform, 2004). The group's recommendations (more commonly known as the Tomlinson Report) included raising the quality of vocational education to ensure parity of esteem, and to develop vocational education 'with the involvement of employers, HE and other stakeholders to offer coherent delivery of the knowledge and skills needed by different employment sectors' (Working Group on 14-19 Reform, 2004, p. 8).

Taken as a whole, this range of activity sought to balance concerns relating to excellence, equity and human capital. There was an explicit aim to create a system which, through a focus on standards, would achieve excellence for all. Added to this, whatever the limitations of schools' abilities to address wider inequalities (see Cummings et al., 2011 for a full discussion), some serious national-level efforts were implemented to challenge inequalities arising out of socio-economic conditions. There was, furthermore, some government-initiated consideration of the potential to broaden the curriculum and to recognise a wider range of capabilities and human capitals.

However, balancing these priorities in practice often proved problematic. Some schools were undoubtedly supported to pursue their internal improvement, while also developing innovative and wide ranging responses to disadvantage and providing pupils with a wider range of curriculum experiences. But it also appears that more often than not, market place principles cut across wider reform efforts. For instance, it has been widely reported that in disadvantaged neighbourhoods where schools tended to be under greatest pressure to improve, there were considerable incentives for schools to manipulate their local circumstances to their best advantage, and often to the detriment of the most vulnerable. For example, with regard to open enrolment, Burgess et al. (2005) found that 'even for the poorer kids who live near a good school, something is happening in the system that makes them travel further to go to a worse school' (Burgess, cited BBC News, 24 February, 2005). Submissions to the Academies Commission (2013) suggest that some schools were employing tacit selection processes which were dependent on families' social and cultural capitals. It also appears that the range of curriculum opportunities made available to learners were often restricted in practice, limiting the system's potential to 'recognise' a diverse range of learners and to foster a wide range of capitals. As Mick Brookes, the then general secretary of National Association of Head Teachers argued 'the testing regime has narrowed the curriculum to disastrous effect ... having an effect on creativity and innovation in schools' and leading to 'a disconnection from learning by a 'distressingly large' number of young people' (*The Guardian*, 11 June 2008).

Current challenges

In 2010, a Conservative-Liberal Democrat coalition government took office, giving way in 2015 to a Conservative government. Together, these governments have pursued a policy direction which, rather than seeking, at a national level, to reconcile tensions between academic excellence, family and neighbourhood interventions, and the development of wider capitals and capacities, have sought to allow greater school autonomy and greater diversity within the educational market place. For instance, whereas Labour governments introduced academies as a means of raising attainment in disadvantaged areas, the Coalition extended the policy to all schools, with this seeing a rapid increase in the numbers of academies nationally. It also introduced 'free schools' (NUT, 2016), which are independent state-funded schools that can: employ their own staff and set their own pay and conditions; decide their own curriculum; determine their own admissions criteria and operate independent of local authorities. Any 'suitable sponsor' including private businesses, parents, teachers, and faith groups, can apply to the Secretary of State for Education to open a free school. A 'slimmed down' national curriculum has also been introduced for state schools which is intended to ensure greater rigour in teaching and learning in English, maths and science, while also allowing schools greater flexibility beyond these core subjects.

Insofar as addressing the wider disadvantages which children experience outside school remains an explicit concern, the same principle of allowing schools greater freedoms to determine their own responses, rather than to centrally prescribe these, has been applied. Thus, while government support for extended services has been withdrawn, schools now receive 'pupil premium' funding (DfE 2014b)—additional funding attached primarily to pupils who receive a free school meal—which they can use flexibly to address educational inequalities.

On the one hand, this has created a situation in which schools have considerable opportunities to develop locally-tailored and innovative responses to educational inequalities (for examples, see Dyson et al., 2012). On the other hand, the corollary to higher levels of school autonomy is that schools are required to use their freedoms to achieve higher standards and the pressure to raise attainment has in no way lessened. For example, while guidance from the Department for Education (2014b) states that the pupil premium is 'paid to schools as they are best placed to assess what additional provision their pupils need' it also states that schools will be inspected on how their use of pupil premium 'affects the attainment of their disadvantaged pupils' and that schools will held to account 'through performance tables, which include data on the attainment of the pupils who attract the funding, the progress made by these pupils, the gap in attainment between disadvantaged pupils and their peers'. Therefore, even when funding is made available explicitly to address the needs of disadvantaged pupils, there is a considerable incentive for schools to interpret pupils' needs narrowly, and to pursue short-term gains in attainment through internal school improvement measures (Carpenter et al., 2013).

A further distinctive feature of the English context post-2010, is that the economy is only recovering very gradually from the effects of the global economic crises of the late 2000s and associated deep national recession. Economic growth is a major priority and there is a strong policy discourse linking the nation's economic recovery to high standards of attainment—with reduced inequalities seen as a by-product of this. As Aghion et al. (2013, p. 16) explain:

> Evidence suggests that increasing UK school standards moderately … could put us on a growth path that would more than double long-term average incomes compared with current trends … There is a double dividend from improving human capital since many of the gains from growth would accrue to the less well-off, thereby reducing inequality. Increasing the quality and quantity of skills of disadvantaged children will make growth more inclusive through reducing the high levels of wage inequality in the UK. (Aghion et al., 2013, p. 16)

Coupled with this (and even more strongly so than during Labour's time in office), there is a preoccupation with England's position in the international PISA (Programme for International Student Assessment) rankings, which place the Eastern 'Tiger economies' in the highest positions. The government has, for instance, announced a series of initiatives to improve attainment in mathematics in English schools by adopting teaching methods from Shanghai

(Coughlan, 2014a). At the same time, questions have been raised about whether improvements in measured attainment are an accurate reflection of improvements in the quality of education. There has, for example, been some speculation about whether year-on-year rises in attainment have been the result of grade inflation, with calls to make examinations more demanding (Coughlan, 2014b).

Concluding comments

As suggested at the start of this chapter, the English education system has, since the 1940s, been constantly seeking ways to reconcile competing demands for excellence, equity, and the human capital needs of the economy. This has resulted in an ongoing programme of educational reform, with various efforts being made to change the context of the system itself, the outcomes from the system, and the impacts of pupils' social contexts on the system. There have, nonetheless, been some important points of continuity. Most significantly, notions of excellence within the education system have always been overwhelmingly equated with high attainment in relation to an academic curriculum, and there has actually been remarkably little debate over time about whether 'excellence' in this sense— whether for the many or the few—should be the system's central goal. Even now, although there are only one hundred and sixty-four grammar schools remaining in the UK, there is still a sense that they offer a 'gold standard' and a means of escaping disadvantage. For instance, there have been recent calls to change grammar school admissions procedures to ensure that poorer pupils are not disadvantaged in the competition for places (Cribb et al., 2013).

This emphasis on academic excellence has also framed the way in which market place principles have been applied to the English education system. Schools in England, whatever the backgrounds of the pupils they serve, and however much autonomy they may be granted, are nonetheless competing to achieve the same centrally-determined standards of attainment, and they face punitive sanctions if they fall short of these. In this situation, even if national initiatives are introduced to support schools to engage with wider issues of disadvantage, or if schools are given greater freedoms to determine their own responses to the needs of disadvantaged pupils, a more narrowly focused concern with academic standards may well dominate.

This increasingly strong central narrative—that excellence will lead to economic prosperity, and will pay a 'double dividend' in reducing inequalities—is not without its critics however, even if their influence on policy has been slight to date. For example, in 2012, the Confederation of British Industry (CBI) argued that the English education system still:

> Seems to fail Callaghan's test [of improving outcomes and prospects for all children] despite thirty-five years of initiatives... On average, standards have risen—as the annual increase in average scores of GCSEs and equivalent qualifications shows. But ... [t]here is a long tail of low achievement among young people in our schools ... disproportionately made up of those from disadvantaged backgrounds.
>
> (CBI, 2012b, pp. 21-22)

Elsewhere, the CBI has argued that the education system is failing to equip many young people (many of whom are likely to be concentrated in what Savage terms the 'precariat') with the skills demanded by employers in twenty-first century. These not only include improved literacy and numeracy skills, but also a much wider range of capabilities in self-management, business and customer awareness, communication skills and attitudes to work (CBI 2012a). Reflecting its members' concerns, the CBI has called for the:

> Development of a clear, widely-owned and stable statement of the outcomes that all schools are asked to deliver. This should go beyond the merely academic, into the behaviours and attitudes schools should foster in everything they do. It should be the basis on which we judge all new policy ideas, schools, and the structures we set up to monitor them.
>
> (CBI 2012b, p. 33)

Other organisations, including, for example, the Institute for Public Policy Research, are also once again focusing attention on the need for high quality vocational education to match the current skills shortfall in skilled trades and the predicted growth of employment sectors which require vocational skills (BBC, 2014). Such aims, however, may be considered to sit somewhat uneasily with the pursuit of a narrow definition of academic 'excellence'.

In conclusion, perhaps what this exploration of historical and contemporary inequalities in English society and education has most clearly demonstrated, is that it is possible to engage in an ongoing programme of education reform—changing school structures, curricula and governance, the implementation of successive initiatives—and yet, overall, only to have narrowed the gap between more and less advantaged pupils a small amount on a tightly defined set of indicators. This is, of course, not to undermine the value of such gains as have been made over time—and it is important to acknowledge that there are limits to what educational reforms might realistically hope to achieve in the face of wider societal inequalities. However, it also suggests that to move the system in markedly more equitable directions, national policy makers need not only to learn from schools' ongoing efforts to balance competing priorities, but must also engage in meaningful debate about what a more equitable society would look like, and what the education system in such a society should actually be setting out to achieve. What it means for the education system to be at once excellent and equitable, and supportive of the economy, must be revisited. In the light of Savage's analysis that England is 'splintering' into an increasingly unequal society, this is a particularly pressing priority.

Chapter 5

Researching equity and inequity: The voices of marginalised people

Inger C. Berndtsson

There are many groups of students and citizens who may be acutely marginalised in education systems through systemic or structural issues around poverty, class, place, gender, ethnicity, migrant status, age and through disability. The methods chosen to research these people's experiences are of great importance. In relation to a more qualitative approach, the lifeworld approach (Bengtsson, 2013a) will be outlined and scrutinised as methodology and theory, putting forward the lived experiences of marginalised people. The lifeworld theory puts aside the separation of individual and society and instead views them as intermingled, both dependent on each other. The examples given in this chapter are from people with visual impairment and blindness and how they experience marginalisation in everyday life and society.

Introduction

Inequity is a reality for many children, teenagers and adults in human life, schools and society. However, the processes that lead to inequity are often hidden in social life. In this chapter it will be argued that one way to explicate processes that lead to inequity is by understanding this phenomenon through people's narratives, accessing the voice and experiences of marginalised groups and people. This is comparable to what Murphy (1990) took note of when, as a professor in social anthropology, he experienced paralysis in his own body. 'I looked for human beings reduced by physical incapacity to a struggle for survival / ... / and I found Society. / ... / the paralysed are 'marginal' people, and the study of their tenuous position at the edge of society will tell us much about all of social life' (p. 5). When it comes to understanding the living conditions for children, teenagers and adults who tend to be marginalised, there is need for qualitative research approaches and methodologies, which have the possibility to take the perspective of underprivileged groups instead of primarily relying on more traditional methodologies and approaches.

Regarding disability studies there are two branches; one more narrow with either a idealistic version where disability is researched as constructed through discourses and languages, or a materialistic version where disability is researched as socially created by socioeconomic factors and discrimination (Söder, 2009). Some of these studies are also often 'tightly connected to the political activism of disabled persons' (p. 67). This has been more common in the UK than in Scandinavia.

In the broader branch of research, disability is studied within social sciences and humanities. Quantitative methods and statistics are often used with tendencies to isolate the impairment to individuals (not focusing disability). In other cases research is more theoretically oriented, focusing creation of disability in relation to the environment (Söder, 2009). There is a growing interest in gender and intersectionality here, but also a more elaborated theoretical awareness, not least in terms of cross-disciplinary approaches. This deeper theoretical development in the field of disability research is much needed (Söder, 2013).

In inclusive research two approaches to empirical research have been identified; a macro-oriented and a micro-oriented perspective, both being found to be too narrow for the study of inclusive education, defined as a relational concept and phenomenon (Haug, 2010; Söder, 2013). The lifeworld approach, as outlined in this chapter, might here contribute to the further development of a relational perspective encompassing both bodily and societal aspects as intermingled.

In relation to qualitative and interpretative research approaches, in a wider sense, there are some interesting methodologies that have been developed and refined that utilise creative approaches. For example, in England inclusive team research has been developed where a number of collaborative inclusive research groups work together with academic researchers in this field, ensure that research undertaken is of value to the lives and experiences of disabled people, but also that disabled people should be in control of research agendas (Townson, et al., 2004). Also in Sweden there have been initiatives taken from the disability organisations to further their influence in disability research (Söder, 2013). In Sweden an example of innovative strategies using a lifeworld approach for empirical research has emerged (Bengtsson, 2005, 2013a); that links to the tradition of relational perspectives in Nordic disability research (Gustavsson and Tøssebro, 2005, p. 37). In this chapter this lifeworld approach will be presented and methodological possibilities and implementation within inclusive education and disability studies will be discussed. As an example, results from lifeworld empirical studies will be presented where blind people's lived experiences of marginalisation and aspects of inequity have been researched.

Understanding disability and inequity

In the Nordic countries there has been a long tradition of disability research since the 1960s (Gustavsson and Tøssebro, 2005). One branch of this research stresses 'the complex and situated interaction between individual factors and the environment / ... / sometimes called the relative definition of disability' (p. 33). Here disability is seen as emerging both between a person and his or her environment, as well as between different individuals. This view contrasts with a more traditional approach where disability is seen in individual, often medical or psychological terms where primarily contextual barriers create disability (ibid.). In the field of special education in Sweden there has been a similar trend, where the discussion has mostly been articulated within different perspectives, such as the categorical and the relational perspectives (Emanuelsson, Persson and Rosenqvist, 2001, p. 22).

How disability and inequity are understood is a necessary baseline for researching these phenomena. Understanding disability as an individual medical diagnosis or functional limitation most often ends up in researching individual differences and similar foci, which also can be compared to the use of a categorical perspective in special education research. The use of traditional individual research methodologies is often the case in these kinds of empirical research. When foremost contextual influences and social structures are identified as creating disability, this is referred to as the social model. Postmodern and constructionist perspectives are apparent here (Gustavsson and Tøssebro, 2005). In the family of relational perspectives, five variations have been identified in the Nordic disability research. The relational model discussed in special education is one of them. Another is critical interpretation (ibid.). However, later I will argue for the use of a lifeworld research strategy as an alternative when a relational perspective is obvious. My view of inequity takes a similar startingpoint, arguing for the relational aspects of defining these phenomena in everyday life, both theoretically and in practice, as characterised by an intertwinement of individual and society.

One approach identified in the family of relational perspectives is the critical interpretational perspective (Gustavsson, 2004; Gustavsson and Tøssebro, 2005), which takes its starting point in 'the interpretation of what phenomena or processes on different levels mean from an insider's and/or an outsider's position' (Gustavsson and Tøssebro, 2005, p. 37), where both individual and social aspects of disability are combined and converge. Here again there are conjunctions with a lifeworld approach, due to the relationship between lifeworld phenomenology and hermeneutics (Bengtsson, 2013a). However, first I will comment on the hermeneutic tradition underlying critical interpretation within the relational perspective.

In the early 1970s a group of educational researchers in Sweden approached the field of underprivileged groups by trying to grasp their situation from their own perspective or horizon (Trankell, 1973) and understand their situation by using field methods similar to ethnographic research in combination with elaborated interpretation processes (ibid.; Ödman, 2007). This qualitative approach was quite innovative of that time and references were made to the hermeneutic tradition (Gadamer, 1960/1995; Palmer, 1969). Researchers in the group focused mainly on migrant groups but also other marginalised groups, such as people with blindness (Johansson, 1974) or learning difficulties (Gustavsson, 2001).

The methodological question that emerged from this research was put as how is it possible to understand people's lives from their own way of seeing and living. Ödman (1995) expresses this approach as comparable to sitting down on the others' chair or jumping into another person's shoes. For the purpose of researching inequity this seems to be an approach of great relevance, offering research tools to understand and interpret the situation of others; to listen to their voices; and the view set out in this chapter will argue for this methodological position and an interconnection between the critical interpretative approach (used within disability studies) and a lifeworld approach as it has been developed in the Gothenburg tradition (Bengtsson, 2013b) and offers a dense theoretical basis for the study of inequity.

Phenomenological theory and philosophy have had various foci during the last century (Bengtsson, 1991). This is also true for the empirical phenomenological tradition during the last decades. The lifeworld approach has since the early 1990s been developed as an empirical research approach within the field of education in Sweden (Bengtsson, 2005, 2013a), primarily initiated by a research group at the University of Gothenburg. Nowadays this approach is an established tradition within the Nordic countries (Bengtsson, 2013b), not the least within the field of disability and inclusive education (Berndtsson, 2001; Carlsson, 2011; Grundén, 2005; Hautaniemi, 2004). Lifeworld phenomenology offers a rigorous developed theory putting forward the sociality and intersubjectivity of the lifeworld. It is of vital importance that we do not have to choose between individual and society, instead they shall be seen as integrated and intermingled in daily life.

The social lifeworld: life and world as intermingled

For the purpose of studying research problems related to people's various life-situations focusing on their lived experiences it has been found that the lifeworld is an extraordinary relevant theory and philosophy. Lifeworld phenomenology is primarily based upon philosophy developed by Husserl (1948/1973), Heidegger (1927/1993), Merleau-Ponty (1945/2012) and Schutz (1932/1967, 1962). Central in it is the concept lifeworld, which in a brief sense can be described as the world in which we live our daily lives (Bengtsson, 2005, 2013a).

The theory of lifeworld challenges the traditional ontologies monism and dualism and affords a constructive contribution to an alternative way of regarding life and world. The concept lifeworld in its profound meaning shall be regarded as pluralistic and constitutes an intertwinement of life and world. The world is always what it is for a living human being. Heidegger (1927/1993) expressed the lifeworld as *in-der-Welt-sein* (being-in-the-world) and Merleau-Ponty (1945/2012) choose the phrase *être au monde* (being-in-the-world), mainly putting forward the lived body as fundamental for everything we do and experience.

In lifeworld theory life and world are in their deepest sense related to each other, in the same way as object and subject, individual and society, body and mind, inner and outer are. In this chapter the relation between individual and society will be specially scrutinised. In consequence, lifeworld theory tries to challenge and put aside the more traditional ways of viewing reality. At the core of lifeworld theory is consequently an intertwinement between various aspects and it is distinguished by 'both and' instead of 'either or' (Bengtsson, 2013a). The lifeworld is consequently always related to a human being—it is always someone's lifeworld. Each person thus has his or her own world as it unfolds from each person's life-situation and body.

Due to the relatedness between life and world, it is of utmost importance to figure out the essence of the subject inhabiting the world. The French philosopher Merleau-Ponty (1945/2012) developed a theory putting forward mind and body as integrated in the lived body. The subject becomes in this theory a body subject, integrating body and mind, which through perception and actions inhabits the world. This body is differentiated from other objects, as it holds a unique position of being the source for all lifeworldly experiences. Further, the own lived body is always something unique for each person. It is through this body that we experience our world, which also means that when our body changes the world changes too, and of course the opposite (Merleau-Ponty, 1945/2012).

This example of how the world is experienced through and by the lived body is perhaps the most intriguing example of the lifeworld phenomenological pluralism. The lived body is therefore neither just object nor just subject and from this theoretical base it has been possible to deeply discuss changes in life due to bodily restrictions (Berndtsson, 2001; Grundén, 2005) where human activity plays a role as taking an active part in the world. It is through engagement and activities that we build up and become absorbed in the world. It is through actions that we also to a great extent change our worlds.

Schutz (1962; Schutz and Luckmann, 1973) put forward the everyday lifeworld as the main world that comprises everything that is possible for a human being to experience and do (Bengtsson, 2013a, p. 6), which of course also contains experiences of restrictions due to aspects in everyday life, either bodily or restrictions set up by others. A lifeworld approach then offers special possibilities to catch up with the phenomenon of inequity as it is lived and experienced by people in everyday life. Researchers have also put forward the usefulness of the theory of the lived body for disability research (Berndtsson, 2001; Hughes and Paterson, 1997).

The lifeworld is social in its innermost essence. We live together with others in a shared world and our lifeworlds slip into each other. We share lifeworlds to varying degrees with others both well-known as well as anonymous people for longer or shorter spaces of time. In this way we are included in each other's lifeworlds and have, as Schutz (1932/1967, p. 165) expresses it, 'grown older together; our experiences have been simultaneous.' This inter-subjective or social aspect of the lifeworld also comprises social representations and attitudes of others, sometimes standing out as prejudices. Lifeworld theory therefore fits well with the challenges and demands when researching disability, equality or inequality, as well as inclusion or participation.

Schutz in particular has contributed to the lifeworld theory by highlighting its social meaning and addressing how we are and tend to be engaged in each other's lifeworlds. In our previous stock of knowledge (experiences), a concept developed by Schutz (1932/1967), we have access to our own experiences, but also what has been passed on from our family, relatives, teachers, schools, et cetera. This gives us a clue to understand prejudices and inequity as it can be experienced in everyday life. In the research related to in the section presenting lived experiences of inequity, the concept 'social body' (Berndtsson, 2001, 2015) is introduced putting forward the social experiences of inequity in daily life.

Methodology

Husserl (1948/1973) expresses the lifeworld as pre-reflexive and pre-scientific, which means that the world is always and has always been there before empirical research as a ground for all of our experiences and actions in the world. One basic starting point, when researching people's lifeworlds, is the challenge to make the often tacit and implicit world visible and noticeable. With some well-known words, Husserl states and highly recommends the importance of going to the things themselves and being flexible when examining various phenomena.

Some branches of phenomenology state that phenomena have to be described; the lifeworld tradition outlined here, however, mostly relies on a statement from Heidegger (1927/1993, p. 61) where he claims that description has the character of understanding and that phenomena therefore have to be interpreted.

One challenge within lifeworld empirical research is how lived experiences can be put into focus and understood. This deals with methods of collecting and analysing data, primarily how we can catch people's lived experiences in research. People perhaps also have difficulties in relating to their own lifeworld experiences and therefore researchers need to take into consideration reflexion, both individual and shared, as well as the researchers' interpretations when studying various phenomena.

Consequently, when using a lifeworld approach, there is no disparate dividing line between phenomenology and hermeneutics. However, there have been some different traditions examining people's lifeworlds. One tradition goes back to the Utrecht school where empirical research mainly was a form of open and unstructured methods (Langeveld, 1984). Another opposite tradition put forward a more rigorous and structured methodology (e.g., Karlsson, 1995). A third is the developed lifeworld approach (Bengtsson, 2005, 2013a) based on an attempt to study the chosen phenomenon as rigorously as possible, but not proclaiming fixed methods. Instead, there is an intention of openness and choosing research methods in conjunction with how the phenomenon is possible to study (Gadamer, 1960/1995). However, tools used within the lifeworld approach are most often related to qualitative strategies and methods,

Lived experiences of inequity: the example of blindness

The empirical example of using a lifeworld approach in this chapter comes from research focusing on people, aged thirty-eight to sixty-one, with severe visual impairment and blindness. It concerns how they have learned to handle their new life-situation and lead an active life again. Two extensive studies have been performed focusing on the lifeworlds of people becoming visually impaired, mostly as adults (Berndtsson, 2001, 2015). In the first study eight people participated and in the second six. Both studies tried to answer questions concerning how life changes due to vision impairment, and how people learn to handle their changed everyday lives. These changes have been identified to dimensions regarding the experiences of time and space, the performance of activities and, as will be highlighted here, social aspects regarding vision loss, which sometimes resulted in lived experiences of marginalisation.

The experienced less value of blind people

Inequity appeared to be a major theme in the analyses of the interviews, expressing the loss of sight as not only physical and perceptual, but also as a social consequence. Maria says: "Yeah, it's all about ... well, being accepted as you are and *equal*. Many people make you feel, like, inferior. I'm not as good, as all the others like me can see /.../ it depends on their attitude." Maria faced blindness when her children were young; she even had a newborn child. She was not only faced with all the practical difficulties that occurred in her daily life such as finding her way around at the hospital and at home, preparing food, taking care of her children, et cetera. She also saw herself having less value than before becoming blind. "It feels like ... I'm being dragged along, I'm not equal."

Lars who has been blind since early childhood has similar experiences to Maria. He says: "Some people like, look down on you, probably more or less unconsciously, but still." For him this has been a reality during his whole life, something he has been forced to handle in constructive ways, not letting these attitudes destroy all his life and career. For Anna, who became blind in her teens, the lower value of blind people appeared in contrast to being actually treated as her workmates when getting a job as a secretary. She also got the same salary as her colleagues, something that amazed both her mother and the consultant. This was very unusual in the middle of the twentieth century. Instead inequity often stands out as a fact in the narratives about the labour market. Lars believes that blind people often get work of minimal importance, having something to do.

Alice has received several qualified jobs in strong competition but in spite of this she still has a feeling of being a second-class citizen. "Deep down I think I've felt that I'm not really good enough as I do not have perfect hearing and have never had it, but I'll prove that I can still do things, anyway—that it's possible." When as a little girl she was at school she was also treated in a special way, due to her early-impaired hearing. This treatment by teachers in her early years created a feeling of low value. "Yeah, you feel that you're not good enough or what I should ... I can't find the right word." Today, as a person with both hearing and vision impairment she experiences her own value being less than seeing and hearing people. This was brought to the fore again when she started orientation and mobility training with a white long cane. The white cane brought about a confirmation of her low self-esteem as an individual—not being a complete person when being disabled.

> Well it [the cane] confirms the original feeling to me æ and that ... when you then have a disability you're not a whole person. You're not complete ... I don't think I'm whole ... I would not say adequate or complete person, as I have these disabilities /.../ that somehow you don't have the same dignity, you become smaller, a little lower, a little ... well, you're not quite a full human being. (Alice)

Alice has to fight these feelings and experiences of low self-esteem when she tries hard to find her human dignity again. Lars stresses that situations where as a disabled person you are dependent can also result in feelings of low self-esteem. Maria has come to the conclusion that she will never become of the same value as seeing people. "But I probably never will, that's just the way it is, I've realised that. I'll never be seen as equal compared to anyone." When we discuss this statement, she makes the nuance that she does not experience this among disabled people, but among non-disabled people she has the feeling of never reaching the same value as others. "Yet in the blind's world, we are all equal," she says. As a consequence of this statement she expresses a need for meeting other people with visual impairment or blindness, as among these people she has a feeling of being equally valuable.

Lived experiences of normality

Due to the experiences of being of less value a desire of being as everyone else emerged among the participants, which became obvious, particularly in the first study. Karin says: "You want to be—just completely normal." Often the focus on normality stands out in relation to using a white cane in public. Starting to use a white cane often comprises feelings of not being normal, being different from other people in society. The white cane symbolises blindness, and can be identified as a symbol of stigmatisation. Lived experiences of stigmatisation most often result in feelings of being different, where blindness seems to dominate encounters with other people. Karin sometimes folds her white cane in situations where she will not be compared with people with vision impairments. "… you want to be pretty normal," she says. Learning to use a long cane also comprises aspects of normality, as exemplified by Maria.

> I remember my first day really well when I sat there in this orientation room along with [the O and M instructor]. She took out white canes that should get the feel of; she described them as that. I then started to howl, I felt that it was the end of everything, holding the cane was like burning your hand, it was terrible, horrifying that was it. /…/ No, it was actually horrifying. / … / It wasn't me anymore, I was just a disabled blind person. It was not me. (Maria)

The white cane transported Maria to a feeling of being primarily blind and disabled. Her identity as being a mother, a woman, et cetera was totally swept away. It should also be noted that her experiences also had bodily expressions where she felt the cane as being so hot it could be compared to a burn injury. Therefore, regarding disability, bodily and social aspects need to be seen as integrated and intermingled in lived experiences. The long cane can in this example be interpreted as being symbolic and a representative of attitudes and prejudices about blind people as not being as capable as sighted people, thus putting normality into focus. Maria, again: "Yeah, I was extremely handicapped. I was DISABLED and BLIND in capitals. I was not Maria anymore, I was just some disabled person." Included is also a feeling of being different. "But it's just that, I'm different, everyone looks at me. That's how it feels."

Something had been intermixed in daily intercourse, something that had to do with one's own value, being different and aspects of normality. The everyday social lifeworld is changed due to this 'something' that had been wedged into encounters with various people. Further, the participants shared experiences of becoming typified where others seem to value them with regard to an idea of a typical blind person. Frequently they did not feel that they had anything at all in common with this kind of ideal type. These processes sometimes resulted in a feeling of becoming another person, thus having a changed identity.

Some respondents did not accept being treated by others as some kind of declassified person. Claes is an example of this: "I'm no less a person than anyone else just because I don't see, and I've said that to myself and I live by that motto. No one should be able to hit me across the fingers just because I can't see." Ingemar also expresses notions of blind people he had faced when as a teenager he became blind. "Obviously when you became visually impaired ... people perceived that someone who's blind can't do much, you become isolated and sit at home, but I didn't feel this way, I didn't give way. I wanted to be everywhere." However, there is one woman in the studies that does not recognise these kinds of prejudices at all. As with Ingemar she became blind as a teenager, Anna narrates: "Something I consider to be really very pleasant, is that you never had to feel pushed out ... no, I've always been involved and not out of pity or anything like that." For her, being vision impaired, has never stood out as something different. She has been treated as everyone else.

Possible alterations of inequity in school and society

Murphy (1990) writes: 'Our society erects walls of discrimination and inaccessibility, both physical and social, but the handicapped keep trying to scale those barriers, to break out of themselves, to escape the web of constraints, to force their way into a full and rounded life' (p. 159). Many of those who have participated in the studies fight for their right to be treated and valued as a normal person. Claes, who is one example of this, says: "But I've been fighting to live as a normal, average person, and that's important." Living with vision impairment in daily life means facing other's prejudices of blindness on a daily basis.

In the first study (Berndtsson, 2001) a kind of pattern was recognised. Being occupied by the onset of blindness most of the participants felt some kind of sadness when confronted by feelings of low self-esteem, not being respected as before, not being trusted to handle simple daily life activities, not being appreciated. Those who have recently become visually impaired generally related to these feelings. The focus here is primarily on themselves and their own feelings. Interaction with others is problematic, as related by Veronica: "And then there's several people standing and talking, several in one room and then I would rather go home to bed. It becomes too much, I cannot deal with it." One example narrated by Karin is when her workmate unlocked the door for her at her own home. At work Karin is very skilled and handles most of the daily routines, yet her workmate did not believe she was able to unlock the door of her own apartment. In this initial first stage the focus is on one's own person and feelings in relation to daily encounters. As a second step some kind of ambivalence to the attitudes of others has been noticed. An excerpt from an interview with Maria will exemplify this. "Sometimes I could be so damn miserable and you think everything is so horrible, then sometimes you become just angry, then I think, what the hell, I'm really fine. I am as good as I am and I can do as much as I can." How persons are viewed and treated by others also influences their activity performance, learning and participation in society; as in schools and workplaces for example. This also deals with processes of identity. When to some degree you have accepted the impaired vision, it is obvious that sometimes when encountering people in daily life they will still see you as primarily a disabled person, with objectifying tendency.

> Must it be like this for another fifty years until people's attitudes ... admittedly, it's not every single person, but it comes up every few days. /.../ When you accept yourself as what you are, why can't other people do it. Which then constantly reminds me that I'm not like everyone else.
> (Maria)

Those participants who have been blind for a longer period of time, sometimes up to fifty years, focus on the other person, trying to understand what is going on. These others tend to assume, in most cases from their own outlook on blind people, that blindness always leads to severe restrictions. When Lars speaks about a headmaster who many years ago did not accept him as a pupil at his school, he says: "But maybe it's not much to speak of, you have to understand that people are afraid of new situations, that's the way it is." Both Ingemar and Anna use humour instead to disarm the attitudes of others.

Through glimpses from the studies referred to above (Berndtsson, 2001, 2015) it has become obvious that people value others very much from their own earlier experiences of disability; otherwise their views often accord with common perceptions in society and prejudices. In general people with impairments are looked upon as typified and become marginalised. This is most often the case when people lack experience of interactions with persons with impairments.

When the participants in the studies talk about friends they instead express that they often forget their vision loss. According to Schutz (1932/1967) the only way to change the common attitudes in society is through meeting people in a we-relation, face-to-face, where both contracting parties see each other in a you-relation, as subjects for one another. These meetings in daily life have to take up the attention of the lived body in the world. First, then, are there openings to changes in attitudes and generalising tendencies, which is vital both for intermingling in schools as well as in society. van Peursen (1977) has an interesting view in this respect where he put forth the concept 'cultural horizon' for a description of the shared horizon of a culture. For the purpose of the discussed theme this could be related to shared common values and notions regarding equity and inequity.

New ways of researching inequity

The examples of lived experiences given above primarily deal with inequity, due to the participants' experiences, similar strategies will of course also serve the purpose of researching equity. Seven strategies have been outlined when researching inequity empirically within a lifeworld approach, even though there is of course a need for each researcher to creatively find their own way into the research. However, these strategies or phases are of an overarching nature, where they very basically discuss prerequisites for lifeworld empirical research.

First, there is a need to try to identify and challenge one's own values regarding disability and inequity for the focused group. This can be compared to identifying one's pre-understanding (Heidegger, 1927/1993). This approach is recommended within hermeneutic research for the purpose of not having prejudices as an unconscious influence in the process of interpretation (Gadamer, 1960/1995; Ödman, 2007).

As a second phase the researcher has to approach the lifeworlds of those people who have been selected for the empirical research. Each person has his or her own world and first of all the researcher needs to establish a good relationship with the participants, built on trustworthiness and a genuine interest for the other person's perspective and world; a we-relation (Schutz, 1932/1967). The researcher also needs to gain confidence from the participants, perhaps mostly characterised by informal meetings and conversations.

The third phase is characterised by openness for having the others lifeworld unfolding and appearing in all its manifoldness. Here there is need for creativity, curiosity and sensitive methods when researching the lived experiences of other people. We need to understand situations of inequity 'in their lived and worldly context as this is where they have their meaning' (Bengtsson, 2013a, p. 8). Research methods used in this tradition are primarily qualitative strategies, such as interviews, narratives, biographical interviews and participant observation, often used in combinations and characterised by continuous reflection (Bengtsson, 2013a; van Manen, 1990; Taylor and Bogdan, 1998). Narratives (Polkinghorne, 1995) in particular are regarded as a most relevant tool for examining people's lifeworlds, where the narratives give us glimpses of the others' world (Berndtsson, 2001). Also observing people's use of tools is a source to the other's lifeworld experiences. Overall, observing people's ongoing activities is imperative when the aim is to gain knowledge about individuals' lifeworlds.

Trying to come close to people's lived experiences and actions in the world can be compared to an 'insider' perspective (Gustavsson, 2001). The forth phase builds on to this. It is the formal analysis and is characterised by processes of interpretation (Ödman, 2007), often with a critical frame of reference (Ricoeur, 1993). Of course analyses start as soon as meeting with the participants, but in the fourth phase the analysis is deepened and more systematised. The researcher must still be aware of his or her own pre-understanding of the studied phenomenon, preventing it from unconsciously guiding the work with clean-cut interpretations and the lived experiences of the researched participants must always be kept in focus, even though different interpretations and descriptions may develop.

As a fifth phase lifeworld theory or phenomenological philosophy may be used in the interpretation with the main purpose of deepening the results still further; 'the significance of *thinking* phenomenologically while *doing* phenomenology' (Berndtsson, Claesson, Friberg and Öhlén, 2007, p. 257). Here phenomenological language can be used in a descriptive way to express and explicate lived experiences (Bengtsson, 2013a, p. 11; Berndtsson, 2001).

The sixth phase consists of an ethical reflection. Ethics guide and are implemented throughout the whole research process, but in step six the ethics of practice are given specific attention. It is of great importance that people's sometime vulnerable situations are respected and paid attention to. Participating in research is also always a free choice. Special attention should be given the presentation of the results, where identification of the persons should be prevented.

As a seventh and final phase the research results hopefully will guide processes of change regarding inequity and equity processes in school and society. The knowledge of the life-situations of others may perhaps lead to a change regarding the situation of marginalised people. However, if there is to be a lasting change, people must change their attitudes through meeting people whose life-situations are valued as less than others. Here the declaration of the human rights is a guiding-star. Finally, it is important to note that the research strategies presented above are just one example of how lifeworld research paying attention to inequity can be executed. A variety of strategies can of course be chosen within the wider frame of a lifeworld approach.

Conclusions

Using a lifeworld approach is a useful and fruitful choice when researching inequity as it takes a starting point in people's lived experiences and lifeworlds. As a result, disability intertwined with inequity can stand out in terms of how it is experienced by people being and acting in the world. Further, through the theoretical concepts and resources within lifeworld theory, lived experiences of inequity can be revealed and brought into focus telling us something important about the experiences of marginalisation in social life, which makes it possible to scrutinise the changed life-situations due to inequity from the person's own point of view. In doing this both bodily and social aspects can appear as can how a perceptual limitation of the body contributes to a feeling of a changed identity in social life, putting forward the inter-subjective dimensions of the lifeworld, expressed in the concept 'social body' (Berndtsson, 2001, 2015). Experienced inequity in daily life can then stand out as critical for activity and learning and as preventing the individual from leading an active life and being treated as an equal member of society.

Section 2, Developing equitable practice: case studies from England and Sweden

Chapter 6

Formation of fundamental values in the Swedish education system—a discursive analysis of policy texts

Inger Assarson, Ingela Andreasson, Lisbeth Ohlsson

Introduction

The purpose of this chapter is to highlight some discursive constructions that can help us understand what is happening in the meaning-making processes related to formation of fundamental values in the Swedish education system. The analysis of the fundamental value text's and preliminary work looks into how standards and values are created in language activities in variations of explanatory models and constructed thought systems.

As such the chapter is focusing a Swedish context and the tradition of seeing school as a meeting place for children and young people with different backgrounds. This approach takes its point of departure from a set of values which are regarded as important for how citizens in society should act towards each other. These foundational values are inscribed into the curricula of the whole Swedish school system. The National Agency for Education is commissioned by the Swedish government to support schools in their work with the realisation of foundational values.

The education system has always been an important instrument in shaping the way citizens think about the world. Education has been a means to spread common values, from antiquity's philosophical schools, to convent schools and the medieval universities up to today's national schools and in doing so forming a national identity. The national identity was also an important element when democracy attained its breakthrough in the west world during the 1900s.

Even Aristotle raised the issue of a system of common values in his speeches about important virtues among equal citizens. Phronesis, virtue of practical wisdom, is a specific form of knowledge that deals with compassionate social and practical judgement to mange situations and meetings as a good social being (Hellspong and Brumark, 2003). Aristotle believed that without this knowledge or virtue among citizens it would not be possible to hold together a political entity such as a country.

Historically, issues such as culture, social political movements and religion have had a special function to convey the fundamental values of society. Today there is in Sweden an ongoing struggle between different interest groups aiming at controlling school causing a tension between, for example, a humanist discourse, a discourse of *Bildung*[1] and fostering and an economic discourse pointing out the importance of employability. In Sweden the workers' history has had an increasing impact especially after 1946 when they became in majority in the Swedish parliament. The labour movement in Sweden has been characterised by the conflict between the liberal labour movement that emerged in 1870 and the socialist groups winning influence mainly in the early twentieth century (Hirdman, 1990). Within the liberal labour movement the idea of *Bildung* and self efficacy were prominent whereas the social democrats emphasised freedom, in the sense of freedom to gain prosperity but also to an amount solidarity through common financed welfare for there members. The social democratic policy since 1920 has been affected by liberal ideas aiming at making the capitalism as free from crises as possible in order to increase production and values available to allocate between the citizens and at the same time promoting the health of the workers (Fredelius, 1977). Leading values were just distribution of the recourses of society, social service and welfare in collaboration between the state and the capitalists. These liberal social democratic values were those lifted to convey to students in the curricula in Sweden after the second world war. Since 1945, the democracy mandate that was previously tied to subject tuition has become an undertaking for schools to work in accordance with democratic values.

The role of the school as a mediator of values then is not new, but when the Swedish curricula was restructured at the beginning of the 1990s (Lp. 94) its undertaking as a mediator of education and values was clarified. In preliminary work and discussion the issue turned up in connection with increasing immigration, questioning what is Swedish and the need of a more clear definition of what democracy could be after the fall of the Berlin wall when its antipode disappeared. A clear unifying direction in citizen fostering was required.

1. Bildung (German for "education" and "formation") refers to the German tradition of self-cultivation (as related to the German for: creation, image, shape), wherein philosophy and education are linked in a manner that refers to a process of both personal and cultural maturation.

Simultaneously the new public management ideology reached schooling and the former state control was decentralised and became target-oriented and subject to competition. Principally the concept of fundamental values began to be discussed by the *Läroplanskommittén* (Curriculum Committee) in its report, School of Education (SOU, 1992:94). The work on values also received further attention when the then Minister of Education Ingegerd Wärnersson declared 1999 as the year of fundamental values (Ds 1997:57; Zackari and Modigh, 2002).

The school's fundamental values, as set out in the policy documents, contain five fundamental values:

> Solidarity with the weak and vulnerable
> Equality between men and women
> All people are equal
> Sanctity of human life and
> Freedom and integrity of the individual.

When value is combined with fundamental to form a fundamental value, the two parts may to some extent be seen as incompatible (Andersson, 2002). Fundamental as a metaphor is something stable, solid, something everything else rests on while the five values above stand as columns on this fundament. The word value expresses a fundamental perception of the desirability of a condition or procedure, that is say, an evaluation that indicates the degree to which something is good or bad. In this regard, it is a question of values that are perceived as good. Accordingly, the five fundamental values deal with the desirable relationships and how these relationships should be organised in our society.

In the introductory chapter of the curricula (Lp. 94, Lp. 94, Lpfö 98, Lgr 11) it states that schools must 'be designed in accordance with democratic values' and that 'the school has an important role to play in communicating and establishing the fundamental values in students on which our society is based' (Chap. 1). The school's mission to promote children's and young people's learning cannot be separated from the democratic mandate (Swedish National Agency for Education, Skolverket, 2007). The fundamental value work of the school creates an ethical order regarding the values that must apply and the school has a citizen-fostering mandate to convey a common platform for both the perception of democracy and all people are equal as in the rights and obligations of citizens. The concepts in themselves can be considered rhetorical and say very little about what they mean in practice. As such they first take on meaning when those who use them create meaning in them (Assarson, 2009a).

The directive and preparatory work on the curricula that are the focus of our study, were written two decades ago. The formulations and significance originate from a discussion that we now understand in a different way than when it originally took place. The new curricula (Lgr 11), which were prepared in connection with the new Education Act 2011 (SFS 2010:800), have retained the fundamental values in accordance with previous descriptions without major intervention. However, when we now consider the text, this must take place based on other currents and a different way of thinking than those that existed twenty years ago. Naturally a contemporary reading of the texts will be critical when reviewed from discourses that were not relevant at the time they were written. Yet it is in the present that the text must be implemented by personnel in the schools and therefore new ways of approaching it will be worthwhile to accentuate in the review of how it originated.

In general official texts and policy documents are written in an attempt to attain uniformity so that they can act as governing for an activity. On the one hand, it can result in difficulties when the uncommunicativeness of the unified policy documents is confronted by the difference, variation and dynamism that the activity is in, and which are characteristic of the postmodern society (Hargreaves, 1998). On the other hand, the aim of political consensus means that policy documents are often compromises and are formulated so that they can be subject to different political trends. There is then a risk of them being too vague and ineffective as policy instruments (Assarson, 2007). The consensus, which on the face of it lies in rhetorical texts, is the result of political negotiations where anything that jeopardises consensus is repressed. This takes the possibility of satisfying the need of nuance and problematics from the text, that the activity requires, and leaves it to the teachers to find their own approach, which can then be interpreted as corresponding with the intentions of the policy documents (Assarson, 2007).

Discursive analysis of preliminary works

The methodology in this study has its base in political and ethical philosophy. An assumption is that the discursive order frames the interpersonal scripts in the context of social roles such as those based on social class, ethnicity, gender and disability (Laclau, 1993). That makes it important to scrutinise how discourses interact in those documents that are supposed to become a lodestar for teachers in their work with fundamental values. In the review of the preliminary work, where the intentions of the fundamental value work in the schools are defined, we have used the term cluster and analysed how these are created through different characters being linked to a nodal point (Laclau and Mouffe, 1985). Thus it emerges how meanings are created relationally. A cluster brings to mind 'bundle' or 'heap', which can be used to show how specific concepts and expressions create significance and show how the different parts of the fundamental values are made to belong together (Andreasson, 2007). Since the purpose is to study how fundamental values are formed in official texts, we have tried to fashion how words relate to such bearing characters as democracy, the other, or equivalence.

In the following, the preliminary work for the curricula has be reviewed with the aim of identifying discourses that form the basis for the understanding of the intentions of the school's fundamental value work. In the review below the focus has been set on the different meanings ascribed to the fundamental values and create both analogies and contradictions. When the texts are reviewed, the specific meaningful units that have created significance in the values and standards have focused on, e.g. democracy, heritage and moral competence. Other characters (words/concepts) have then been linked to each meaningful unit, where the significance has been expanded and problematised. This kind of meaningful unit can be seen in accordance with Laclau (2004), as an empty signifier that gets its function by gathering together something that has divided. Such open expressions are often criticised for their vagueness, yet indefiniteness should not be seen as a failure in the actual expression, for example, 'fundamental values'. Rather, according to Laclau, it is impossible to construct a entirety in rhetorical expressions in a society that is so strongly marked by fragmentation and heterogeneity as the post or late modern society we now live in.

Concepts that can be linked to fundamental values in the policy documents have during the analysis been formed into clusters and by doing so have given meaning to the five areas;

> Democracy and influence,
> The school as a social meeting place,
> Understanding of 'the Other',
> Moral guidance,
> *Bildung* and learning.

Fundamental values are formed

When we speak about fundamental values, we use terms and concepts that customarily have represented what in Sweden has traditionally been associated with a democratic, just and equal society that takes into account all its citizens. All these terms or concepts can be related to what the French philosopher Derrida (2003) would call messianic, as a social common desire and anticipation of something that could occur in the future. They represent visions of how a good school in a good society could be fashioned (Sigurdson, 2002). Furthermore, they can be related to what philosopher Laclau (2004) terms as empty signifiers as they have no meaning in themselves, only first when they are given meaning in talks, discussions and actions. Only as concepts do they give some guidance to the school's personnel about how they should be implemented in practice. Naturally, values and standards that we associate with fundamental values must be understood in the context in which they are formed. It is important to see how the different concepts are brought to the fore in the preliminary work such as reports and propositions in order to create an understanding of the political intentions concerning the work of teachers and school personnel with these issues.

Democracy and influence

In the directive to the Curriculum Committee's work, prominence was given to the school's role to 'strengthen the democratisation process in the community' (Dir. 1991:9). Emphasis was given to importance of students being given the opportunity to exercise influence and take responsibility as part of the democratisation process. In addition, democracy presupposes critically thinking citizens. The school should therefore aim to give students the ability to see context, rather than just explain facts, take a critical stance rather than reproduce the subject matter of knowledge and critically review facts and circumstances. This kind of democratic objective must be reflected in the school's working methods to contribute towards shaping citisens who recognise the consequences of specific behaviour. The role of citizen is made the focal point while the document determines what is meant by this role, what the school should do and what these measures mean for the students, something that later reappears in the planning of the curricula.

Democracy is a multifaceted concept. The proposition (Prop. 1992/93: 220) states the importance of not constricting its meaning to a form of democracy that is based on the majority view being allowed to prevail.

> The school shall, pursuant to the Swedish Education Act, be formed on a democratic basis. Democracy can mean a number of fundamental values necessary for a good society, but it can also narrowly refer to a form of decision where a majority opinion prevails
> (Swedish Government Proposition 1992/93:220, p. 18)

Instead, it is respect for the minority, for each person's uniqueness and individual responsibility that may form meaningful values in the democracy. The proposition states that students' influence must permeate the teaching. Influence is not explicitly linked to the fundamental values, but rather becomes a part of the *Bildung* undertaking that the school must focus on. Fostering and the delegation of knowledge are key in order to uphold a nation. Fundamental values are therefore formed around a common basis of democratic values. Laclau claimed that dominant discourses emerge as a form of homogenisation in each society (Laclau, 1996). The discursive power produces a shared knowledge that is considered to be true, valuable and useful. However, it also creates an ethical, moral order that says something about the values that must apply. In the directives, democracy has the meaning that all students have a voice and that students also have greater scope to form their own schooling through participating in both the planning and evaluation of the teaching provided. Accordingly, this identifies the school's ability to provide the conditions for such democratic values such as regard and respect for others and the opinions of others, the ability to take responsibility for oneself and one's fellow beings, the ability to responsiveness and ability to assert your own opinion. These abilities are assumed to be part of a democratic citizen fostering, which in the proposition emanates from a *Bildung* concept rather than from fundamental values.

The school as a social meeting place

According to Schüllerqvist (1996), a shift occurred during the latter part of the 1990s in Sweden in the public rhetoric, from a school of skills to the school as a social meeting place. The development took place simultaneously with the political concern for increased segregation and heterogeneity in society and the growing discussion of a single common value. In addition to knowledge, children and young in pre-school and school must also receive social training in the community at an early stage.

A part of this education is about democracy. Another is about becoming a social citizen and therein the school becomes a social meeting place, a central incentive and a prerequisite for a democratic school and a democratic society. Today's society is affected to a greater extent than before by influences from many different parts of the world and the heterogeneous give more opportunities than previously to become visible (Dir. 1991:9). The importance of students learning how to live together with peers who have different experiences, abilities and knowledge than themselves is emphasised in the proposition (Prop. 1992/93: 220).

> According to the committee, the school has an opportunity and a responsibility, as a social and cultural meeting place, to strengthen the ability of children and young people to live with this cultural diversity and to perceive it as a positive force.
> (Swedish Government Proposition 1992/93:220, p. 41)

At the same time as this heterogeneity becomes clear, there are counteracting forces that strive towards a homogenisation (Assarson, 2009a). The Belgian philosopher and feminist Chantal Mouffe believes that there is a tendency to overcome discordance in society by seeking solutions that disguise creative conflicts (Mouffe, 2008). One of the basic ideas behind the democratisation of the school has been that people from different social strata, with different cultural and religious backgrounds, must be met. The aim of these meetings is twofold. One is that they need to the increase understanding when engaging the experiences and knowledge of other groups as well as to contribute to smoothing out differences through prioritising, by implication, the Swedish, and by doing so stimulate the harmonisation of society.

> The growing international exchange also has consequences for the school. However, this development not only results in demands of new knowledge but also raises the growing importance of support in their own language, history and culture, through establishment in their native district and of the Nordic dimension.
> (Swedish Government Proposition 1992/93:220, p. 9)

The report also highlights the endeavour that, 'At the same time as we see an increase in internationalisation through contact across boundaries between individuals and groups, and through cooperation and coordination, we can also see a distinct trend in the pursuit of protecting one's own culture, the own group's language and patterns of life' (SOU 1992:94 p. 89).

There is, without reservation, also an idea of the ideal citizen implicitly in the idea of a common set of values. It is difficult to distinguish the question of values from the power relations that lie behind the cultural expressions. The western dominance in the Swedish school is strong. Creating diversity may be problematic if values, at the same time, are considered to stand above all cultures' ways of giving meaning to the good, but also if they are seen as something unchangeable over time (Assarson, 2009b).

One section has been preserved from Lgr 80 (1980) that expresses how children's differences must not lead to the school trying to make all children and young alike. The report therefore identifies that the undertaking is more a question of supporting students to leave school with 'maintained individuality and uniqueness and with an acquired ability to respect the individuality of others' (SOU 1992:94, p. 18). Two parallel inferences are drawn in the proposition (Prop. 1992/93: 220) from the quote taken from Lgr 80 (1980); one that there must be an increase in the choices available to students and their parents and the other, that the *Bildung* concept, 'in its deepest and broadest sense' must be reinstated in school. The *Bildung* concept from the report thus opens up the discussion in the proposition about the values the school must manage and the proposals that are then set.

Understanding of the Other

Particular attention should, according to the original directives, be given to questions concerning cultural heritage and cultural change (Dir. 1991:9). Here the directives presuppose that knowledge of 'our' language and 'our' history can lead to understanding and respect for the 'cultural heritage of other people and nationalities'. This way of thinking was enhanced when the new directive came into force after the change of government in 1991, when a Conservative Government came to power (Dir. 1991:117). In the pursuit of homogeneous values in school, Sawyer and Kamali claimed in a report about 'otherisation processes' in schools, that perceptions are created at the same time of the other, those who are not like us (Sawyer and Kamali, 2006). The values, which the school must be based on in the fostering of growing citizens, are focused on

Swedish society but also on how this society can be considered from different angles. The school is expected to provide knowledge that makes up the student's own identity in the native district, the Swedish language and cultural heritage in the broadest sense, but also augment teaching of the common European cultural heritage (SOU 1992:94, p. 89). The texts include the aim to safeguard common values and to create an understanding of belonging to Sweden and Europe. The danger that such a perspective may be too restricted is recognised through stressing the understanding of 'the other', for both domestic minorities as well as the cultural heritage of other people, which cannot be grouped in the majority society. Therefore, in accordance with the directive, Swedish society must, on the one hand, be characterised by tolerance and openness something linked to the conditions for harmony in society where different people are able to live together. While on the other hand, if the restriction of the role of the citizen is also emphasised in his or her own cultural heritage there is a risk of creating a limit for tolerance, something that schools must counteract.

The rapid changes and development in information technology are underlined in the proposition as a threat (Prop. 1992/93:220). Consequently, the opinion here, is that particular attention must be given to important parts of the cultural heritage that may be challenged by such a development. Thus the idea of *Bildung* is the cohesive force, which gives security and strength in order to face the unknown. Knowledge of technology is combined in this idea with the fostering to tackle this new media in conformity with prevailing standards. Castells (2000) points out that the threat that lies in computerisation is less to do with how citizens are educated than the ability to decode the information it provides. The risk is rather that specific groups learn to master the semiotic tools and resources needed to critically interpret and behave, while others will be referred to the restrictive pre-packaged explanations. Interpreted from a socio-cultural learning perspective, the new artefacts alter the process and structure of the social and mental processes. When the school embraces information technology as a mediating tool, with so much inbuilt culture and acumen, it should therefore also result in the boundaries of who has the abilities changing in relation to the ability to handle the new technology (Assarson, 2009a).

Immigration and increased international exchange are highlighted in the proposition (Prop. 1992/93: 220) as an opportunity for children and the young to gain a broader understanding of the unknown and something that society should encourage. The different knowledge and experiences acquired through language skills are expected to benefit society. At the same time the proposition underlines the importance of the school being able to manage 'the differences in values that can be found e.g. in views about religion, school, gender roles and fostering' (Prop. 1992/93: 220, p. 10) in segregated areas where disputes due to the different backgrounds and mind-sets of the students belong to everyday life at some schools.

The report (SOU 1992:94, p. 92) accentuates the value of primary, lower and upper-secondary schools as the only social institution where everyone, regardless of background, interests and values, can meet for a longer time. Despite difficulties in cultural differences being highlighted, it is to a lesser degree than in the proposition (Proposition 1992/93: 220) subsequently presented to the Swedish Parliament. Emphasis is placed in the report on the development opportunities that diversity provides and the importance of students being able to take advantage of these opportunities and manage these problems. While the section in the proposition dealing with social change and immigration highlights the problematisation and societal benefits of internationalisation the report to a far greater degree emphasises the possibilities of diversity thinking and personal development. However, today's diversity of different cultures and languages are described in both the report and the proposition as a resource.

> In this connection we would like to point out the great resource that people with an immigrant background constitute. A growing proportion of the population has a mother tongue other than Swedish; over one hundred languages are represented in residential areas, workplaces and in schools. More than 100,000 students have knowledge of a 'home language' and then primarily in languages other than English, German and French. There is every reason to utilise this wealth of linguistic knowledge in different ways than has previously been the case(SOU 1992:94, p. 92).

The report signals the importance of students developing all of their languages in connection with managing the perception of the other. A social turning has received more influence over the research being carried out regarding multilingual teaching and the acquisition of language (Block, 2003). Scollon (1998) says that we do not only assert ourselves as individuals in the linguistic processes, but also allow the other to step forward in a context of constant ongoing relationship-building. The language not only becomes a linguistic instrument, nor merely an instrument depending on culture and society, but a process in which the ego forms in relation to others. This process occurs in several languages for many children and young. Today children speak one or more other languages in an increasing number of homes in Sweden. The different cultures they reside in give them different fragments of identities (Assarson, 2009a) a view that can be already discerned in the report about school as a *Bildung* institution.

Moral guidance

Interest in fundamental value issues is explained in the proposition primarily through increased understanding of man's need for an internal compass in a society where external rules are not enough. An ethical compass and moral expertise are deemed as one of the most important proficiencies that a school can give to students, skills that are also considered to be life-long. In these discussions over the importance of standards and morals, fundamental values are considered as abilities to be used by the individual to integrate into the prevailing social order

> There is also a realisation that an ethical compass and moral expertise are one of the most important proficiencies with a life-long value that school can give to a child. Even though ethics is always a highly personal and individual virtue, there is a collective responsibility to communicate and sustain it (Swedish Government Proposition 1992/93:220, p. 3).

In the supplementary directives from December 1991 (Dir 1991:117), the school's normative undertaking is clarified and it is emphasised that the school's teaching cannot be regarded as a value-neutral activity. The values that the school must impart are those anchored in the country in accordance with the 'Christian ethics and Western humanism' and must be governing for all teaching. The wording is based on a document from Anders Piltz that is included as an appendix to the report to illustrate how to interpret the meaning of the concept. In the constantly recurring debate surrounding the issue, an incompatibility between the Christian and the humanist (Andersson, 2004) is offered on the one hand and on the other a historicity in which these concepts are developed in parallel. Piltz (Dir 1991:117) says the values in the Christian message are also found in the secular stories throughout Western history, as a way to elevate man above animals. What we consider today as natural ethical guidelines have been administered by the Jewish-Christian tradition, where the Greco-Roman heritage is also included and has, according to Piltz, never been replaced by any atheistic humanism.

The western ethic can be seen to emerge on the one hand from the Stoics and Plato's and Aristotle's theories and, on the other hand, from the Christian philosophers' further development of these ideas. Thomas Aquinas created a synthesis of the biblical interpretation of morality and the view of morality that emerged during antiquity by uniting faith and reason. He based his theory on man's natural desire for happiness and to act reasonably. It is precisely through her sense that she is able to understand the divine law as expressed in the Bible and thus achieve success (Spjuth, 2006).

The notion of man's potential to become a free, considerate human through *Bildung* was strengthened during the Renaissance and later the Age of Enlightenment. The desire of the proposition and the report to unite knowledge and moral fostering in the *Bildung* concept included a wish and expectation that value issues must permeate both teaching and teaching-free time. Therefore all school personnel, including cleaners, canteen staff, caretakers, clerks, student health staff are elevated to be aware of their role and responsibilities (Prop. 1992/93: 220, p. 32). The latter point is the responsibility of the Vice-Chancellor so that the school's personnel are aware of their obligations, but could it also be interpreted as the school having a responsibility for how the school's service personnel are offered participation in school's activities.

In a post-modern approach to ethics there is a reaction against the Age of Enlightenment's idea that there is a metaphysical universal ethic that can be understood in rational terms. If anything, such a view must be regarded as impossible as well as undesirable (Grenholm, 2003). Without an ethical pluralism and without an ongoing discussion and questioning of how good is constructed socially there is a risk of the exercise of symbolic violence against dissidents. The philosopher Derrida problematises the relativisation of the good values that may result when they lose their metaphysical basis and are seen as socially constructed. In a deconstruction of Kant's philosophy, Derrida emphasises the possibility of a common social good. In longing for the good, man presuppose some kind of unifying basis of the collected documents, which throughout history still exist as good. The history of what has been good is stored in man's social consciousness and linguistic documents and is transferred to new generations (La Caze, 2007). It would be possible therefore to refer to a general perception of what historically has been proven to be good for man. Such a way of thinking can also be suspected in how the risk of relativisation of the good values is addressed in the governing documents for the school, drawn up after the proposition.

The significance of the fundamental value's standards is exemplified by the sanctity of human life, individual freedom, solidarity with the weak and vulnerable, respect for the individual's uniqueness and integrity and the equal values of everybody. The standards are justified as their content is such that most people in Sweden can accept them even if they are regarded from different perspectives and cultural backgrounds. The school has a responsibility to provide students with knowledge of how these values have materialised historically. This knowledge must be communicated in such a way that students develop a personal approach to them and can wittingly decide on various issues.

The investigators behind the proposition believe that many children and young people live in a tough environment and in a rootlessness on account of the social development over the last decades, which is why the school must provide students with the 'social and moral skills to acclimatise themselves among many impressions, to ignore the harmful from the fun in youth cultures and to progress unmarred and unharmed' (Prop. 1992/93: 220, p. 7). While the curriculum committee in its report (SOU 1992:94) considers such social changes in the light of the consequences for learning and the approach to knowledge, the proposition gives greater prominence to the importance of taking advantage of traditional values. The proposition (Prop. 1992/93: 220) here speaks of the family's renaissance while the report stresses the school in its social context and the family as a changing entity. Consequently, the family is described in the report based on the changing society while in the proposition the family is portrayed as a more permanent institution:

> Contact between children and adults has changed both in terms of quantity and continuity and thus the contact pattern between young and adult has become fragmented ... The family has been destabilised and its functions changed. (SOU 1992:94)

> In recent years, there has been a tendency for young people to start families earlier and prioritise the family higher than a few years ago. Qualitative objectives in life—to find someone to share life with, sexual and emotional fidelity, to accomplish something that is important to others, to be a good mother or father, to spend time with their children— have a greater standing in youth's dreams of the future than in the past (Swedish Government Proposition 1992/93:220, p. 5).

In the proposition young people are seen as isolated from the adult world, while in the report a social awareness is attributed, especially with regard to global issues and the environment, which previous generations of young people did not possess. Grenholm says, in a changing world it is difficult to defend the values as universal and consistent. More often it is based on one's own and others' varied experiences and what society considers to be an acceptable human outlook (Grenholm, 2003).

The proposition highlights three perspectives that must characterise the work of the school, the ethical, international and environmental perspectives. These must not only be found in all subjects, but are also expected to result in 'consequences and responsibilities of the school's personnel in their behaviour and attitude outside of the teaching sessions and the teaching itself' (Prop. 1992/93: 220 pp. 14-15). The proposition asserts that it is not only in teaching and the fostering of students that the school's moralistic view is expressed and becomes visible. These fundamental values are also staged in how the school confirms the different status of different categories of personnel or in the management of the students' differences in gender, experiences, circumstances, cultural and ethnic background.

Bildung and learning.

Education and *Bildung* are regularly the subject of discussion in society. The debate at the time of drafting the proposition can be considered as a backlash against the requirement of an effective school and the employability of pupils and students. Meanwhile, in *Bildung* there is a belief in what we inherit and the tradition we are enrolled in and which act as a disciplining force. *Bildung*, irrespective of how we look at it also signifies a forming and its importance not uncommonly has the identifying individualisation character where uniqueness and originality are highlighted (Assarson, 2009a). The term is given weight in the curriculum committee's report (SOU 1992:94) by providing the title for the entire study, 'School of *Bildung*'.

The *Bildung* concept was taken from Germany and in Sweden it has strong historical roots in the Swedish adult education movement. Initially the term represented the objective, what should be achieved, as well as the process. Eventually an ideal image emerged of the educated man who seeks inner change and regeneration to a more humane man (Gustavsson, 2001). *Bildung* is thought to form the personality, but also to create the possibility to see through the perceptions of the world that exist, to pave the way for a true perception—

that is to say, *Bildung* as a modern rational notion. A central question is what distinguishes the educated, cultured man. Biesta (2002) considered the answer to lie not in terms of discipline, socialisation or morality. Rather, it is an expression of a cultivation of the inner life, which enables man to grow and live.

In the report the classical *Bildung* notion is defined in its culturally significant but also fostering and forming function:

> The transfer of knowledge and values belonging to the school's central and unavoidable mission. The school must provide students with access to knowledge traditions. The classic *Bildung* notion has nothing in common with the concept of free fostering in the form of unbridled development of abilities, which nature has given the child. Such a concept is at odds with the perception that man is a being who forms itself.
> (Swedish Government Proposition 1992/93:220, p. 13)

The school's fostering and educational missions are merged in the report. Biesta (2002) links together the *Bildung* concept with the existential responsibility of ethics philosopher Levinas. As humans, we can only be born and live, experience and learn with others. *Bildung* can then occur anywhere and not necessarily be something that occurs within the pre-established framework of the school. Instead *Bildung* will be both a lifelong challenge as well as a lifelong opportunity. A description is given in a report from the National Agency for Education with comments on Primary and Lower-Secondary School of Education (1996) of a retrospective report's view on *Bildung* and knowledge:

> The school's increasingly complex knowledge mission lies behind the expression 'School of *Bildung*'. The term *Bildung* refers to a knowledge dedication, which not only sits on the surface but also becomes part of the personality.
> (Skolverket, 1996, p. 9)

Such a *Bildung* approach, in relation to the 'social turn' also becomes visible in relation to knowledge and learning (Block, 2003). Within a socio-culturally inspired theory, the appropriation of language and knowledge is considered to be woven into the context dependent activities, which affect the individual's objectives with, and approaches to, learning (Lauesen, 2001). This means that the concepts of action, operation and activity are understood as interacting processes, and it is in the individual situations that arise that the students assimilate knowledge and language. Seen in a school setting, it thus becomes important to see the student as an actively acting subject with others in all the various situations in which learning is expected to occur. One of Vygotsky's main claims is that the social interaction between people has a crucial importance for the conceptual development and for the creation of the structures of thought.

> Every function in the child's development appears twice; first on the social level and later on the individual level; first between people (interpsychological) and then inside the child (intrapsychological). This applies equally to voluntary attention, to logical memory and the formation of concepts. All the higher functions originate as actual relationships between individuals. (Vygotskij, 1978)

The report recommends in such a spirit a transition to a sociocultural view of learning and knowledge development. The committee leans towards learning research that emphasises learning as part of a greater social and cultural context. To learn means acquiring other, new ways to think about and to relate reflectively to phenomena in the surrounding world. The school's mediation of knowledge and fostering mission merge and the proposition emphasises that there can be no conflict between them both. Fostering must be a part of teaching. The school has the importance of a culturally significant arena for culture creation and as a meeting place an important socio-bearing mission (SOU 1992:94).

Collision between values

Policy governing documents are usually drawn up in negotiations between different interests and therefore not uncommonly include different compromises in the wording. This section reviews some of the anomalies, i.e. parts where there could be difficulties in reconciling different values. At the same time it is not possible to establish an unambiguous meaning in what we see as the good values and can therefore be problematic to manage.

In the Swedish Education Act chapter 1. § 2 (SFS 2010:800) the democratic values have the status inalienable. This means they cannot be negotiated away, while in the proposition they are presented as something that has validity within a given culture circuit. These values are applicable in all circumstances within this cultural circuit and do not need to be explained, nor proven to be 'economical, efficient, practical or useful' (Prop. 1992/93: 220 p. 18). However, the same values are portrayed at the same time as unstable. They must be explained, confirmed, understood and developed. There is an inherent difficulty in the drafting between, on the one hand, seeing the values as non-negotiable and at the same time as cultural dependent in a changing world. Cultures are constantly being recreated and when cultures meet a negotiation immediately occurs where cultures mix. Cultures and languages do not live in parallel but are interrelated with each other. As cultural actions they are associated with power and status, which positions languages and cultures in the school's activities. This phenomenon has subsequently been addressed by inter alia Pirjo Lahdenperä (2004) under the concept of interculturalism as something cross-border, challenging and changing.

The directives contain some difficulties for the curriculum committee to manage before writing the report. One of these is the risk that the starting point in one's own cultural heritage makes the other unfamiliar. The responsibility of the school is defined as to strengthen the independence and self-esteem of the students. In the directives this is assumed to occur when the student finds their context and then preferably in what is Swedish or European. Students with a different cultural heritage instead become the one's expected to be strengthened by encountering understanding of their otherness. Here there is an inherent difficulty in the encounter between students with different backgrounds. Another difficulty is that teaching on the one hand must be objective while on the other hand, it is emphasised that it cannot be neutral in terms of value. A third difficulty may be to balance factual, comprehensive knowledge with the normative and fostering mission. An additional dilemma is to manage the balance between the school's and student's responsibility. In this context, it is expected that students will be strengthened by taking over more and more responsibility for their own learning with increasing age. This demands an organisation of the learning environment so that this becomes possible.

The democratic values have different significance in the report and in the proposition. In the report these are a part of the *Bildung* notion and are based in Dewey's' pragmatic ideas about the transfer of the democratic cultural heritage while those in the proposition more often rest on the individual's freedom of choice and personal responsibility. In the texts about democracy, the social power dimensions are also more accentuated in the report than in the proposition where power is seen more as responsibility. Freedom of choice and responsibility as democratic values become difficult for the school's personnel to relate to without further discussion about power and about people's different opportunities to choose and take responsibility, or about how different choices are construed and by whom. The proposition leaves many decisions to the schools and therefore it is also emphasises that 'management by objectives means that politicians relinquish power in many issues' (Prop. 1992/93: 220 p. 28). The question is how this power is then constituted in schools.

The relationship between the majority and the minority risks being contradictory when the fundamental values on one hand are based on values such as 'most people who live in Sweden can accept,' while on the other hand, the minority and the individual must be respected. At the same time it is emphasised that schools cannot see each opinion and position as being as good as another. The school must not be value-free, but must actively counteract opinions and forms of expression that 'encroach upon someone and that conflict with fundamental values regarding human equality and women's and men's equal rights and opportunities' (Prop. 1992/93: 220 p. 20). In the same way as the starting point in terms of cultural heritage is described as our relation to the others, here the majority can become ours which is presumed to be prevalent and where minorities will be the other that must be understood in order to be respected, but without some form of participation being secured. These fundamental values are formulated in the proposition as a social majority construction, which is why xenophobia could be an indication that some of those belonging to the majority feel threatened, by the different way of thinking, by the others. In such a conflict, it is difficult to see that the fundamental values could be negotiated. Rather there is a risk of the consequence being the elimination of threats by immigrants being urged to embrace the majority culture.

Chapter 7

Using inquiry to shed light on and respond to inequities identified within a network of English high schools

Sue Goldrick

Despite the widely held belief that one of the key purposes of education is to improve equity and opportunities for all, we know that education is becoming increasingly inequitable, both within and between national education systems (OECD 2007). As other chapters in this volume have testified, over the last twenty-five years, the English education system has come to be characterised by substantial inequities in terms of access, participation, engagement and outcomes, in particular for students from backgrounds of poverty or ethnic diversity. Despite evidence of overall improvements in English education, the most disadvantaged children, in general, attend the lowest performing schools (Lupton 2005), and the performance and qualities of one school often impact directly on other schools in the same area. In addition, the gap in attainment between the most and least advantaged continues to widen (Ainscow et al., 2006b, 2012).

Tackling this problem clearly involves ever more powerful national and regional policies. However, the idea of teachers as policy-makers (Ozga, 2000) suggests that real change also requires the deep engagement of teachers and school leaders in making their own practice, within and between schools, more equitable. National educational policies shape and constrain teachers' beliefs and practice but, even within such a context, teachers can create enquiring spaces where they can reappraise and truly deepen their understandings of their students, and how they need to respond to their learning needs, so that all students may benefit.

This chapter draws from evidence from a study of a network of secondary (11-16 or 19) schools (known locally as 'high schools') within one local authority area in England. It reports on a potential way of achieving this kind of change through collaborative enquiry between teachers and university researchers in context.

For many years, researchers in the Centre for Equity in Education (CEE), at the University of Manchester, have worked closely with networks of schools, forming collaborative inquiry partnerships with the aim of better understanding and tackling equity related issues experienced within schools. The CEE is committed to doing research that makes a difference with respect to educational equity. Researchers work alongside practitioners such as teachers, teaching assistants and senior school leaders and together they seek practical solutions within their complex local education situations (Ainscow et al., 2009, 2012).

The CEE approach builds on its members' previous work, including the projects *Improving the Quality of Education for All* (Hopkins et al., 1996) and *Understanding and Developing Inclusive Practices in Schools*. The latter is particularly relevant. Operating between 2000 and 2004, *Understanding and Developing Inclusive Practices in Schools* (Ainscow, Booth and Dyson, 2004, 2006a, Dyson et al., 2003, Howes et al., 2004, 2005), involved twenty-five schools and three universities in three different regions of England. Together, school inquiry teams and university researchers explored issues in inclusion and sought ways of making participating schools more inclusive of their diverse populations. This approach has been developed 2006 to the present with schools elsewhere and with a somewhat broader focus on 'equity'. In the first instance, this development took the form of a five-year project with a network of schools in a single local authority area. It is from this project that this chapter draws its evidence.

Research setting

The project was located in an area characterised by socio-economic disadvantage, and social and ethnic segregation. At the centre of the area is a large town of about 82,000 people, which was once prosperous in the manufacture of heavy textile goods. Now, however, most of the old industries have disappeared and unemployment is high. Housing is segregated, with old cramped terraced housing near the town centre and large sprawling isolated social housing estates on the outskirts. The town centre residential district is inhabited mainly by low income Pakistani heritage families, while the social housing is inhabited mainly by low income White British families. In between the social housing estates and scattered across the hills and along the valleys are small towns and villages comprising renovated housing occupied by relatively affluent professionals who commute to work in the three nearby big cities.

At the start of this project, the local authority's secondary school system comprised a hierarchy of sixteen non-fee-paying state secondary schools, including two selective grammar schools, two selective faith schools, eleven comprehensive schools and one special school. Two out of the sixteen high schools did not have provision for 16-19 year-olds, both of which served economically disadvantaged communities. Central and local government identified the exam performance of all these schools as varying considerably. One of the schools was one of the lowest performing schools in England, while the two selective schools were among the highest. Ten of these high schools, including the ones at either end of the performance spectrum, were clustered within a five-mile radius of each other.

Unfolding process

The project was set up in 2006 between four of these high schools, three of which were seen as being at the bottom of the school performance league table and within the main geographical cluster of schools identified above. The fourth school was about seven miles from the others and half way down the league table. All four were comprehensive schools and had previously worked together. The headteachers from these schools approached the University to work with them on a collaborative project focused on improving practice in equitable directions. The heads agreed a fee their schools would pay to the University to design, facilitate and support inquiry-based developments across the four schools for one year, with the possibility of continuing at the end of the first year.

It became clear that issues of inequity existed in each of the four schools but with different meanings in each one, especially when defining how inequity was experienced by different groups of children. In discussions with the university researchers, the heads therefore decided to create the agenda as a set of broad research questions through which each school could decide on a focus specific to their context. The three questions were as follows:

> Which learners are most vulnerable to underachievement, marginalisation or exclusion in our schools?
> What changes in policy and practice need to be made in order to reach out to these students?
> How can these changes be introduced effectively and evaluated in respect to student outcomes?

It was felt that this agenda, with its focus on groups of learners, would enable the school staff to respond more meaningfully to the complexities of their individual school contexts. There was a risk that the questions might lead the school staff to focus on deficit views of their students, rather than looking at the learning context of these students. In nearly all cases, however, the inquiries sooner or later opened out to explore contextual factors that might be contributing to the students' marginalisation. In addition, student outcomes were nearly always seen as being synonymous with attainment scores, and while improvements in these rightly remained a key goal, other student outcomes emerged as also being valuable, such as improved self-esteem, confidence, independence, tolerance and life chances.

Over five years, fourteen of the sixteen schools in the area joined the network, some for one year or five years, but many for two to four years. For these schools, the agenda worked at two levels—within each school and across the schools as a group.

Within-school developments

In each school, inquiry teams were set up, generally consisting of between four and six staff members, representing different perspectives on what was going on in their schools. This was to encourage critical and constructive dialogue within the teams. Typically, teams comprised a combination of teachers, senior teachers, teaching assistants and behaviour support assistants. In addition, at least one team member was required to be from senior management to enable access to resources. A researcher also worked closely with the school teams, supporting them in gathering and making sense of evidence and acting as a critical friend.

At the start of the year the inquiry teams took part in introductory workshops where after analysing their local education system, and the inequities therein, they analysed their own school contexts in terms of groups of students they regarded as vulnerable in some way. They speculated over possible reasons for these perceived vulnerabilities by trying to see them from different perspectives. Sometimes, they could not articulate the reasons, or they explained them in terms of perceived deficit characteristics of the students and their communities. Examples of some of the student groups identified and initial 'hunches' about these groups, over the five years, are given in table 1.

Table 1: Starting points: Identified groups of learners and initial hunches about why they lose out

Equity issue identified	Initial hunches about identified groups of marginalised learners
Mobility	Students who change school between the normal starting and leaving dates. Hunches: They often change schools before they are 'pushed' for challenging behaviour and they are not interested in learning in their new schools. They are more interested in establishing new identities with their peers. Little is known about their backgrounds.
Permanent exclusions of Asian heritage young men	A disproportionate number of Asian heritage boys are permanently excluded for serious misbehaviour. Hunches: This could be because they have little respect for their parents and the older generation, and they are often distracted by 'dubious enterprises' they are involved in outside school.
'Invisible', 'ghost', 'wallpaper' students	Students who are quiet, middle ability and do not present challenging behaviour. Hunches: They appear to have a 'disappointing time' at school.
Non-participants in-out-of-school-hours (OOSH) activities	Students, mainly girls from disadvantaged backgrounds, who choose not to participate in out-of-school-hours activities. Hunches: Peer pressure and general lack of interest in school are seen as possible causes. Participation in OOSH activities would ultimately improve their attainment scores.
Poor attendance	A very high number of students (18%) persistently choose not to attend school. Many go to school but choose not to attend lessons. Often they present challenging behaviour. Hunches: Families and communities have low expectations of school.
Middle ability, underachieving with challenging behaviour	A large number of middle to low ability students are underachieving, and present challenging behaviour. Hunches: They have little parental involvement and little self-discipline.
Difficult children to engage with due to behaviour and / or communication skills	Students who have extremely challenging behaviour with severe learning difficulties and/or disabilities. Hunches: They are very difficult to support and engage with.
Newly arrived and learning to speak English as an additional language (EAL).	Large numbers of mainly Eastern European students with English as an additional language often speak their first language with friends in class. Hunches: They are reluctant to mix with other students. Tensions between these and other students exist.
Underachieving White British boys	Boys who are not making enough progress. They are not motivated but not challenging. Hunches: They suffer from 'estatism' (social housing culture). For example, they happily coast along, letting their mothers and sisters take care of them.
High drop-out rate of students in post-16 schools	A disproportionate number of students who transfer from schools without sixth forms to schools with sixth forms drop out. Hunches: At their new schools, they are found to be lacking 'good' academic or independent learning skills.

In general, the inquiry teams then engaged in a process of gathering a range of evidence to explore and clarify their hunches about who exactly their identified students were, and their experiences of school and learning. As they found out more they formulated and refined exploratory-oriented open-ended research questions.

The university researchers supported the school teams in gathering and engaging with evidence to explore the nature of their students' experiences. Methods for gathering data included using existing school statistical data, mutual observations; student, teacher and parent surveys; video recordings of lessons; student shadowing; focus groups and interviews with students and teachers; student-led inquiries and participative photography.

Researchers also acted as critical friends when the teams were making sense of their evidence. Many of them said they were taken aback by what they found. Often these were unexpected insights into their school contexts and their own taken-for-granted beliefs and values, leading to shifts in their assumptions about the groups of students and the nature of their assumed marginalisation. This then spurred them on to collect and engage with more data to explore their situation more deeply and in different directions, which, in turn, often led to more surprises and more reappraising of assumptions. Sometimes these surprises were uncomfortable, and the staff members voiced their dissatisfaction about what was happening for these young people in school. Many of them felt a sense of responsibility to do something about these situations. In contrast, one or two school teams persisted in blaming the children for these less palatable experiences.

In some schools, the teams shared their evidence and insights with their colleagues at whole school meetings, which, to varying degrees, challenged and stimulated staff's thinking. In other cases, they shared their insights through informal interactions, coaching activities or joint practice developments. Some of the inquiries led to whole-school or department developments in policies and practices. In contrast, some other teams found it difficult to find a voice in their schools, leaving them feeling like 'secret societies'.

Towards the end of the school year, each school team was assisted in producing a collaborative account of their inquiry developments, and these were disseminated at a conference held at the end of the school year. Senior leaders were invited to these conferences, alongside representatives from schools outside the network, and other professionals from related disciplines in children's services.

Alongside the accounts and notes generated through the process of working with the network, semi-structured interviews were carried out with participants at the end of the year. This was to generate evidence of what the network, its focus and its activities meant to them as individuals. Below are examples of four schools' experiences of carrying out inquiry-based developments as a way to tackle inequities identified, and how this process impacted on how they saw and responded to these inequities.

Four examples of within-school inquiry developments

School A was a small 11-16 high school with about four hundred and fifty students on roll, around ninety per cent of whom were from White British families. The number of students eligible for free school meals (FSM) was twice the national average and a higher than average number of students were identified as having learning difficulties. Ten per cent of students did not attend school regularly. The school was under-subscribed. Consequently, it had a very large number of feeder primary schools, twenty-seven in all, with thirty-five per cent coming from the north of the town to the south, involving long and sometimes difficult journeys to school. Most of the students came from neighbourhoods characterised by socio-economic disadvantage. There had also been an unexpected intake of Eastern European students and there was growing concern about ethnic tensions. In total, thirty-four per cent of students joined the school after the normal starting date. There were new arrivals virtually every week. At the same time, a large number of students left the school before the normal finishing date, transferring to other schools when places arose, as this school had not been their first choice.

The inquiry team were keen to investigate issues around this mobility, in particular, in-coming mobility. They discussed how little was known about their previous schooling experiences, whether these had been in different countries, or in England. In the case of those from other English schools, some, but not all, of the older new arrivals had been advised to leave their previous schools and go elsewhere to avoid possible permanent exclusion. For most of the young people, it was difficult to gain information about the curriculum they had studied or their ability levels, and it was difficult to place students because of timetable restrictions.

The team were encouraged to explore their mobile students' experiences of learning. In Year 7, the first year of high school, twelve per cent of 11-12 year-old students joined the school after the normal starting date, but what shocked the team was that by Year 11 this figure had risen to fifty-one per cent, the year when 15-16 year-olds sit GCSE (General Certificate of Secondary Education) exams. They then looked at the percentage of mobile students who had gained five or more A*-C GCSE grades (the national benchmark of success in secondary school) over the previous two years. They were even more shocked to find that while this figure was twenty-one per cent and eighteen per cent for those students who had started in Year 7, (still low compared to other schools), this figure dropped to three per cent and four per cent for students who joined in Years 7 to 9, and dropped further to zero per cent and three per cent for students who joined in Years 10 to 11. Mobile students were making very little progress in terms of attainment scores.

The inquiry team discussed how the students joining higher up the school seemed not to be interested in learning. They were more concerned about social aspects of schools—about fitting in or alternatively gaining an identity, possibly a reputation of notoriety with their peers. However, through conducting focus groups with Year 11 mobile students with support from the university researcher, the team were genuinely surprised to find that this was not the case.

While many of them commented that they found the school friendly and welcoming, most of them were not confident in their academic subjects. They were not clear what their expected grades were, most of them had not been able to take their first choices in subjects, they were not fully aware of the range of choices they had, and some of them felt they had been put in classes in an ad hoc fashion. Many students felt frustrated that their coursework from their previous schools was not acknowledged, and sometimes they felt they were viewed negatively for not having done this work and were not given support to catch up. They struggled with how to act in class and around school, and missed their old friends and home. Most of them had rich experiences of life, of which the team were unaware.

The team went on to shadow some newly arrived students in class. They discussed how most of the students seemed awkward in class but eager to please both the teacher and peers. On-going negotiation of friendships was evident, on occasions resulting in their being drawn quietly into off-task activities. When given appropriate attention from teachers, such as being asked easily answerable questions, providing extra one-to-one support, and being named, students evidently grew in confidence. In contrast, they were sometimes completely ignored.

The team reflected on the inquiry process and one of them commented:

> I think transcribing it is really effective. Your initial reaction is to laugh. You read something and you think 'oh gosh, that is terrible' and then you go back to it and start to think about it and discuss it. Having it actually written down, some of those things that they raised make you focus on some difficult things. It really brings them to light.

Another teacher explained teachers' views of mobile children coming into their lessons and how they needed to change it:

> We've looked at from the point of view that it's not fair on the teachers, 'It's not fair on me as a History teacher to have these students come in half way through Year 10 and to expect me to be able to get them to their grades' … There's this unrelenting drive to increase standards. These teachers are saying 'Oh good grief! I've got more kids arriving part way through. The data says that they're bright enough to get a grade C or a B or an A, how do I get that grade? How am I supposed to do that when they have been doing a different History course … and then actually lose sight of the child. We only see that potential grade and how we get them to that grade … [We need] to focus on whether we are being fair for that child. [We need to ask,] 'Hang on a minute, what does it actually mean for that child walking through the door, being new to the school?'

A clerical officer in the inquiry team, responsible for monitoring data about new arrivals, argued that the inquiry had changed her understandings of the needs of the students. Consequently, she made a point of finding time to meet with the students rather than just knowing them as names on the computer screen or parent voices on the phone.

The team went on to develop a number of procedures to support these students when they first came into the school. However, at the end of the first year the headteacher left the school, and despite the team's wishes to share their findings and develop responses with other teachers in the school, this did not happen. Indeed the team struggled to have their voices heard over the following years as four new heads came and went over the following four years and the school entered a period of turbulence and close scrutiny by central government.

School B was a large 11-18 high school with about one thousand and four hundred students on roll, of whom three hundred were in the sixth form (Years 12 to13). It was situated some seven miles south west of the main town centre. It served a mainly socio-economically advantaged community, mostly White British, with forty per cent of parents having higher education qualifications, and many of these leading 'alternative' lifestyles. It was over-subscribed and mobility was low. Nevertheless, a small number of children, coming from a nearby housing estate, experienced disadvantage. These children struggled to compete socially and academically with their peers. The school was designated as a training school for newly qualified teachers and other aspects of teacher development.

The school's sixth form had a different profile as many students from other schools in the area transferred to this school for Years 12 and 13. Spaces arose because a number of pupils from School B transferred to a nationally reputed sixth-form-only college in a neighbouring local authority area. In the sixth form at School B, a higher than average number of students were eligible for FSM. About thirty per cent of the students were Asian British, having transferred from High School C at the end of Year 11.

The inquiry team's hunches were that some children were having a 'disappointing time' at the school, that they did not feel they belonged to the school, nor were they very interested in learning. Through these discussions they realised they did not actually know much about these students or indeed who they were, other than that they were 'those grey, middle ability kind of student'.

They used existing data from their whole school behaviour system to identify a group of Year 9 students to focus on. They used the school's system for recording approval and disapproval—known as 'credits' and 'sanctions'—to help them in this. They looked for students who had received less than ten credits, when others had received over a hundred, but who had no sanctions, and had full attendance. To the team's surprise, twenty-five per cent of students met these criteria, and were 'invisible' to the system. What surprised them more was that they were from across the 'ability' range. This stimulated 'some serious and honest reappraisal' of how they viewed and interacted with these students. They had assumed being invisible was connected to ability.

They decided to shadow some of these students in lessons with support from the university researcher. They were taken aback by how similar the observed students' experiences appeared to be. They found that many of the students were rarely named or approached in class. They either tended to work through their tasks quietly, often finishing before other students but not then demanding attention, or they were quietly off-task occasionally distracting other students.

When reflecting on this analysis, the team speculated that the students probably did not want to be noticed or picked out. However, when the students were asked during subsequent focus groups, how they felt about lessons, they unanimously said that they wanted to be noticed, acknowledged and praised, but not necessarily in obvious upfront ways. They were acutely aware that other students did get noticed and that these students determined the pace and focus of learning. One of the students reflected, 'being good isn't enough'. Once more the staff were taken by surprise and committed to share their findings with their colleagues.

The team ran a whole-school teacher workshop to explore the evidence and its implications. Following these discussions, a programme of school-based staff development activities was designed. These comprised trios of volunteer teachers observing students in each other's lessons and then reflecting on the learning experience together. During a second round, the volunteers asked the students what they felt about the lesson and what they felt they were learning. The discussions with the students seemed to indicate that when they felt they were learning was less about the activities they were doing, and more about their relationship with the teacher. One of the inquiry team reflected:

> It's been a real eye-opener, especially in our school where we focus a lot on teaching approaches, methods, and techniques, and on classroom organisation.

Another teacher added:

> We thought we were looking for approaches—classroom methodologies ... but these don't appear to have been so important. What has emerged is the strength of relationships. There's nothing really surprising about this, it's just it's not given the priority it perhaps deserves. It is not so much about the three-part lesson, interactive white boards, exam schemes, which text books you are using, assessment processes or anything like that. There are more fundamental issues around social cohesion and what both students and teachers come willingly to school for.

School C had a student population of about six hundred and fifty 11-16 year-olds. Eighty five per cent of students were British Asian, coming from different localities but mainly from the community living around the school where over seventy per cent were British Asian. This community was characterised by high levels of socio-economic disadvantage. The school was oversubscribed, though this popularity had not always been the case. Five to six years previously, it had been a 'failing school' with the number of students getting good GCSEs plateauing at around fifteen per cent. However, the then new head radically changed the organisation of the school, with the focus becoming about 'attainment and results rather than equity' (head teacher of School C) and within a few years the school was identified as one of the most improved schools in England, and the head received an award from the Queen and Prime Minister. Attainment in five A*-C GCSEs had soared to fifty-one per cent. The head had reorganised the students into academic, vocational and learning support strands at the end of Year 9. The academic strand comprised only those students who were seen as likely to get five A*-C grades in their GCSEs. Once placed in these strands for Maths, English and Science, students could not move for the rest of their time in the school. Their curriculum and the teachers who taught them were different from those of their peers.

The inquiry team decided that they wanted to investigate students in the vocational strand, that is those expected to get low grades in their GCSEs, who were underachieving and presenting challenging behaviour. They identified these students from their attainment progress and behaviour records. Their hunch was that these students did not have good independent learning skills, had unrealistic expectations for what they might achieve in their exams, had little parental support and struggled with their British Asian identities.

The team observed the students in lessons. Most of the team members discussed how they were not surprised by what they said they saw. They mostly interpreted the students' interactions negatively. The students tended to arrive late, were generally disengaged from lessons, and had no urgency to complete tasks. Students also appeared to have problems with understanding instructions and concepts, resorting to copying answers from the board or peers, and chatting. They got bored quickly and often disrupted the lessons.

However, when the teachers, with support from the university researcher, went on to conduct student focus groups, the same students who had been observed in lessons talked about how they liked having tasks explained to them, having their worked checked during lessons, having teachers help them individually, giving presentations to the whole class, debating, doing structured activities in groups, and talking through tasks before writing, and how these interactions did not always happen. There were clearly two very different sets of viewpoints about what was going on in the classroom.

The students also talked at length about the strand system in the school, and the vocational strand within which they were all placed. Some comments were positive, for example, 'it's easier so you learn better', or 'I'm happy where I am'. However, many comments were negative, such as 'they don't think much of us lot', 'it's unfair', 'they get more opportunities', 'everyone should have an equal shot at the exams but you can't', 'the vocational strand is for those who basically messed up their [earlier school exams]', and 'we are like the low group, the lower people'. These comments led them to investigate further, through a survey and teacher focus groups, how the staff interacted with students regarding target setting for progress and exam results.

The teacher focus group and survey data revealed that teachers' discussions with students in the vocational strand about target grades tended to be 'less focussed and honest' than with more able students. Teachers found it hard to say to students that if they worked really hard they might still not achieve the benchmark grades. This lack of clarity often resulted in the students believing they were going to get higher grades than they did. Through a subsequent staff survey, the team found that many staff did not have a 'sound understanding' of the value of lower GCSE grades, and of the pathways open to students if they left school at 16. One of the inquiry team reflected, 'we get wrapped up so much in the A*-C culture'.

The team decided to investigate what the students said their achievements and activities were outside the classroom but still in school. They found that these students did very little in contrast to other students in the academic strand, even though these activities were rarely related to the students' academic studies. One teacher reflected, 'it's not necessarily because these students are excluded, more that the academic students volunteer', and argued that they needed to 'positively discriminate for these students' in the vocational strand. She felt that the academic-vocational divide 'was creating an underclass' of students with low self-esteem, and they have 'no way of tracking' these students' experiences even though they had a 'wonderful tracking system for academic progress'. She concluded that the head's 'grand plan' for getting the school 'very good results' had worked, but added,

It's really having a detrimental effect on half the school. We're more or less saying that [we] have created our internal [selective] system, which then has a totally demotivating effect on my kids.

The inquiry team shared their evidence with the head teacher and the senior management team, and then small discussion groups of teachers. The findings from these discussions contributed to the decision to hold a curriculum review to widen the range of skills that were explicitly developed in school, to develop ways of demonstrating to students that they were making progress, that they could be successful beyond academic subjects, and to widen staff and student knowledge about 'realistic post-16 options' and 'different ways of being intelligent'. It is also interesting to note that at the end of the second year of the inquiry network, the head announced he was leaving the school to become an advisor for an initiative that looked at creating a fairer, more coherent system for children and young people across the whole local area.

During a reflective discussion with the head at the end of the first year of the inquiry, he explained that initially he 'only went along' with joining the inquiry network because of his colleagues in the other schools, but he had seen it as 'potentially enabling' his staff to investigate an equity issue which might have 'useful messages' for them. He reiterated his rationale for creating the academic strand, of wanting to create an academic group and a culture of academic achievement, which he felt had paid off for those students and those at the top of the vocational strand. However, the headteacher acknowledged that the curriculum for most of the vocational strand was 'a bit of a trudge', and 'not very inspiring'. He wanted to provide 'more genuinely experiential and motivating' courses, not the 'current classroom based options'. He wanted to 'worry less about exam results, and think more about the experience of education' and the motivation [students] gained from it, to 'continue feeling good about themselves' and to feel that 'school matters', more than 'squeezing the next grade out of them'. He also felt that encouraging students to do GCSEs was not motivating. Being pushed to go from a low grade to one that was only marginally higher 'did not give a very positive message'. When asked how the students might feel about doing different qualifications from GCSEs, he said it was crucial that they 'needed to feel confident in the knowledge' that the course they were doing was of 'equal value in terms of providing genuinely equitable opportunities', adding that this '[needed] to be true', and the pupils '[needed] to feel it was true'. Assessment offered students a 'passport' to post-16 education in the 'current target driven culture', but something needed to change, 'we need to give a better deal to those kids'.

School D had just over five hundred students on roll. The school was undersubscribed and student numbers were declining. Over twice the national average of students were eligible for FSM. Many children arrived at the school in Year 7 with attainment scores in numeracy and literacy well below national averages. Most students were White British and most came from two nearby housing estates. The communities on these estates to the north of the main town were some of the most socially and economically disadvantaged in England with life expectancy being seven years less than in neighbouring areas. Attendance was one of the lowest in England at eighty-two per cent. Outward mobility was also high, with many students transferring to School A, given that it too was under-subscribed. The school was also at the bottom of the area's school league table. Within two miles of the school, were the area's two selective grammar schools, the two selective faith schools, and School C, whose students were mainly British Asian.

The school had also had a huge amount of media and central government attention over the previous ten years. Some years previously a collapse of discipline was identified, teachers threatened to walk out unless a large number of students were permanently excluded, and the school was briefly closed. National and international press broadcast the whole episode, and after that, they and central government had kept a close eye on the school.

The inquiry team comprised a newly employed History teacher and two teaching assistants (non-teachers who work alongside teachers in classrooms) who both lived locally and whose children had or were attending the school. The team felt they had to tackle attendance because if the students were not in school they could not help them. In their initial discussions they wanted to focus on the causes. They discussed, for example, parental and community attitudes, teacher attitudes, and home life difficulties, and the fact that perhaps the students 'just could not be bothered'.

One of the team members monitored attendance closely. What prompted them into action was the finding that over a four week period in the first half term of the year, two thousand five hundred and twenty-two lessons were missed across the school. Finding this 'pretty mind blowing' they decided to ask the students what they thought. They devised their own method for generating students' views. These were fast-paced interactive workshops for about fifteen students, a cross between lesson-type activities and a focus group format. All three members of the inquiry team evidently had good relationships with the children, and this was particularly noticeable on other occasions when the two teaching assistants were working closely with students identified as having challenging behaviour.

The team ran several of the workshops with a variety of groups of students from across their school and found that their 'hunches turned out to be wrong'. The students told them overwhelmingly that they attended some but not all lessons. The ones they chose not to attend, they said, were boring and were not planned well; students often had to copy out of books; the teachers did not often interact on a one-to-one basis in the classroom; they did not care; they 'had your card marked'; the students could not trust some teachers. When the team tracked more closely the students' truancy patterns, it became clear that, in general, these students missed or presented challenging behaviour in classes with teachers they did not like, and in particular, classes with 'cover teachers', those teachers who are brought in to cover for teachers who are absent. On the other hand, most of these students participated relatively well in classes with teachers they liked.

Just after the team started carrying out its workshops, the school was visited by Ofsted, the national schools inspectorate and was judged to be inadequate. It was therefore placed into 'special measures' and inspectors started to monitor the school on a regular basis. School staff relations deteriorated and some staff threatened to go on strike again. The media were also trying to persuade children and parents to speak out against the school, offering money outside the school gate. The atmosphere was tense. One team member commented that it had been 'awkward' for her. Another added,

> If you go up into the school staffroom, you will see the divide in the staff, the ones who are interested and the ones that are not bothered. They're not in for trying to help us get over the barrier that's blocking us get out of the media spotlight.

The collaborative inquiry activities seemed to reinforce the team's moral commitment to enhancing the experiences of their students. Their challenge was to stimulate others in their school to work together to reappraise their assumptions, values and practices, whilst also keeping their morale up to continue doing their best to help the young people in the school. The team shared their evidence with the whole school, and used this as an opportunity to introduce 'non-confrontational mutual coaching', which they called 'learning conversations', across the school to encourage staff to work together to develop their practices. They had considered carrying out mutual observations but they felt their colleagues had been 'observationed out' through close scrutiny from Ofsted. Participants from the network and the university also attended the meeting to show that the network inquiry approach was bigger than just School D. Unfortunately, at the start of the fortnight when the learning conversations were due to take place, Ofsted announced they were coming in again to carry out another inspection and so the coaching sessions were postponed. Despite all these disruptions, one of the team members reflected,

> The first half term of this year was like a battle between the Old and the New. The negative 'These kids are the problem', lots of copying-out, no-proper-marking-of-books, being-rude-to-the-kids, type teachers lost ... People came out of hiding, and said, 'Right what can we do?' In a way it gave people who had almost been intimidated by the problems the confidence to come out.

A year later the school was judged by Ofsted as 'good with outstanding features', in particular for some of the teaching and the pastoral care. During this time, the student workshops continued across the school in every department and the students' views were drawn on to help shape teaching and learning. Learning conversations between staff finally went ahead. By this time, the inquiry activities had been incorporated into the school's general practices and the school organised these initiatives for itself.

Despite all of these developments and the positive feedback from Ofsted, central and local government determined to close the school. Students transferred to other schools in the area in the final two years of the school. Many of them transferred to School A, despite its long distance away, resulting in mixed experiences. While School A benefited from no longer being under-subscribed and some of the students settled in well, others did not. Some struggled at their new school with the new systems, teachers and bullying, and some had to be moved on to other schools. In its last term, a small group of sixteen students remained at School D, unable to secure places at the faith school they wanted to attend nearby. It was felt they might present too many challenges for the receiving school and adversely affect the school.

Cross-school developments

At the cross school level, the teams came together about six times a year, including the introductory workshop and the end-of-year conference. At the interim network meetings the teams shared each other's experiences of their inquiry activities. Initially, the first four school teams were reluctant to work together as they felt they had nothing in common, that their school contexts were unique. However, they came to look forward to these meetings. As one inquiry team member commented, the space and dialogue enabled them to reflect on their own school circumstances:

> It gives us time to reflect and it offers us a mirror to our schools with critical ears and eyes from other places, we don't exist in isolation.

They borrowed each other's ideas for inquiry activities, and they inspired each other to keep going through difficult situations, and supported one another to try out new ideas.

In most cases these cross-school interactions and activities appeared to deepen understandings of the issues of equity being experienced both within and across their schools. As one teacher reflected,

> It shouldn't really matter which school [the students] go to, they are all equally deserving … I now feel that I have a responsibility to all students in [the area].

Another added,

> I think there is inequity within and across schools in [the area]. It's something we need to tackle head on, not sweep under the carpet because not all students get a fair chance in our education. Across the country it's the case but this is our patch and we need to make sure we tackle it, and this process seems to shine a light on what's going on.

A number of the participants witnessed first-hand how one school's good fortune was another school's misfortune. At one of the cross school meetings, a teacher from School A expressed some relief because their school was no longer taking in large numbers of students after the normal starting date. They were at full capacity given the imminent closure of School D, and students having transferred across to their school. Team members from School D reacted with resigned smiles to each other. A teacher reflected,

> It was like kicking a dog when it's down. If the staff are feeling undervalued and vulnerable, what's that doing to the kids?

Conclusion

The evidence from the inquiry process reinforces many of the more negative findings from other chapters about the English school system in this volume. We see clearly the effects in the education system of social inequalities and of the concentration of disadvantage in particular places. We see how schools are faced with challenging, if not insuperable, difficulties which make it extremely difficult to achieve equitable outcomes for their students. We see how spatial segregation coupled with a system which encourages competition between institutions creates local hierarchies of schools in which the winners act to protect their interests and the losers are vulnerable to punitive sanctions and even to closures. We see also how the focus in national policy on attainment targets distorts the ways in which schools work with their students and what they try to achieve on their behalf. Time and again, schools seem to be driven to act in ways which protect their own institutional interests, but which marginalise particular groups of students. Perhaps most troubling of all, we see how school leaders and teachers appear to be enlisted in these marginalising agendas and see the inequities which arise from their practices as inevitable, or even beneficial. Students from disadvantaged backgrounds, along with their families and communities are routinely seen as authors of their own misfortune. Time and again, teachers cast themselves as safeguarding the interests of those who are able to achieve and as moral guardians to the most disadvantaged, showing them how they might do better—if only they would.

Nothing in the inquiry process changes the fundamentals of this situation. There are no radical changes in school organisation and practice, and the process is in any case incapable of troubling the national imperatives out of which those practices arise. Even at a local level, the process is not good at challenging forms of inequity that lie outside the immediate control of teachers. Faced with sources of inequity beyond the school, teachers continue to focus primarily on the within-school issues over which they can have some immediate influence. At no point is there any sense that they are going to work collectively across the schools to tackle systemic or wider societal issues. Moreover, the process is heavily dependent on external support—more accurately, critical friendship—from the university team who help inquiry teams and their schools to examine their practices and to explore different ways forward. Whether such a process could arise and be sustained purely from within a school's resources is far from clear—and, if it could not, the prospects for taking this approach to scale are limited.

Nonetheless, things do change in these schools as a result of their engagement with inquiry—and they change despite the apparently overwhelming pressures of national policy and societal inequalities. Some teachers at least, whilst remaining focused on their schools and classrooms, nonetheless begin to think differently. They identify the ways in which inequities arise out of their own practices, and find ways to change them. They are, in some cases at least, able to carry their colleagues and headteachers along with them, and there is some indication of the process becoming embedded in schools. Crucially, they begin to think in terms of evidence rather than presupposition as the basis for their practice. English schools are rich in particular kinds of data in that they know a great deal about the measured attainment of their students and know something about a range of demographic indicators through which the attainments of particular groups of students can be interrogated. For the most part, these data are used to inform a narrow focus on attainment and processes of segregation and marginalisation (Ainscow et al., 2007). However, we see in the schools here how they can also be used to identify groups of students who are doing badly in a range of ways, and/or who are somehow excluded from the life of the school. They can then form the basis of new kinds of practice aimed at generating more equitable practices and outcomes rather than reinforcing the status quo. Moreover, we also see in these schools how teachers can begin to elicit and build upon the voices of their students. The notion of data widens to include what children and young people say and think, rather than simply how they perform in tests.

The inquiry process, then, provides teachers and other school staff with some space in which they can deepen and widen their understandings of equity, and, at least in terms of their own practices, can re-form policy. Although the process in its current form cannot easily be taken to scale, the examples above suggest that some of the change processes can become incorporated and embedded within schools' practices and, as such, can become sustainable. The key challenge for the future, therefore, is to find ways of engaging more teachers and more schools in processes of this kind. It may be that universities need to change what they understand by educational research and therefore how they engage with schools. Initial teacher training and continuing professional development may offer larger-scale opportunities for injecting a more critical and ethical dimension into teacher development. It may also be that school-to-school networking offers a promising way forward with schools providing critical friendship to each other. All of these could be facilitated considerably by supportive central government policies. However, none of them is entirely dependent on such facilitation. Even in the most unpromising of circumstances, it seems there is something that schools and teachers can do for themselves to develop more equitable practices.

Chapter 8

Constructions of student identity in talk and text: A focus on special educational needs in Sweden and England

Ines Alves, Ingela Andreasson, Yvonne Karlsson, and Susie Miles

Introduction

Defining, organising and responding to student diversity, in terms of culture, ethnicity, language, and ability, is a major feature of modern schooling, yet education systems respond in different ways to this challenge. The significance of this chapter is in its analysis of the way teachers in England and Sweden, two remarkably similar countries in many ways, respond to individual children categorised as having 'special educational needs' (SEN). With a relatively small percentage of children (one to two per cent) being educated in special schools, and fluid boundaries existing between mainstream and special schools, the English and Swedish education systems can be characterised as having developed sophisticated ways of responding to the complex individual needs of students through a continuum of equitable educational provision. In this sense, a policy emphasis on inclusive education has led to blurred and permeable boundaries between special and mainstream provision. In asking questions about the way in which schools construct and respond to difference, we consider how teachers' conceptualisation of children who have difficulties in learning tends to replicate the boundaries that national policies aimed to erode.

Following Dyson and Millward (2000, p. 37), we use the theoretical perspectives of two scholars—Thomas Skrtic in the USA and Mel Ainscow in England—considered to have articulated 'a theoretical account of the relationship between inclusion and schools as organisations'. We present and interrogate our findings from school-based research in the two country contexts. Skrtic (1991) has theorised schools as 'bureaucratic' organisations, which resist change. They perceive children who struggle to learn within their established practices as anomalous, and instead of rethinking their practices to include such children, they establish separate sub-systems such as special education to accommodate these children. This can only change if and when schools seek to become 'adhocracies' in which teachers pool their expertise and resources to change established practices so that 'anomalous' children can be included. Ainscow (1999) likewise draws a distinction between 'stuck' schools which preserve their established practices, and the 'moving' school which 'is continually seeking to refine and develop its responses to the challenges it meets' (p. 12) through effective leadership, enquiry and reflection, and collaborative planning. It is these moving schools which, like Skrtic's adhocracies, are able to include children who find it difficult to learn within established practices.

Drawing on these perspectives, the question of how learners 'with difficulties' are categorised and labelled, and how these processes inform schools' responses is both an indicator of and a driver of the extent to which schools are operating in a 'stuck', 'bureaucratic' manner or in a 'moving', 'adhocratic' manner. By exploring this issue within schools in different national systems, moreover, it becomes possible to gauge the status of the systems as a whole in these respects and to gain some insight into the extent to which system characteristics shape school and teacher practices. With this in mind, this chapter reports research that was conducted in English and Swedish schools to better understand how teachers construct, and respond to, students' differences through the language they use to categorise and label individual learners, and plan to meet their needs.

In the first study, interviews were conducted with fifteen teachers and five teaching assistants in two primary and six secondary schools in the north of England, and case vignettes of twenty-three children were compiled (Alves, 2015). This research in English schools formed part of a comparative study of English and Portuguese schools which took place between 2009-2012, and was funded by a Research Fellowship of the Foundation for Science and Technology (*Fundação para a Ciência e a Tecnologia*, Reference SFRH / BD / 61437 / 2009). The second study involved the analysis of documentation in fourteen Swedish comprehensive schools of the difficulties experienced by eighty-six boys and fifty girls, which took place over a three-year period (Andreasson, 2007). This study was financed by the National Agency for Education. A third study, also based in Sweden, took the form of a one-year ethnographic exploration of how students attending a special unit in a comprehensive school were described, categorised, and organised. The data collected includes video recordings of everyday activities and interviews with students, teachers and head teachers, and the study was funded by the Swedish Research Council and the University of Linköping (Karlsson, 2007).

We begin by introducing the national policy contexts in England and Sweden and their impact on responses to the individual educational needs of children identified as having SEN. We then introduce examples of teachers' spoken and written language to illustrate their conceptualisations of students perceived to be different, as well as some of the interventions and processes that take place at an organisational level (in schools and classrooms) when teachers construct students as different. We consider the role of written and spoken descriptions of individual children identified as having SEN, including assessment processes, and categories used to organise children according to their characteristics and perceived differences. Finally we reflect on some of the significant similarities and differences between the two country contexts in relation to the theoretical positions developed by Skrtic and Ainscow.

The Swedish context

As we see elsewhere in this volume, policy rhetoric has a strong democratic theme in Sweden, and the concept and key principle of 'a school for all' has had a long history, with support from across the political spectrum. Individual freedom and integrity, the equal value of all people, equal educational opportunities, equity between genders, and solidarity with the 'weak', are values promoted through education policies for the majority of the twentieth century (Arnesen and Lundahl, 2006). The 'school for all' plays a key role in providing students with the knowledge and values they need to be active citizens, as individuals and as members of a democratic society.

The two-track system of special and mainstream education and the terminology used to describe so-called 'problem children' can be traced back to the beginning of formal education in Sweden in the nineteenth century (Berhanu, 2012). However the first framework was introduced in the 1960s to guide the provision of services to children identified as having 'special needs' in mainstream schools. Since then, international guidelines, and the Salamanca Statement, in particular, have influenced policy development (Berhanu, 2012). The Education Act (SFS 2010:800), for example, has incorporated key principles from the United Nations Convention on the Rights of the Child (UN, 1989), specifically, that children have the right to be involved and heard in matters affecting them. It establishes that education is to consider the child's perspective, give them a voice, listen to them and take them seriously. It has reinforced the integration of all students, irrespective of disability or difficulties in school (SFS

2010:800), and has also given parents and students the opportunity to appeal against decisions regarding the provision of special support.

Despite this strong political commitment to equal education opportunities, regardless of gender, social class, religion, ethnicity, SEN or geographical location, there have always been groups of children who do not have the same access to education as the rest of society. Approximately two per cent of students are eligible to attend special schools, based on a medical diagnosis of disability, and are excluded from the 'school for all' philosophy (Börjesson and Palmblad, 2003; Persson, 2003). This includes students with developmental disabilities, sensory, physical and/or intellectual impairments.

The key principle of 'a school for all students' was re-enforced by the 2011 Education Act (SFS 2010:800), alongside a needs-based ideology in which the broad category of SEN is used instead of detailed disability categories (OECD, 2005a). The Act also stresses schools' responsibility to give all students the guidance and encouragement they need in their learning and personal development, based on individual circumstances. The school mission is to promote learning by stimulating the individual while developing both knowledge and democratic values. Despite the intention of the Education Act to move away from a category-based system of special support, medical diagnoses such as ADHD, Asperger syndrome, and labels such as social emotional and behavioural difficulties (SEBD) are commonly used in schools (Giota and Emanuelsson, 2011). A medical diagnosis is commonly required before children are entitled to specialist teaching.

It is estimated that seventeen to twenty per cent of all students in the ordinary comprehensive school system are defined as having SEN and so in need of special support (SNAE, 2003; Cameron et al. 2012; Giota and Emanuelsson, 2011). The reasons for being defined as having SEN vary, but students at risk of not achieving the expected educational targets in one or more subjects, and those who have behavioural difficulties, are most likely to be provided with additional support. Following the introduction of inclusive education, the number of pupils described as having SEN has increased, possibly because teachers have found it so difficult to meet the needs of individual students (Berhanu, 2012).

The Education Act (SFS 2010:800) stipulates that organisational solutions in the form of segregated teaching should be avoided whenever possible within the comprehensive school system. In many schools it has been considered as the best way to provide support for some children by separating them from the other students. However, there are substantial within-country variations in the proportion of students who receive special support. These depend upon academic attainment, geographical location and other demographic factors (SNAE, 2003; Giota and Emanuelsson, 2011). Municipalities reported that, on average, they had about four special teaching groups in which students spent more than fifty per cent of their time—it seems likely, though, that this number may be under-reported Göransson, Nilholm and Karlsson (2011). Karlsson's (2007, 2012) studies, for example, have shown that students in special teaching groups experience marginalisation despite the existence of a democratic ideology encompassing equal educational opportunities and children's right to be heard in matters that concern them.

National education policy has been strongly influenced since the 1990s by international attempts to raise educational standards and introduce school reforms, including deregulation and the marketisation of the educational system, largely defined by school choice and increased competition (Englund, 2004). These trends raise questions about the impact of such policies on the education of children with SEN, and on school policy and SEN services. Little evidence is available, but Cameron, Nilholm and Persson (2012) have speculated that outcome and efficiency will come to dominate the discussion, and that, 'We are also likely to see the re-emergence of older organisational solutions involving training in basic skills and an expansion of segregated services' (p. 213).

The English context

National policy on special educational needs in England must be understood from the perspective of the Warnock Report (Department of Education and Science, 1978), which provided a framework for the SEN system. Translated into law in the 1981 Education Act. Warnock continues to underpin the practice of special needs education, and this framework has five significant elements: (1) SEN is defined in general terms as a 'difficulty in learning'; (2) a large minority of children (one in six at any one time) was deemed to have these needs and many would be maintained in mainstream schools; (3) the assessment of SEN was to take place on an individual basis by teachers, educational psychologists, doctors, and other professionals; (4) SEN assessments would lead to the meeting of needs by local education authorities; and (5) provision could be in mainstream or special settings (Dyson, 2005). In the English context, therefore SEN continues to be identified on the basis of difficulties experienced in school, rather than simply on the basis of impairments or medical conditions (Department for

Education and Skills, 2001a), although medical assessments are often involved in determining the level of SEN (Department for Education and Skills, 2001b).

The election of the New Labour government in 1997 brought with it a commitment to support the development of inclusive education, with the endorsement of the Salamanca Statement at policy level (Department for Education and Employment, 1997). This was unusual because English governments do not usually align themselves with international declarations in education or look elsewhere for models on which to develop policy (Dyson, 2005). In 2001, legislation was passed to protect students against discrimination on the grounds of their disability. The Special Educational Needs and Disability Act also strengthened parents' rights to choose a mainstream placement. At about the same time, the national schools inspectorate, the Office for Standards in Education, issued guidance on how to inspect the inclusiveness of schools (Ofsted, 2000). It is true that the New Labour governments were never entirely comfortable with their commitment to inclusion and their early enthusiasm waned as their period in office progressed. Moreover, the Coalition government returned in 2010 promised to remove what it characterised as the 'bias towards inclusion' in national policy, instead placing the emphasis on parental choice (DfE, 2011, p. 5). Nonetheless, the introduction of the principle of inclusion into the national education debate ensured, if nothing else, that placement in regular schools is seen in England as the desirable outcome for all but a small minority of children identified as having SEN. That small minority, moreover, is likely to be identified on the basis of parental preference more than on the capacity of regular schools to educate these children.

Alongside support for inclusive education, policy pressure has increased on schools to raise academic standards, and to ensure that all learners reach a minimum standard of attainment. Teachers are required to pay greater attention to the individual differences of all their students in relation to raising academic attainment. A government strategy, 'Removing Barriers to Achievement' (Department for Education and Skills, 2004), brought special needs education into closer alignment with the mainstream standards agenda, and promoted personalised learning in order to meet the diverse needs of all children, and reduce reliance on separate SEN structures and processes. Inevitably, tensions exist between the parallel agendas of inclusion and standards. However, one of the positive outcomes of the interaction between the two agendas is that teachers in England have been required to take a closer look at the individual outcomes of students who had previously been overlooked because of low expectations, associated with common assumptions about difficulties with language and literacy, and social backgrounds (Ainscow, Booth and Dyson, 2006a, 2006b). In addition, schools have developed sophisticated managerial systems to respond to these new policy pressures.

These new systems have led to the creation of a more universalised approach to individual provision, in which every student is in receipt of target setting, and allocation to particular groups or individual tasks. This universal provision is usually quite distinct from the more formal approach to the planning of individualised education for students identified as having SEN, students who have disabilities, and students who speak English as an additional language (EAL). The process of determining who needs individual planning leads to the construction of notions of difference and of SEN, with respect to individual students, and groups of students.

Schools are expected to deal with a wide range of different levels and types of individualisation and differentiation. Each school has a designated Special Education Needs Coordinator (SENCO) who is responsible for the identification and management of individual children identified as having SEN, and who works in close collaboration with teachers, support staff and external support services, such as Educational Psychologists. In the majority of cases, it is members of staff working at school level who are involved in identifying and making decisions about appropriate interventions. Although terms such as MLD (moderate learning difficulties), ADHD (attention deficit hyperactivity disorder), SEBD (social, emotional and behaviour difficulties) and dyslexia are used when providing written feedback to the local authority, they are not necessarily perceived as medical labels. Rather, they provide a way for parents and professionals to make sense of the difficulties that children experience with their school work.

It is important to note that the study reported here was conducted prior to the introduction of new legislation, introduced at the beginning of the new school year in September 2014 (DfE and DfH, 2014). The new legislation responds to some extent to the call to reverse the 'bias towards inclusion' noted above, but focuses principally on strengthening the position of parents in the decision-making process and making the planning of provision more coherent and effective. However, the fundamental philosophy underpinning the conceptualisation of SEN as outlined by Warnock, the acceptance that most children identified as having SEN will be placed in regular schools, and expectation that their teachers' efforts will be focused on academic achievement are all set to continue.

A Code of Practice provides guidance for schools and local authorities on the identification and assessment of SEN. Although this has been updated in line with recent legislative changes, it is the earlier version (DfES, 2001a) which was in force at the time of the research reported here. Under the provisions of this earlier version, schools were legally required to 'have regard to' the Code in providing services for children regarded as having SEN. At the time of the study, within school support was known as 'School Action', and if children required external support, this was provided through 'School Action Plus'. A 'statement' secured a legally-enforceable entitlement to assessment and appropriate provision—usually involving some additional financial or other resources—for children whose needs were seen as demanding more than the resources routinely available in and around schools. Children who are seen as likely to need a statement have a fuller assessment of their needs than school staff alone could provide. Parents have the right to see all copies of reports and the right to appeal against decisions. Like all other parents in England, parents of children with SEN also have the right (with certain restrictions) to choose a school for their child. The rights allocated to parents of children with SEN has, over the years, had a considerable impact on special needs provision, with conflict arising between parents who want to secure additional resources by having children's needs recognised, and those who manage the ever-decreasing budgets. The sometimes bitter disputes arising around statements of SEN have posed a major challenge to the English special education system.

Constructing difference through talk and text

In this section, we provide some illustrative examples from the English and Swedish studies, and then consider some of the similarities and differences between the two contexts. In both contexts, individual education plans (IEPs) are used to manage individual planning and provision for students. In England, IEPs are amongst other forms of individualised planning which include 'individual behaviour plans' and 'individual learning plans'. Whereas statements are documents with legal force produced by local authorities, mapping needs and provision for the long term, IEPs are school-level documents intended to guide provision on a more practical and short-term basis. They tend, therefore, to be relatively short despite containing a wealth of information. This includes: 'areas of need' (cognition and learning; behaviour, emotional and social difficulty;

communication and interaction needs; sensory and/or physical needs); targets to be achieved (such as, 'to increase...; to develop...'); students' strengths and views; suggested class strategies; and additional support provided by the school. They also contain information about how parents and carers can support students at home; and how the progress will be monitored and assessed, when and by whom. In some schools, students are encouraged to participate in reviewing their IEPs and to attend review meetings, although the actual level of student participation varies considerably from school to school.

Some English schools were moving away from using 'traditional' individual planning, as a way of responding to diversity, towards more whole-school approaches. For example, 'provision mapping' was used extensively in one of the primary schools studied. This is a system of linking all interventions available in a school context and assigning pupils to these interventions on the basis of perceived benefit, rather than SEN status or label. Student 'tracking' similarly is a complex system of checking the desired progress of all students against national targets, and of allocating existing resources and interventions to students who 'are falling behind'. These systems have been developed in order to decrease the amount of bureaucracy that teachers have to deal with.

The English study involved compiling a series of pupil case vignettes, and identifying the way differences were conceptualised (through the labels and descriptions teachers used), and the explanations offered for individual planning and provision. The language used to describe students included terms related to notions of average and expected achievement norms, such as: 'being average', 'below average', 'booster child', 'being where they should be', 'being behind'. Being 'below average' was considered to be a warning sign for SEN, and sometimes linked to pupils with 'gaps in their knowledge' and to 'poor attendance'. The following excerpts further highlight the teachers' discourse (Alves, 2015):

> Now I've only got two children that are below where they should be, and these are the two SEN. [They] are going to go through school with special needs, and we have to help them achieve *different low-level targets*.
>
> She [is] a very low average, she's border[ing] on the special education needs but she's not quite there.
>
> He's what you call a booster child, (...) just below average but it's not because he's special needs, it's because of his English.

The terms used to organise the SEN system, 'School Action', 'School Action Plus' and 'Statement', were also widely used by teachers to describe, and so conceptualise, students and their 'needs'. For example, 'He *is* School Action'; 'They are statemented'; 'SEN children'.

In Sweden, standardised tests of various kinds are used to identify cognitive difficulties. By contrast, students with behavioural difficulties tend to be assessed by teachers, based on what they consider to be 'normal' (SNAE, 2003; Andreasson, 2007; Karlsson, 2007, 2012). In this way, the identification and definition of students as being different from school norms is a highly subjective process. If students do not 'reach the minimum knowledge requirements', or 'present other difficulties in their school situation', for example as a result of social, emotional and behavioural difficulties, the Education Act (SFS 2010:800) requires the school principal to be informed and an assessment carried out, usually involving the student health team. If a student is deemed to be 'in need of special support', this is provided through an IEP.

The IEP process starts from the perspective of individual students, specifying students' needs, how they will be met, and how interventions will be monitored and evaluated. It then focuses on learning and teaching to ensure that plans are of practical support in teachers' daily work, school organisation and management. Students and guardians are given the opportunity to participate in the development of the IEP. Research in Sweden has shown, however, that IEPs are not generally accepted as being effective, with discrepancies having been identified between policy and practice: IEPs seem to be used as administrative, rather than education and development tools for the benefit of the students; and parents' and students' participation needs further exploration (Andreasson, Asp-Onsjö and Isaksson, 2013).

In the studies by Andreasson (2007) and Karlsson (2007), the Swedish teachers use similar language to the English teachers, commonly describing students' ability as being 'average', 'behind', or a 'slow starter'. They have also made judgements about the students' mostly negative attitudes to school: 'not collaborating', 'immature', 'not wanting to do repetitive skills training', 'not wanting to practise and train', 'willingness to work'. The teachers' identification of students' 'lack of ability' and 'lack of standard behaviour' sometimes led to them being conceptualised as 'deviant', as the following examples illustrate:

> He is of average intelligence, and so why is he not reaching the goals then? But of course you cannot reach the goals if you do not do your English

homework, or if you do not practise multiplication tables. / ..... / He has an immaturity as well, so he is behind. He doesn't like that..
(Karlsson, 2007)

Most of the time he pokes around with his pen or eraser or a piece of paper. It takes a long time for him to get started with the simplest possible tasks. (Andreasson, 2007)

In Sweden all students, and particularly students identified as having difficulties, are increasingly subjected to assessment and follow-up processes. This is carried out in everyday practice, in talk and in interaction through meetings and in the classroom, and is recorded in written assessments, including IEPs. The education system requires students' individual qualities and abilities to be monitored and evaluated from year one (age seven) to upper secondary school (age nineteen). The broad label 'student in need of special support' tends to be the preferred response to difficulties experienced in school. In theory, this means that school difficulties are related to the school environment. However, several studies have shown that teachers and schools often look at students' school difficulties from an individual perspective, holding the students responsible for the school's problems (Isaksson, et al., 2007; Nilholm, 2007; Isaksson, Lindquist and Bergström, 2010). Teachers' discourse seems to be based on assumptions of 'the normal child' being academically and socially well-adjusted, and of students taking responsibility for their school work, being motivated, and becoming more independent and aware of their own learning process (Andreasson, 2007).

Responding to difference through interventions

In England, the main ways of responding to student diversity in mainstream schools include organising students by ability, differentiation, interventions and the provision of additional resources. Grouping students together for certain lessons, usually according to their level of attainment in literacy and numeracy, is a common practice both at primary and secondary school level, and is often referred to as 'setting'. Schools make use of a variety of grouping practices, but the commonest is a mixture of setting for most or part of the curriculum, with 'mixed ability' grouping for the remaining subjects taught. Differentiation involves dividing the whole class into levels when planning lessons, but also introducing a range of structured activities. Distinct targets are formulated to be achieved by the students, either working individually, in pairs, or in groups, and with appropriate materials.

The term 'interventions' is used to refer to extra support in most cases by teaching assistants—that is adults who work alongside teachers but are not themselves qualified teachers, and who may or may not have any training for their role. Figure 1 helps conceptualise the way interventions are delivered; they can take place both in and out of the mainstream classrooms, and can be offered to pupils individually or in small groups. In-class support is mainly aimed at breaking down activities into smaller steps, repeating instructions, and making sure the students stay on task. Teaching assistants can be assigned to individual pupils or be assigned to groups of pupils. Out of the classroom, interventions may take the form of packaged programmes, some of which are developed and purchased commercially. Most are delivered in small groups and are aimed specifically at literacy difficulties (e.g. *Reading Recovery, Beat Dyslexia*), numeracy difficulties (e.g. *Every Child a Counter*), and social difficulties (e.g. *Social and Emotional Aspects of Learning*).

Figure 1: Modalities of support (Alves, 2015)

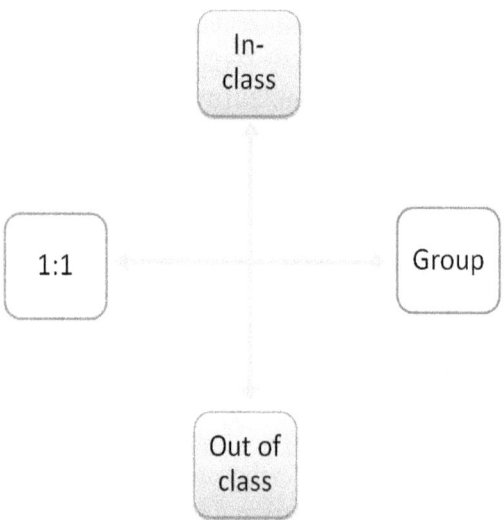

Within these structures, English schools have developed a complex repertoire of responses and tools for intervening in, children's learning. These include: a wide range of human resources, such as teaching assistants, higher level teaching assistants, SENCOs and EAL coordinators; additional physical resources, such as a 'learning support area', accessible buildings, radio transmitters for students with hearing impairments, visual timetables and home-school diaries; and support from external services, such as Child and Adolescent Mental Health Services, Ethnic Minority and Traveller Achievement Service; and nearby special schools, which act as resource centres and sources of knowledge for mainstream schools.

In Sweden, it is the special education teachers who play a pivotal role in developing interventions for individual students, including specific training; adaptation of working methods and of learning materials; extra homework; organising students by ability; and providing extra resources in classrooms (SNAE, 2003; Giota and Emanuelsson, 2011). Extra support is often delivered both in class and outside, and involves the adjustment of teaching materials, breaking learning down into smaller steps, repeating instructions, and helping students to stay on task. Students' difficulties tend to be understood as individual problems, rather than difficulties in the school or teaching environment (Isaksson et al., 2007; Lahdenperä, 1997; Persson, 2003; SNAE, 2003, 2008). This means that interventions tend to be individualised, rather than addressing the difficulties in the school environment. Students are often organised into groups with those who have similar difficulties, and taught by the special educator in a separate room outside the regular classroom. This can have profound implications for students' self-esteem and identity construction.

In her ethnographic study, Karlsson (2007) explored the organisation of a special education group for five boys (seven to twelve years-old), defined as having SEN and 'social, emotional and behavioural difficulties', whose placement varied from eight months to three years. As other researchers have documented, boys from low socio-economic status are more likely than girls to be identified as having SEBD and found in special teaching groups (Daniels, Hey, Leonard and Smith, 1999; Giota and Lundborg, 2007), and their lack of success in school and in later life has been well documented (Landrum, Tankersley and Kauffman, 2003).

Karlsson found that teachers often focused on the boys' individual shortcomings or deficits, without considering the impact of organisational barriers within the school. The boys came to be identified and associated with the category of SEN and SEBD, and there was more focus on social care than on academic learning. Although schools are emphasising the importance of developing behaviour for inclusion in the regular classroom, the boys experience a decline in their agency and responsibility in relation to their behaviour and feelings. This raises questions about equity, and about students' rights and voice in special teaching groups. The study highlighted the invisibility and marginalisation of the special teaching group, both centrally in the municipality and in the context of local school activities. More recent research has highlighted the possibility that everyday school practice may portray particular boys as having a deviant and problematic identity (Evaldsson and Karlsson, 2012; Karlsson, 2012).

Discussion

The aim of this chapter was to analyse the way educational differences/SEN are conceptualised and constructed through teachers' talk and text in two contrasting policy contexts. National policies in those contexts are broadly based on social-democratic principles and have been influenced by progressive international trends and policies such as the Convention on the Rights of the Child and the Salamanca Statement. National commitment towards greater inclusion of children with disabilities and those with difficulties in learning in mainstream education indicates the equitable principles on which the education systems are based. Both education systems are highly developed, with sophisticated services being provided for individual students according to perceived needs. Indeed our small comparative study of teachers' practice in England and Sweden is interesting precisely because of some notable similarities.

Special education has been created as a separate sub-system in order to respond to students identified as having SEN. This is consistent with Skrtic's (1991) view of schools as bureaucratic organisations that resist change. In this context when faced with a group of students who may need responses different from those already available, educational systems create subsystems. The perception of these differences amongst pupils leads to a series of dilemmas related to student identification, placement and curriculum (See Norwich, 2002, 2007, 2010), and the classification of students into categories and eligibility procedures (Florian and McLaughlin, 2008). The concept of SEN sits uneasily alongside principles of participation, equity, rights and ethics (Dyson, 1999; Pijl, Meijer, and Hegarty, 1997; Thomas and Vaughan, 2004), and the situation of students identified as having SEN represents a tension between the 'desire to treat all the children as the same, while also treating them as different' (Dyson, 2001, p. 25).

Although the ways in which SEN is determined within the two education systems are distinctive, the countries share more similarities than differences. For example, the influence of medical definitions is strong in both contexts. Although, the language used is less overtly medicalised than in the past, the practice of attributing children's difficulties to their own characteristics remains. As we have seen, Swedish teachers have proved resistant to the idea that difficulties might arise from organisational barriers and instead tend to focus on the child's characteristics. In England, too, there is no real attempt to understand the interaction between the child and the learning context. Instead, the term SEN is often understood normatively, indicating students who fall below the attainment levels expected of their peers and have more difficulties than the majority in following what is taught at school. The concept of SEN is thus constructed as part of a continuum of difficulties in following the content of the 'mainstream' curriculum, where the nature of that curriculum goes unchallenged. 'Relatively slow progress' (Ofsted, 2010) and low achievement are often considered an indicator of SEN (McLaughlin, et al., 2006; Dyson and Gallannaugh, 2008). A student who has SEN is defined as having 'a greater degree of difficulty learning' than the majority of their peers, or as requiring 'some special intervention to ensure that he or she can access or benefit from the education' (DFES, 2001; McLaughlin, et al., 2006).

This focus on the norm is connected to the fact that in both contexts schools tend to have standard aims and teaching practices for their students, with students organised in classes, assuming a hierarchical progress underpinned by the acquisition of knowledge and progress towards the desired norm (Roldão, 2003: 153; Andreasson et al., 2013). Attainment, particularly in literacy and mathematics, is seen as the key outcome against which students will be assessed. Those children who do well in these relatively standardised systems are regarded as having 'normal', or average needs. Those who do less well are likely to be regarded as having 'special' needs and as needing some kind of additional support. As we have seen, this support is often organised through some form of individual planning. IEPs in both countries are therefore individually focused, with students' difficulties being defined and described mainly as individual shortcomings and deficits. The plans tend, therefore, to describe what will be done differently or additionally for struggling students, and say little if anything about how the standard practices of the school and school system might change.

The identification process involves professional judgements on individual students (Dyson and Millward, 2002; Asp Onsjö, 2006; Karlsson, 2007; Ofsted, 2010). As a result, it is not based exclusively, or even largely, on the application of objective criteria, but instead tends to be a 'messy process influenced by many individuals and conducted in an environment of rationed resources' (McLaughlin et al., 2006, p. 46). As we have seen throughout this chapter, children's needs are constructed by teachers (and, we might add, by others involved in the assessment process) rather than simply identified. Not surprisingly, therefore, the proportion of children and types of need identified have changed over time, in ways that may be more related to the pressures on schools than to any actual changes in children's characteristics (Dyson and Gallannaugh, 2008). Similarly, identification may be related to characteristics of children which, on the face of it, should have nothing to do with special educational needs. So, it has been reported that a disproportionate number of students from certain social groups and ethnic backgrounds are identified as having SEN (Dyson and Gallannaugh, 2008; Berhanu, 2012). The influence of social class on SEN has also been observed in the way decisions are made about grouping students by ability (Muijs and Dunne, 2010). Humphrey et al. (2006) likewise report that the main ways in which children are allocated into groups according to their learning needs are: cultural (EAL; migrant); SEN and disability; and failing to achieve, especially in literacy.

In many ways the English and Swedish education systems are less rigid than many other national systems, and are characterised by fluid and permeable boundaries between special and mainstream education. Yet, boundaries are being re-created on a daily basis, as teachers respond to student diversity within their classrooms, and construct notions of who is different and who is 'normal' through their practice. The concept that most children are 'normal', and a minority are 'different', and therefore do not fit easily into a standards-focused education system, is deeply entrenched in both countries. Teachers' knowledge and expectations have profound impact on the outcomes for their students.

The picture we have portrayed does not appear to be one in which national systems or the schools within them are embarked on a process of radical change. Although there are doubtless exceptions in both countries, there is little evidence in the studies we have reported here of 'adhocratic' or 'moving' schools rethinking their practices in order to include learners they might otherwise find problematic. Rather, the picture which emerges is of the perpetuation of boundaries by teachers' daily practice. Although policy has moved away from historical forms of medicalised categorisation, the thinking remains the same. Despite efforts made to erode the category-based system, it has not been possible to leave it behind completely, partly due to the ingrained beliefs about normalcy, partly due to the reinforcement of those beliefs by education policy focused on standards of achievement, and partly due to the emergence of new forms of categorisation.

Conclusion

This chapter began by focusing on national policy in England and Sweden and on exploring ways in which schools and teachers determine who is eligible for extra support, the construction of notions of difference, and responses to students identified as having SEN. The national policy regarding SEN in each country is, of course, influenced by the wider cultural and political context. Yet despite differences such as a somewhat stronger social democratic tradition in Sweden and the different forms of the neoliberal marketisation of schools in the two countries, student identification processes have considerable similarities. These seem to be underpinned by a resistance to change the way education systems work—in other words with the self-preservation of bureaucratic institutions identified by Skrtic (1991). Responses and discourses about pupils with SEN tend to be individualised and based on an assumption of within-child factors to explain difficulties. Practitioners seem to have an implicit notion of what is 'normal' or 'average' and the aim is to get all pupils as close as possible to that assumed 'expected level'. The responses to pupils 'with SEN' take place both within and outside the mainstream classroom with a special focus on literacy and numeracy. This ensemble of factors is problematic when trying to create equitable responses to all pupils insofar as it functions on an assumption that all pupils should be working towards a desired norm, and it works by singling out some pupils as 'being below average' and 'needing something different from or additional to' what is made available to the majority of pupils.

The research from both countries indicates that the way student identity is constructed in talk and text shows that schools and teachers still struggle to respond to pupil diversity. The pursuit of more equitable responses through the creation of an 'adhocratic' (Skrtic, 1991), 'moving' (Ainscow, 1999) school ethos in which all practitioners, pupils and parents work collaboratively to problem-solve and create inclusive responses that benefit all pupils requires a radical change that continues to prove elusive.

Chapter 9

Consequences of differentiated policies and teaching practices in the Swedish school system

Joanna Giota and Ingemar Emanuelsson

In this chapter results from two longitudinal and nationally representative studies will be highlighted and discussed. The first study describes the extent and forms, integrated versus segregated, of special education support offered to students in the Swedish compulsory school over a period of twenty-nine years. The relationships between special education support, background variables and goal attainment in Grade 9 were studied as well. This study is based on about thirty-five thousand students born in 1972, 1977, 1982 and 1987. The second longitudinal study aimed to explore how head teachers (n=683) for older students and head teachers (n=250) for younger students in the Swedish compulsory school handled a range of special education issues in their schools. The results show that difficulties in school are still seen as being caused by student characteristics rather than shortcomings of the school and teaching practices. Some students do not receive equal opportunities to learn and flourish in school and thus run the risk of becoming socially excluded and marginalised in a here-and-now and a future perspective.

Introduction

A basic idea behind the introduction of a common nine-year compulsory school in Sweden in the early 1960s was that the curriculum goals should be individualised, that is, adapted to all children's prerequisites and needs within the framework of the regular class/group. Classroom instructions adapted to 'a mean level of ability' were assumed to cause problems and lead to insufficient achievements for both the 'weakest' and the most 'talented' students (Lgr 62).

In the 1980s the curriculum (Lgr 80) emphasised even more that 'if a student is facing difficulties in school it is necessary to begin by examining whether the school practices can be changed' (Lgr 80, p. 54). This was suggested also by the Salamanca Declaration (Svenska Unescorådet, 2001) developed by representatives of nine-two governments and twenty-five international organisations, which Sweden signed in 1994. In other words, the inclusive ambition of the special education support policy in Sweden is based on a perspective of 'a school for all' and decisions taken on democratic ideals about the right of all individuals to fully participation in regular school classes as well as in society as a whole (see also Haug, 1999; Dyson, 2005).

Research studies in Sweden show that the reasons for difficulties and failures in school are often explained as shortcomings of individual children. Most often they are expressed in diagnostic and/or disability labels (Emanuelsson, Persson and Rosenqvist, 2001). The shortcomings of the school or the ways that school meets and handles individual prerequisites and needs of special education support are used to a much lesser extent as explanatory factors of children's difficulties and failures in school.

In Sweden, the previous Education Act (1985:1100) that allowed neither ability grouping nor organisational differentiation formulated equity. By referring to a conditional extension in the School Regulation (SFS 1994:1194) stating that 'if there is a special reason' schools have been able to bypass this organisational principle that guarantees equity in school, and students in need of special education support could be placed into special education classes/groups outside their regular class; and still are according to the present Education Act (SFS 2010:800) and School Regulation (SFS 2011:185).

As shown by several research studies (Nilholm, Persson, Hjerm and Runesson, 2007; Giota, Lundborg and Emanuelsson, 2009; Giota and Emanuelsson, 2011a, 2011b) and national evaluations (Skolverket, 2006, 2009) the segregated and 'tradition-bound-way' of organising support in general and special education support in particular still persist. Students receiving instruction outside their regular class/group or in special education classes/groups is nothing unusual today. In fact this 'trend' has steadily increased since the early 1990s even though the inclusive approach to the teaching of all children in compulsory school is the recommended key educational policy (Skolverket, 2005) for ensuring that all students stay in education (or training) until the age of nineteen.

The usually individual-bound or diagnosis-based/disability categorisation underlying the support measures outside the regular class/group however has consequences for the 'special' students both in terms of knowledge attainment, self-beliefs and motivation to learn. Most often these consequences tend to be negative, and particularly in a long-term perspective (Emanuelsson, Persson and Rosenqvist, 2001). In other words, the education career of students receiving special education support in special education classes/groups tends to be a special one alongside, but not equal to, the education career of these students' former classmates in the regular class. Emanuelsson and Persson (2002) show that these students often get a continued alternative education career in individual programs at upper secondary school with similar consequences to special education support outside the regular class in compulsory school. Students in individual programs show the highest dropout rates from upper secondary school. Alternative education careers of students lead in other words to insufficient qualifications and thus unequal opportunities with negative consequences for quality of life.

For instance, Emanuelsson (1974) has followed students who had received special education measures in their regular class compared to students who had received instructions in special education classes/groups. After controlling for individual characteristics and social background, Emanuelsson could show that support outside the regular class did not increase these students' possibilities to successful participation in society. This type of support measure was instead clearly related to long lasting learning problems and thus subsequent marginalisation in many different ways also in adulthood (cf. Sonnander, Emanuelsson and Kebbon, 1993).

Studies on the long-term consequences of special education are, however, rare both nationally and internationally. Nevertheless, the occurrence of difficulties in school and the difficulties to manage these are shown to largely depend on what is taking place in 'regular' school situations and are not caused solely by the 'flaws' or individual characteristics of the 'special' or diagnosed students (Giota, Emanuelsson and Berhanu, 2013). National (Skolverket, 2003, 2005, 2008, 2009) as well as increasing international evidence (Booth and Ainscow, 1998) show that many children in need of special educational support, for different reasons, do not receive equal possibilities for learning and thus run the risk to become socially excluded and marginalised. A prerequisite for attaining equity in education is that the professionals in school are knowledgeable not only about the consequences of different support measures for individual and groups of students, but also of the implications of different definitions of school difficulties, assessment practices and teaching practices for these students' possibilities for living a good life. In order to prevent academic failure for 'vulnerable' young people, and in the long run to avoid social exclusion and marginalisation, we have to understand upcoming student difficulties in school in broader and also more inclusive perspectives.

In this chapter, national evaluation studies and research conducted within the research project *Special education in comprehensive schools: Extent, forms and effects* (henceforth abbreviated as the STOFF-project) will be presented in order to highlight prerequisites for equality in the Swedish education system. The Swedish Research Council of Education financed STOFF. One of the main aims of STOFF was to search for relations between school profiles, as these were expressed in answers from head teachers, and students' success or failures in the same schools, here-and-now as well as in a long-term perspective. STOFF is part of the ongoing Swedish longitudinal research program called *Evaluation through Follow up* (henceforth abbreviated as the ETF-project). In close cooperation with Statistics Sweden, ETF has, from its start in 1961, followed up nine nationally representative samples of students, born between 1948 and 1998, each comprising about 9.000 (see Emanuelsson, 1979; Härnqvist, 2000; Svensson, 2011).

School reforms and drops in achievement

In the early 1990s the Swedish school system went through a series of educational reforms. These reforms are historically the largest since the 1940s and are to be interpreted as the beginning of a paradigm shift in the Swedish school system. The implementation of these reforms turned the Swedish school system from being one of the most centralised school systems in the world to become one of the most decentralised. At the same time as school was decentralised in 1991/1992, a new curriculum (Lp. 94) was introduced and a new grading system.

> The decentralisation of school implied that municipalities and schools took on greater responsibility and autonomy to organise teaching with their students' needs and interests in focus. In addition, parents had the possibility to choose among schools—community governed or independent schools—other than the one closest to their home, and schools have had to prove to parents that they are 'good' schools, which most often means that their students have attained high marks. Until very recently, marks were officially not been given until Grade 8 in compulsory school. Since the fall term of 2012 marks are assigned starting in Grade 6, according to a new grading system that came into force, along with a new curriculum. (Lgr 11) in July 2011

This curriculum (Lgr 11) puts a strong emphasis on assessment and students' individual test scores in school. In practice, this is another expression of the same individual-bound diagnosis of 'special' students' weaknesses as previously. Given the fact that today schools in Sweden are actually forced to compete with each other for their existence there is a growing risk that students who are not 'good' achievers, or are somehow perceived as disruptive, are placed into different groups outside the regular class. This can be practiced more or less intentionally by schools in order to be able to show a high average level of performance in the regular class as measured by test scores.

Already in 2003 the results of the national evaluation of the Swedish compulsory school (Skolverket, 2004) showed that the achievements of Grade 9 students had dropped in almost all school subjects as compared to the achievements in 1992 and that gender differences had increased in favour of girls. It appeared that in mathematics and in the area of reading comprehension the knowledge of the fifteen-year-old students was in particular low, especially among boys. In 2000 and 2003 the PISA education ranking (The OECD's Program for International Student Assessment survey in mathematics, reading comprehension and natural sciences) showed that Sweden was above the OECD average in mathematics, while in 2006 and 2009 the results dropped to an average level and in 2012 fell below the OECD average. Considering the PISA-results it can be concluded that no other country had fallen so abruptly as Sweden in mathematics over a ten-year span (Skolverket, 2009, 2013).

In the late 2000s the Swedish National Agency for Education commissioned researchers to investigate the reasons for the observed drops in achievement, both in national and international assessments from the beginning of 1990s and onwards. In their report, these researchers concluded that the increasing differences in student achievement and the larger drops in achievement for some student groups took place at the same time as the educational reforms were introduced into the Swedish school system (Skolverket, 2009). Four main reasons for the drops in achievement were suggested as a) the increasing segregation in living, along with the free school choice, which has resulted in an increasing school segregation; b) the decentralisation of school, which has resulted in big differences in resource allocation and how resources are used by different schools; c) increases in ability grouping, along with an increase of special solutions outside the regular class; and d) individualisation, defined as an increased proportion of independent work, where students have been left alone to plan and take responsibility for their own learning with no active support from the teachers.

This high proportion of independent work has resulted in some students becoming less interested and engaged in school work and that the 'vulnerability' of already 'vulnerable' students, such as those in need of special education support or from homes with low socio-economic resources and ethnic minority, has been accentuated. At the same time, from 2000 onwards teachers' collective expertise, both with respect to subject knowledge and didactic skills, has declined. Changes in teacher competence and practices have resulted in socio-economic factors having an increasingly importance for students' opportunities to succeed in school (Skolverket, 2009; see also Vinterek, 2006). This development is not compatible with the idea of individualisation as a means and goal of 'a school for all to provide an equal education for all its students' (Giota, 2013).

Individualisation in policy

In 2011 Giota was commissioned by the Swedish Research Council of Education to investigate the idea of individualisation from a broader point of view than individual work. In her research review, Giota (2013) concluded that individualisation has different consequences for different students and student groups depending on how teachers have interpreted differentiation in the curricula and practiced individualised teaching.

In the following, the focus will be on individualisation, which is a complex concept, because of its different interpretations. Most often it refers to how teachers can adapt the learning content, materials or the degree of difficulty in the school tasks in order to meet each student's prerequisites and needs. Individualisation has also to do with students' possibilities to make choices or to make their voices heard in matters concerning them, their education and school life. Furthermore, it includes questions about the amount of responsibility that teachers may demand from the students concerning their own learning. Individualisation in school can refer to one or several of these aspects and to different degrees depending on the purpose of individualisation.

The purpose of individualisation, or the selection of a specific aspect or aspects of individualisation, is not always clear or easy to interpret in the various curricula and especially in Lp. 94. It's not either clear what advantages or disadvantages different aspects of individualisation may have for individual or groups of students. Individualisation in a certain way may have positive consequences for some students and at the same time negative consequences for others, depending on their needs and interests. Some needs and interests may also end up as more important and emphasised in the classroom according to different circumstances (see also Vinterek, 2006).

Independent of these difficulties, Giota's (op. cit.) analyses of the different curricula for the Swedish compulsory school during the last one-hundred years (from 1919 to 2011) show that individualised teaching is much broader than a simple choice of a method or a 'work form' for teachers to apply in their work with the students. Individualisation is not just a question of prioritising a specific content in teaching either. It is a view and refers to the idea that school shall be a place for all its students, where each student shall be valued, treated equally and met with respect in all circumstances, and in spite of differences in knowledge attainment. School shall help all students to develop as individuals and into fully-fledged and active democratic citizens, working for the 'good' or making things better for other people and society. The purpose of individualisation in school thus is to help all students to become individuals and collectivists at the same time.

Seen from this perspective, placing students with disabilities in a regular class does not mean that they are *included* unless they get a place in the group in their own right and their weaknesses are seen as an asset to the class and not a problem. A 'school for all' refers thus to a quest of individualising teaching for all students based on democratic ideals. Individualisation and inclusion as an organisational principle for special education support is both a means and a goal to build a better society and thus part of a society's democratic transition. However, the analyses of individualised practices in Sweden, show teachers and head teachers to express a quite narrow understanding of this principle, and practice individualised teaching increasingly as a way to organise teaching in 'special groups' (Giota, op. cit.).

Individualisation in practice

In order to develop into fully-fledged citizens, students shall be given possibilities to participate in decisions that concern them. These decisions include the content of their schooling and ways to reach educational goals. These rights to influence were established as early as 1979 by the Government (SFS 1979:717) and later on in the Education Act (1985:1100) and the curriculum (Lgr 80). In the 1992 interim report *About students' right to influence, participation and responsibility* (SOU 1996:22), a school committee noted that the right to influence did not work in practice. Three reasons as to why students should have influence on decisions that concern them were emphasised. Among them was the UN's Convention on the Rights of the Child from 1990, stating that children have the right to secure their upbringing and opportunities to develop. Applying and strengthening the rights and interests of all students in this matter was seen as a prerequisite for school to succeed in educating all children for lifelong learning (Giota, 2013). The analyses of Swedish research studies in the field of education, published between 2000 and 2010 (forty-three in total), by Giota (op. cit.), show that student influence is one of the main aspects of individualisation in Swedish schools that has to be improved.

The lack of influence on matters of importance to students appears to be one of the main reasons that many of them experience school content as of no use to them and lose their motivation to learn. Teachers seem to view student participation in democratic processes more as a 'form of work' or something students shall have in order to practice for a future citizenship. Democracy for students on the other hand seems to be more about justice and having a say on matters of direct importance in school, such as the planning of major tests and homework. Expressed differently, for teachers it may be more important that democracy becomes 'effective' so that students' voices are heard, rather than about *what* seems to be less important. If students in special education classes/groups have a say they choose social inclusion and being together with their friends and classmates in the regular class rather than catching up on schoolwork by being in a 'special' group (Giota, op. cit.).

The wish to work alone is more often expressed by high-achieving students, while 'weaker' achievers prefer more often to work with others. It appears that high-achieving students do not feel challenged in school and 'weaker' achievers are not straining themselves to the fullest. Thus, the teaching offered by school between 2000 and 2010 does not seem to fit either of these student groups at the same time as the curriculum (Lp. 94) advocates that all teaching shall be individualised (see also Vinterek, 2006). So 'to whom has teaching been adapted?' The answer to be given is to the 'middle' or 'average-achieving' students' implying that during the 2000s school in Sweden was actually not a 'school for all' but rather 'a school for no one' or maybe 'just for a few' to use Swalander's way of putting it (op. cit., 2006 in Giota, 2013).

The results presented in the research review by Giota (2013) imply that the old problem to differentiate or individualise the internal work of school according to all students' prerequisites and needs is far from being solved. Meanwhile individualised work in school seems to have taken expressions other than those intended in policy, where some student groups appear to become 'the losers'.

Resource allocation and special education support

It is almost impossible to discern from the available reports or statistics exactly what resources have actually been used for ordinary and special education respectively and what specific problems and difficulties are to be supported. This is a national and international phenomenon (Skolverket, 2002a) implying that it is difficult to measure accurately various consequences of special education, particularly the longer-term ones. As already mentioned, the studies conducted within STOFF to be presented in next are parts of the Swedish longitudinal ETF-project. ETF has, since 1961, used a cohort-sequential design to create a database, located at the University of Gothenburg, with a rich amount of information about individual educational careers from early grades in compulsory school to adult life. Through combining different kinds of data collected within the project with register data about processes and outcomes at later points in time, a powerful longitudinal design to study a wide range of scientific issues, including consequences of special education, has been created.

By referring to results obtained within STOFF, among others, the National Agency for Education (Skolverket, 2009) concluded that the proportion of students receiving special education support has increased from the mid-1990s; in particular the support given outside the regular class. The need of special education support measures seems to be relative, however. It is harder to get such support in schools where the needs are actually greatest, such as in segregated city areas. One explanation to the increasing number of students being defined as in need of special education support, given in the report, is that the ability of schools to adapt teaching to all students has declined.

A study within STOFF by Giota, Lundborg and Emanuelsson (2009) investigated the issue of resource allocation and special education support. The focus of this study was on investigating the extent and forms of special education support given to four student cohorts (born in 1972, 1977, 1982 and 1987) by the use of administrative data collected by Statistics Sweden within ETF. The results show that the number of students who have received special education support in some part of their compulsory education (that is, in Grades 3 to 9) varies from thirty-eight per cent for cohorts 1972 and 1982 to forty-five per cent for cohorts 1977 and 1987. About 40 per cent of the students born during the 1970s and 1980s received thus some kind of special education support for some part of their schooling in compulsory school. This proportion has been rather constant over the twenty-nine-year period studied here, and as shown by additional ETF-cohorts of students, over the last forty years in Sweden, with an increase of about five per cent during the 2000s. Boys were found to be over-represented among the different ETF-cohorts and groups that have received special education support, as are students from home backgrounds characterised by low educational attainment and students with non-Swedish backgrounds. This finding is in line with findings in international research (see Berhanu, 2008; Berhanu and Dyson, 2012).

There has been a rather substantial increase in provision of special education support between the 1982 and 1987 cohorts. The proportion of students who received support in more inclusive forms and for a short period of time increased noticeably between these cohorts from thirteen to twenty-one per cent. The increase concerned mainly the number of girls receiving support, students whose parents had a high level of educational attainment, and students with Swedish backgrounds, and was most notable in Grades 3 and 4 in the years 1992–1993. These were the so-called 'crisis years' characterised by economic cutbacks and resource reductions also for schools. Noteworthy too is the increase in numbers of girls who received support in more segregated forms in Grade 5, in particular.

Students in the 1987 cohort were in Grades 3 and 4 during the years 1997-1998. The national economy had begun to revive and extra resources were allocated to municipalities (the so-called 'Persson' funding) with the stipulation that they should be used for education purposes, among other things. In other words, the increased special education support among students from more 'privileged home backgrounds' in the 1987 cohort may be because this student group was not prioritised when resources were cut back at the beginning of the 1990s and was now being compensated. However, the increase could also be a result of the resourcefulness of their parents in arguing for their children's rights to receive special education support when encountering difficulties in school.

In another study within STOFF, Giota and Emanuelsson (2011a) investigated through the use of a questionnaire how head teachers (n=683) for older students and head teachers (n=250) for younger in the Swedish compulsory schools described handling procedures of special education issues in their schools. On the basis of head teachers judgments it was concluded that one fourth of the 7-9 grade schools in 2008, when this investigation took place, did not allocate sufficient resources to provide special education support to those students who were considered as being in need of such support. A similar pattern was repeated for the younger students. Here, every fourth head teacher in the 1-3 grade schools estimated that more than twenty per cent of the students in their schools were in need of special education support, while only one of five schools actually provided support in line with the estimated proportion of students who needed that. These proportions are almost identical with those identified in two earlier questionnaire studies in Sweden (Nilholm et al., 2007; Skolverket, 2003). Notable here is also the high importance given by head teachers to medical diagnosis for the identification of a student's special education needs and for the allocation of special education support, for older as well as younger students.

In an attempt to study long-term consequences of special education support, Giota, Lundborg and Emanuelsson (2009) analysed the relations between different forms of special education support and goal attainment in Grade 9 for students in the 1982 and 1987 cohorts. The results revealed students who received special education support at any time during Grades 3-9 to achieve goals in core curriculum subjects to a lesser extent than students who had never had such support. Moreover, students who received special education support at an early stage of compulsory school reached such goals to a lesser extent than students who received support at a later stage. These relations are most evident for students who received support over more than one or two years. The results are in agreement with similar findings in previous research in Sweden (Emanuelsson et al., 2001). Further analyses aimed to investigate whether the negative relations between special education support and goal attainment would 'disappear' if students' results on aptitude tests were controlled. It was found, among other things, that students with low scores on the aptitude tests in Grade 6, and whose parents had post-upper secondary education had a relatively high degree of goal attainment in Grade 9, whilst this was not the case for students whose parents had a lower level of education (Giota et al., op. cit.).

The results of these nationally representative studies (Giota, Lundborg and Emanuelsson, 2009; Giota and Emanuelsson, 2011a, 2011b) indicate that the consequences of special education support are not necessarily the same for all groups of students. Differences in the amounts of success may rather be the consequences of school economy, ways of organising and giving special education support, and parental involvement than differences between individual students. In other words, the allocation of special education support is clearly related to factors other than ability/intelligence alone; a conclusion which is in line with previous research findings (Österling, 1967; Stangvik, 1979; Emanuelsson,

1997; Sonnander, Emanuelsson and Kebbon, 1993; Emanuelsson et al., 2001; see also Skolverket, 2009).

In short, analyses within STOFF show special education support given in more inclusive forms to be more favourable for successful learning and participation in school as well as achievement. More segregated forms of support given—and especially so for longer periods of time—were related to special need students' academic long-term failures.

Special solutions

Today the majority of students in need of special education support, with or without a medical diagnosis, attend regular schools in Sweden. As noted already, according to the Education Act (1985:1000; 2010:800) separating students in difficulties and/or with disabilities into special classes/groups should be exceptional. The inclusive ambition of special education support policy seems to have been difficult to accomplish however and is has continuously been both discussed and questioned (Emanuelsson et al., 2001; Nilholm, 2006a, 2006b; Persson, 2008; Giota, 2013).

One reason as to why inclusive education in Swedish compulsory school has been met by 'tendencies of exclusion' is related to an increasing frequency of neuropsychiatric and other medical diagnoses given to students in—or causing—difficulties. This is especially so since the beginning of the 1990s. An increase of segregated forms of support, like special schools and special classes, has been noticed as part of the same pattern (Tideman, 2000). Considering special schools, the proportion of students in such schools increased from 0.8 per cent in the early 1990s to 1.4 per cent in 2005/2006, rising to 1.5 per cent in 2007/2008, which is almost a doubling over a period of twenty years. The percentages varied widely between municipalities from zero to five percent, however. These percentages can be compared to those showing that the proportion of students with identified learning difficulties/disabilities, who were 'integrated' in regular classes, increased from twelve per cent to fifteen per cent over the same time period (Skolverket, 2008).

During the 1990s many parents demanded that their children ought to be examined by physicians and psychologists because such an expert-given diagnosis was thought to increase the chances for the student to receive the support needed from the school. The increased demands for 'objective' assessments and diagnoses that 'confirm' the needs of the students probably had, at least partly, to do with the 1990s financial crisis and cutbacks of resources in the majority of municipalities and also in the school budgets (Isaksson, Lindqvist and Bergström, 2007). The study among head teachers by Giota and Emanuelsson (2011b) showed parents in general, of both older and younger students, to have limited opportunities to exert influence upon the ways in which classes are composed in school, or on how students are divided in groups, and thus the kind of special education support that their child may need and get. This is in line with findings obtained by Persson and Andreasson (Skolverket, 2003) in their study, comprising about 20 per cent of all compulsory schools in Sweden.

According to Haug (1999) two trends have steered the development of special education in Sweden from its introduction and onwards: a desire to achieve equality and at the same time to maintain high achievement standards in the regular class. These trends have often proved to be contradictory. Even though head teachers tend to advocate that support shall be given within the framework of the student's regular class, in reality it is special solutions that are practiced. The main reason for such solutions seems to be that other students should have the right to be 'released' from classmates who, according to head teachers and teachers, might disturb teaching and 'peace' in the classroom (Skolverket, 2008).

The findings by Giota and Emanuelsson (2011a) show that one quarter of the head teachers for Grades 7–9 practice ability grouping or organisational differentiation and, although to a somewhat less frequency in Grades 1-3, this practice is common even in early ages. Further, twenty-seven per cent of the head teachers for older students and nineteen per cent for the younger state that instructing students in need of special education support in special instruction classes/groups is very common or rather common in their school. The emerging picture, when putting these proportions together, is that ability grouping, or organisational differentiation, and segregating forms of support are practiced in more than every second school for older students (fifty-two per cent) and every third for younger (thirty-nine per cent). A study by Nilholm et al. (2007) among all municipalities in Sweden show that 1.2 per cent of all students in the Swedish compulsory school receive their main education in special instruction classes/groups (see also comparisons with independent schools, Giota and Emanuelsson, 2011b).

International research reviews show no support for permanent forms of group differentiation leading to better attainment in the early years (Slavin, 1987) or in the final years of compulsory education (years 7–12) (Kulik and Kulik, 1982; Slavin, 1990). On the contrary, a substantial amount of research points to the negative consequences of segregated organisational solutions, such as stigmatisation effects and negative effects on students' self-beliefs and motivation (Hallam and Toutounji, 1996). American studies show that children who are placed in special, low-achieving classes encounter both lower expectations and receive instruction from less experienced and less competent teachers (Oakes, 1990).

In line with international studies, national studies indicate that students in special solutions feel 'stigmatised' and marked out as less worthy. They feel that they do not fit in school (Hemmingsson, 2002; Ljusberg, 2009; Hjörne and Karlsson, 2011 in Giota, 2013). Karlsson's (2008) study involving seven to twelve year-old boys in a special education group shows that their teaching was not entirely individualised. They did the same tasks regardless of their age and what school difficulties or needs they had. What they would do, when they would do something and why something would be done was vague to them. These students related the causes of their school difficulties to themselves, inscribing thus themselves a moral responsibility for not being able to concentrate, or waiting for the teacher's help in the regular class (op. cit. in Giota, 2013).

In such a group, where students with various difficulties in school have been put together, there is a risk that those who have some certain needs or difficulties get help before others, while the rest are 'falling behind' even in this group. When these students are then going back to their regular classes, they have 'fallen' even more behind compared to their classmates, while their negative self-image has been reinforced and will to learn has dropped even further. In this way, they 'become losers' on multiple levels, reinforcing their problems even more. Given the fact that students from homes with low resources such as immigrant students are over-represented in these groups (Giota, Lundborg and Emanuelsson, 2009) the marginalisation and social exclusion of already 'vulnerable' students is strengthened. As mentioned already, parents with high educational attainment seem to manage to ensure that their children receive the support and assistance they need in the regular class (Giota et al., op. cit.; cf. Giota and Emanuelsson, 2011b) contributing to the increasing social inequality between groups in the Swedish society (Skolverket, 2009).

In short, although placing students in special classes/groups is said to be done with the students' best interest in mind, the consequences often turn out to be the opposite. Repeated and longitudinal studies over forty years in Sweden, using ETF-data, show that in general it is impossible for a student who exhibits difficulties in managing school work to both overcome the knowledge gaps and 'catch up' with his classmates by receiving special support in various forms of more or less segregated solutions (Emanuelsson, 1974, 2003; Giota, Lundborg and Emanuelsson, 2009; Persson, 1998a, 1998b, 2001). Further analyses within STOFF show on the other hand that students in schools, where supporting students in difficulties by an additional teaching resource in the classroom was according to the head teachers a common practice, attained not only higher achievements in Grade 9, but also a higher degree of access to upper secondary national programs, stating at the same time that they thrived better in these schools.

In the study by Giota and Emanuelsson (2011a) practically all secondary level head teachers (i.e. for the later grades in the compulsory comprehensive school) attribute the reasons for a student's need of special education support predominantly to the student's own shortcomings and individual characteristics. This differed significantly from the response of the head teachers for the primary level (i.e. the earlier grades), which was far more in line with curriculum based measures or interventions aimed to enhance inclusion as stressed in the formal curriculum (see also comparisons with independent schools, Giota and Emanuelsson, 2011b). A challenging question that emerges here is whether school should try to adjust the curriculum goals to meet the student's needs, or 'adjust the needs' of the student to suit a given curriculum and established ways of teaching demands. This is an example of a dilemma that has been discussed for many years as a kind of paradigmatic challenge (Haug 1998; Emanuelsson et al., 2001).

Equity

In Sweden, equity in the early 1960s referred to equal access to education as a right and as a means to reduce educational inequalities between different groups in society by increasing opportunities for further education, employment, income and quality of life. Already in the late 1970s, Härnqvist (1978) noted that the common nine-year compulsory school, which was introduced in the Swedish school system in 1962 to achieve equality in education, did not fulfil its purpose. The educational level of Sweden had risen when all students went into 'a school for all' instead of the parallel school system that was practiced previously. But as Härnqvist showed, by using ETF-data, the educational inequalities had remained (op. cit., in Giota, 2013).

This traditional way of evaluating equality and justice has been challenged by the Indian economist Amartya Sen (1984) who suggests that the emphasis should instead be on what people can do, what they have the ability to become and what they consider to be quality of life for them and thus on removing barriers so that people can have more possibilities to live the kind of life that they value. This 'capability approach' to equality and justice is based on the idea that what we consider to be core human abilities have universal value and can be seen as an extension of human rights. These rights are to be treated in a certain manner, the right to health, to have resources to own life projects, and the possibility to make decisions about how to design ones' own life (see also Nussbaum, 2000, both in Giota, 2013).

Research studies such as the one by Härnqvist (1978) and new approaches to equality had according to Wallin (2002) as a consequence that the political debate about the 'equality generating functions of the Swedish school system' shifted from the 1980s and onwards to be about *equity* and people's *equal worth*, as stated in the UN's Convention on the Rights of the Child from 1990. In a school context this implies that children and young people shall be treated with consideration and respect. This shift is also a recognition that children and young people are different and that their life projects differ and will continue to differ, but that they, regardless of that, have the capabilities to acquire what school has to offer on their own terms. What school has to offer thus shall be of *equal worth* or have the same *value* for each and every individual student, but teaching does not need to be designed in the same way in every single school. Teaching should be individualised in order to meet every student on the basis of her/his capacities, needs and interests (op. cit., p. 206 in Giota, 2013). Another conclusion here is that although equality, equity and equivalence are inextricably intertwined they have some different interpretations to be noted.

Given the increasing inequalities in the opportunities for learning of certain student groups, and the risk they run to become marginalised and socially excluded, the political debate in Sweden today is about how much variation in equity that can be tolerated or to what extent this variation can be of advantage or disadvantage for students and the Swedish society (Skolverket, 2009).

Concluding remarks

Although the overall objectives in the policy documents have not changed significantly since the introduction of 'a school for all' in the early 1960s, recently or more specifically during the last fifteen years, the demands for having access to segregated special education have increased again, in line with the requirement of schools to show high test scores and secure a status as 'a good school' in the increasing competition between schools over students. The need to 'keep away' students that may be considered as a risk for a school's status increases thereby, resulting in an increased need for a segregated special education (Giota and Emanuelsson, 2011a, 2011b). This need is rarely pronounced explicitly in the political debate. The rhetoric is rather, just as in the 1960s, only talking about how to provide help and support to 'weak' students. The substantial increase of segregated solutions in the early decades of the Swedish comprehensive school was justified as the needs of 'special' students for 'special' support rather than the school's need for organisational differentiation. Nevertheless, a clear differentiation is once again the case.

The knowledge acquired within special education research and evaluation studies about what may cause various difficulties for students in school influenced, nevertheless, the organisation of school's inner work and the teaching processes during the 1980s. Schools could provide the necessary special education support to students without separating them from their regular classes.

In addition to the negative consequences that segregated forms of special education support have for students' learning and overall development, this practice ignores one of the school's most fundamental missions. Students are in school to interact with other people and learn how to be 'a good democrat' and that people are equal although they are different. The question that emerges here is how students can develop a social and democratic competence in life when students in regular classes or certain schools are becoming more and more similar, while the 'others' are becoming more and more different and are left on the 'outside'.

On the basis of results presented in this chapter, we can conclude that special education research faces great and challenging tasks. It is important to carefully study and analyse the implications of the later changes in the Swedish education system. This is particularly important as regards the situations and possibilities given to students, who traditionally have been described as 'weak' or 'disadvantaged'. There are an increasing number of students who are sorted out, or for other reasons leave school as 'dropouts' at different stages in school. This is not primarily a particular special education problem, but rather a general educational dilemma, common to all who have responsibility for the Swedish school system and its conditions.

In an analysis of organisational and pedagogical differentiation from a historical perspective and individualised teaching as a key principle in an inclusive pedagogy approach, Giota, Berhanu and Emanuelsson (2013) reflected upon the political debate of today. In the same way as other voices, they concluded that no traces of 'lessons learned' from the nearly seventy years of school experiences that have been made since the introduction of the school reforms in the 1940s can be found. For experienced special education teachers, other teachers in the field as well as scientists, it feels like it would be a case of 'starting all over again'. Even more serious is the downgrading of the aspirations for the goal of 'a school for all', which has become so clear, especially since the turn of the millennium. What are the reasons for 'disarming' the Swedish education system, which during the 1980s had 'a worldwide reputation', and what can be done to resume the faith to equity in the Swedish society?

Acknowledgment

Some of the issues reported here will be examined further within the framework of a new research project, *Consequences of individualised teaching for students' motivation to learn and achievement over 50 years: educational reforms and societal changes*, financially supported (2015-2018) by the Swedish Research Council of Education.

Chapter 10

Extending the role of the school: A case study

Harriet Rowley

At a national and local level, policymakers in England have introduced a range of initiatives, which have sought to tackle inequalities in society and in the education system. One example has been efforts to 'extend' the role of schools so that they are able to offer additional services, activities and opportunities to their students, to students' families, and to the communities that the schools serve. Such attempts have typically started from the premise that by tackling some of the causes of poor educational outcomes, more general socio-economic inequalities would also be alleviated, at least at local level. Although such attempts in some cases have been directed at a national level—for example a series of Extended Schools and Services initiatives (DfES, 2005)—they have been administered at a local level. Despite this relatively low level approach, they have been expected to achieve transformational impact. Unsurprisingly however, they have typically achieved limited impacts, and at best have ameliorated existing inequalities, meaning that they have acted as a substitute rather than enhancing policy efforts to bring about more fundamental change. Thus the benefits of such approaches have been questioned whilst governments' levels of commitment to tackling inequality have remained in doubt (Rees et al., 2007).

This chapter presents a case study of one such school, situated in a deprived area in Northern England, that sought to have transformative impacts by extending its role in the community. Interestingly, the school was part of the Academies Programme, which removed schools from local authority control and placed them under the control of a non-governmental sponsor (see Salokangas et al. in this volume). In this case, the sponsor was a local social housing trust so that two community providers—the school and the trust—came together at a local level to offer a joined-up approach to tackle the causes of poor educational outcomes and broader socio-economic outcomes in an effort to create a sustainable community. The chapter charts the development of the school, Weston Academy (all names are pseudonyms), together with views from community members through family case studies. By using empirical evidence,

I aim to identify a number of factors which seemed to limit the impact the school was able to have. In this sense, I situate the case of Weston Academy in line with so many other similar attempts that have achieved limited impacts but recognise there is much can be learnt from such examples. In particular, I seek to show how and why this case achieved limited impacts in an attempt to move the debate forward from simply recognising that transformational impact is unlikely when working at a local level. Critics (see, for example, Dyson et al., 2010) recognise that in the present neoliberal climate, macro structural policy adjustments that would enable transformational change currently seem unlikely. Thus, I consider what can be learnt from this case and how actors might work at a local and national level to ameliorate the effects of inequality more effectively in the future.

Situating the case study in the policy context: The New Labour years

During their thirteen years of office between 1997 and 2010, the New Labour governments introduced a variety of policies which aimed to modernise public services, narrow socio-economic gaps and raise outcomes particularly in terms of health and educational outcomes for disadvantaged groups (Lupton et al., 2013). Their ambitions had a distinctive social justice flavour and in particular aimed to tackle social exclusion of distinct spatially located communities, which were plagued by the multiple, reinforcing effects of deprivation. Perhaps most noteworthy in terms of the overriding concerns of this chapter, they arguably aimed not merely to achieve incremental progress but 'to do things that were radically different and to achieve a step-change in levels of socio-economic inequalities' (Lupton et al., 2013, p. 16).

For the purposes of this chapter and the case study in question, two aspects of New Labour's education policy are important: Extended Schools and Services and The Academies Programme. In the case of the former, this was a set of policies which sought to extend the role of schools in their community. The rationale behind such efforts posited that the effects of deprivation were clearly related to students' often-poor educational outcomes, and therefore it was logical that schools should become involved in tackling such issues due to their position in the local community and the resources that they possess. In this sense, it was recognised that schools should not simply concentrate on teaching and learning but also conditions 'outside' the school gates. Thus, efforts were directed at improving standards of education but also at tackling wider issues which beset local communities. For example, holding out-of-hours activities for students and their families attempted to broaden experience, increase social interaction or even reduce crime but also aimed to improve attitudes to learning or enable the development of new skills (Big Lottery Fund, 2006). Therefore, it was hoped that offering these opportunities would enhance what was available for students and their families but also improve the achievement of learners inside the classroom.

In 2005 the government showed significant commitment to the approach when they embarked upon a 'remarkable experiment' requiring all state-controlled schools to offer access to a 'core offer' of extended services (Cummings et al., 2011, p. 6; DfES, 2005). This Extended Services initiative was built upon earlier pilots where a selected number of schools were given additional funding to offer a diverse range of activities and access to services for children and their families. The nature of the provision was decided by the school themselves in an effort to encourage them to tailor the services to local community's needs whilst they were expected to work with other service providers to offer out-of-hours opportunities and a multi-agency approach. The government had great expectations of what the initiative would achieve and though it formed one part of whole litany of educational policies which aimed to improve educational outcomes, it was described as a 'key vehicle' for eradicating child poverty and improving outcomes for children and their families (HM Government, 2007).

Another policy introduced by the Labour governments significant to this study was the Academies Programme. An important element to the policy was how the governance of such schools was dramatically changed in that they were independent from local authority control whilst they were not duty bound to follow other state mandates such as the national curriculum, teaching and pay conditions (Gunter, 2011). The programme has now undergone significant changes and under the subsequent Coalition government expanded rapidly. However in its original form academies were required to have a sponsor who was expected to contribute both financially and to the school's governance arrangements (DCSF, 2008). Sponsors came from a range of backgrounds including commercial businesses, faith communities, individual philanthropists and universities (DCSF, 2008). Initially, the programme was directed at 'failing' schools which were struggling to maintain adequate standards of achievement and were therefore often located in urban deprived areas. These changes to the public accountability of schools were dramatic. However, such radical moves were deemed necessary due to the cycle of low achievement levels. Significant pressure was thus placed on schools converting to academy status to improve attainment results quickly. As David Blunkett, the then Secretary State for Education argued at the opening speech for academies, such an improvement in standards for all pupils was vital in building a successful and inclusive economy and society in the twenty-first century with a vision of excellence, diversity and transformation. (Blunkett, 2000).

A product of its time: Weston Academy

It is within this context that Weston Academy was born. The school opened in 2008 and was formed from two previously failing secondary schools. Situated on the outskirts of a large conurbation in the North of England, the predecessor schools consistently struggled to break the complex links between social and economic issues in students' backgrounds and their poor educational outcomes. Like some similar communities in England characterised as 'deprived', the area served by Weston suffers from a high employment-low wage economy with pockets of intergenerational worklessness, whilst other compounding factors were also in existence such as poor health, low level crime and racial tension. The school population itself had a higher than national average proportion of students who are eligible for free schools meals, whilst the number of students with special educational needs also exceeded the national average. Furthermore, around a third of pupils who attended the school came from homes where English is not the first language.

Perhaps one of the most interesting things about Weston Academy was the school's sponsor—Weston Housing Trust, a local not-for-profit social housing trust. Whilst critics have questioned the motivations of some academy sponsors, Weston Housing Trust presented a more favourable alternative. For instance, Chitty (2008) expresses concern over the possible self-interested gains of some sponsors on commercial, religious, or entrepreneurial grounds whilst others have raised concern in terms of financial exchanges and leveraging of budgets between state education budgets and the private sector (Beckett, 2011). However, in the case of Weston Academy, although improving the local school in the area was in the Housing Trust's interest in terms of attracting residents, their motivations were much broader than this. The company's strapline—'great homes, great neighbourhoods, great people', recognised its commitment not only to managing 'bricks and mortar', but also to developing neighbourhoods that people want to live in and of which they are proud. The Housing Trust had already gained a reputation for investing heavily in the local area to improve living conditions whilst sponsoring the Academy was seen as extension of these efforts to enable residents to improve their life chances.

The executive board of Weston Academy, formed of directors from the school and Housing Trust, had a distinctive vision for what they hoped the school would achieve. As one member of the board explained:

> We see providing a school with a good reputation for educational standards as central. For us though, it's not just about improving learning but creating a sort of 'community hub' where everyone can benefit. We see the Academy as not just improving educational chances but life chances; improving employability, aspirations, health and general wellbeing of our residents. We want community members to be proud of where they live, turning it from somewhere which is considered as deprived to a socially and economic sustainable community.

Therefore, the board did not want to just improve standards of education but also extend the role of the school. Similar to the rationale behind other such attempts, Weston recognised that their efforts would need to extend beyond their students and thus would involve their families and the wider community at large. To this end, the school set about offering a wide range of services and mechanisms of support, which were over and above the core business of teaching and learning activities on which a school would typically focus. Therefore, the initiative was very much in keeping with the direction of New Labour policy at the time due in terms of the social justice undertones of aiming to improve levels of attainment for all and access to extended services for community members. Furthermore, the vision was one of transformative change rather than just incremental improvement.

Development and research partnership

Weston Academy's distinctive approach meant that the school offered a particularly interesting research opportunity. Weston Housing Trust was also keen to track the progress of the school and use research evidence to inform their work. Therefore, in 2008 a three-year 'development and research partnership' was formed between Weston Academy and a team of educational researchers from the University of Manchester. Under the aegis of this partnership, the research team collected evidence and acted as a critical friend by asking searching questions and engaging in reflective conversation about the progress of the

Academy (Ainscow, 2002). A key element of the partnership was the sponsorship of a doctoral studentship of which I was the holder.

A longitudinal case study was conducted in order to track the development of the school. This involved an ethnographic approach, which included attending meetings with various stakeholders and conducting regular qualitative interviews with members of the executive board over a three-year period. Ten family case studies were also conducted in order to assess the impact of the academy on their lives. The families were tracked during the second year of the fieldwork for a period of twelve months. Data collection with the families consisted of recurrent interviews as well as observations conducted on an opportunistic basis, for example when the families participated in activities or accessed support offered through the school or Housing Trust. I also interviewed a number of teachers and support workers in contact with the families during the twelve-month period in order to provide further contextual information.

The sample of families was purposively selected and contained two broad groups or 'types' of families. The first group comprised of five families who were considered as particularly vulnerable and were already in receipt of a number of support services provided by Weston and other community services. The children in these families tended to be identified as having learning and behavioural difficulties and consequently struggled to achieve. The five families in the second group were less vulnerable and had limited outside support. In contrast to the other half of the sample, children in these families tended to achieve at an average or above average level. Broadly, the sample also aimed to be reflective of the Academy's intake, containing children of different ages, genders and ethnicities. With the one exception, the families lived in houses which were either owned or located on an estate managed by Weston Housing Trust.

Tracking the development of Weston Academy

Promising starts

There were a number of positive initial signs for how Weston Academy would develop. Firstly, it is important to recognise the significance of the partnership—although housing and education are rarely associated with one another, both sectors are forced to contend with a variety of social and economic issues in deprived areas. A number of processes have contributed to the concentration of poverty in particular spatial areas in England whilst society has become polarised (Dorling et al., 2007, Hills et al., 2010). For instance, social housing has become residualised as disadvantaged and lower-income families have become concentrated in a reduced stock of affordable properties, meaning that providers have found themselves increasingly dealing with socially excluded and vulnerable sections of society (Gregory, 2009). Similarly, schools and other service providers serving these areas have been forced to deal with a range of social and economic issues, which plague the community. However, due to their endemic nature, attempts to alleviate these problems have often struggled to make significant impact.

To this extent, the unusual partnership between Weston Housing Trust and the school symbolises how the academies policy created space for interesting alliances between local service providers to emerge. Thus, despite the well-founded earlier criticisms of the role of sponsors within the academies programme, Weston Academy shows that it is possible for schools to be governed by organisations that are outside the education system but that have complementary aims and interests. Moreover, in the case of public education and housing, their fundamental principles of social responsibility and democratic accountability, which their foundations were built upon, need not be compromised. In fact for Weston Academy, there was potential for such efforts to be extended and in turn the possibility that more equitable outcomes for children and their families would be achieved by the joint venture. Such signs thus seemed to bode well for the level of impact that the school would be able to achieve.

Another promising initial sign was the decision made by the executive board to second a member of staff from Weston Housing Trust to the academy and create the new innovative position of 'Community Director'. Parveen Gupta, the post holder, formed the third point of the leadership triangle with the other two points occupied by William Pugh, the Head and John Burgess, the Deputy Head. The creation of the post was significant since in the English context it is unusual to have a member of staff employed at this level who has experience outside of the core business of schools. Furthermore, the post signalled an intention by the sponsor to ensure that someone acted as a bridge between the two organisations in an effort to create a strong partnership.

The third and final promising initial sign that is worth noting is how the executive board, alongside the research team, engaged in some thought-provoking discussions about their vision for the school and what they hoped to achieve. Within the early stages of the formation of the Academy, time was set aside where the executive board were able to share their experience of working in the area whilst engaging in some blue-sky thinking to build an innovative but contextually sensitive vision for the school. Thus, the school and the housing provider acted as two key local drivers that aimed to shape the ways in which the effects of deprivation would be tackled at a community level. In the past, like so many other deprived areas, such attempts by local service providers had been relatively weak and uncoordinated. However, Weston Academy offered an opportunity for a more joined-up approach whilst the research team were uniquely placed to track what happens when a school in this context attempts to improve social, economic and educational outcomes at a local community level.

Facing reality and experiencing difficulties during the development of Weston Academy

Three themes from the data

Despite these promising initial signs, the executive board soon encountered a number of issues. In this section, I summarise three main themes from the data which were significant during the tracking of the development of Weston Academy. Each theme also forms part of the explanation as to why Weston Academy struggled to achieve transformative change and why the impact of their efforts to extend the role of the school was limited.

Firstly, despite the executive board engaging in lengthy discussions concerning the vision of the school and what they hoped to achieve, they found translating this into practice increasingly difficult. Parveen, the Community Director was in charge of this task whilst the rest of the executive board were expected to support her. However, Parveen was relatively inexperienced in strategic planning whilst there was limited national guidance available that could help direct their efforts at a local level. One of the executive board members explained the problem as follows:

> In many ways, what we are trying to do is ground breaking so we have got to expect to do a bit of a trial and error. It would be useful if we had some kind of framework or at least some policy guidance. There is very little support available or accountability measures for setting up community initiatives yet a lot of government policy seems to be encouraging this sort of work.

In practice, this lack of strategic direction meant that whilst a 'community improvement plan' was produced, it did not act as a working document which was used to guide the executive board's actions. Furthermore, unlike the original vision where efforts to improve standards of achievement and efforts to improve broader outcomes for children and their families were mutually reinforcing, the former became separated, as the plan did not contain details of these strategies.

The second significant theme, related to this point, is concerned with how efforts to improve teaching and learning became increasingly separate from those concerned with the broader educational outcomes and community engagement. Furthermore, not only did they develop separately, those which were primarily focused on improving standards of attainment were prioritised. So, the more distinctive broader, community goals were side-lined, as the following example that Parveen gave shows:

> I have been trying to get some funding so we can employ some more support staff, which are designated to supporting Asian families but it feels like the money keeps getting pushed in other directions. At the end of the day, it's considered as additional. If we need another maths teacher that's what the money will spent on because levels of achievement matter more.

Some local factors contributed to the development of this theme. As previously mentioned, the executive board found putting their vision into practice difficult. This meant that rather than following a detailed plan, efforts directed at providing extended services and mechanisms of support were predominantly offered on an opportunistic and ad hoc basis. Furthermore, William Pugh, the Head and John Burgess, the Deputy Head were experienced in putting in place tried and tested, relatively straightforward school improvement strategies. In contrast, Parveen was less experienced and was increasingly expected to co-ordinate the community efforts, which in many ways were more unpredictable. Thus whilst the management team was intended to function as a three point triangle co-ordinating different parts of the original vision, Parveen became increasingly isolated.

Although these local factors did contribute, national policy imperatives seemed to dictate the direction of the Academy to a much greater extent. Despite the significant commitment shown by the government to tackling the effects of socio-economic disadvantage by extending the role of schools, exactly how offering additional services would contribute to alleviating such issues was left unclear (Cummings et al., 2011). Furthermore, as demonstrated by the earlier quote, schools were often at a loss as to what to do as a consequence of the limited nature of the national guidance available. At the same time, they also put intensive pressure on schools to raise educational standards in the form of narrowly conceived attainment targets. Regardless of the challenging circumstances of some communities, all schools were measured and judged by the same standards and penalised accordingly. These pressures meant that schools had to prioritise such efforts whilst they were forced to wrestle with the contradictions that resulted from an incongruent policy context.

The challenges that Weston Academy inherited from the predecessor schools together with the pressure to improve standards due to academy status meant that the executive board had little choice but to concentrate on narrowly focused attainment targets. Furthermore, the strict accountability measures enforced by the government also meant that the price of failure was high. This was particularly the case for schools that had converted to academy status, whilst sponsors were keen to show that new governance arrangements and increased freedom from traditional local accountability frameworks were enabling them to produce good results. These factors meant that the executive board of Weston Academy were under significant pressure to show that levels of attainment were increasing despite the challenges they faced. As one member of the executive board poignantly put it, 'I think it's best if we play it safe.' Thus, standard school improvement strategies increasingly became the favoured course of action rather than experimenting with broader community-focused initiatives where limited guidance was available and impact uncertain.

The third and final theme is the diminishing role played by Weston Housing Trust in the development of the school as a result of the national policy pressures to improve standards of attainment. Although, as identified earlier, Weston was a promising sponsor for the school in terms of being a key local driver with plenty of context-sensitive expertise, they had limited expertise in how to improve attainment. On the other hand, William was au fait with school improvement strategies, and so it was preferable to leave such efforts in 'his capable hands' (board member). As time passed, the sponsor's position of relative power diminished as the pressure to improve standards increased. This meant that the Trust found it difficult to exert any meaningful force to steer the school's efforts back to the original transformative vision. Therefore, the focus became increasingly narrow and limited to the core business of raising attainment.

Assessing the impacts on students and their families

Four themes from the data

As identified in the previous section, Weston Academy's efforts to improve educational standards and broader community initiatives became separated, and so the impacts of each upon families will be discussed separately. For the purposes of this chapter, two themes will be discussed in relation to each. In this section, I seek to foreground the experiences of the community from the family case studies that I conducted. These insights into how individuals experienced attempts to moderate the effects of socio-economic disadvantage by extending the role of the school are important and unusual since few studies have had this type of access at the local level whilst others have mainly focused on the views of professionals (Dyson et al., 2011).

In terms of the impacts of Weston Academy's efforts to improve standards of attainment, it became clear that students' educational experiences were very different between the two broad groups of families in the sample. Students from the families who were considered to be in less need of support were likely to report that their attainment had improved. For example, two of the boys in the sample who were nearing the end of compulsory education, said that as a consequence of the predecessor schools changing to Weston Academy, they had achieved better grades in their final exams. As Asjad Nissar explained:

> The teachers' expectations are much higher since the school became an Academy, which has meant that we have had to work much harder and attend more revision classes.

However, students in the other half of the sample who had intensive support and were considered as vulnerable to varying degrees tended to think that Weston Academy had not positively impacted their levels of attainment. Instead, these students often struggled with the pressures of the mainstream classroom, as Kaleem Malik described:

> The teachers are constantly on at me, 'you didn't reach that target', 'you are below your age range' … If anything, that has got worse since the school became Weston Academy. It makes me feel like I might as well give up because it feels impossible.   (Kaleem Malik)

Kaleem Malik went onto explain how he often misbehaved, and as a consequence teachers often sent him to the behaviour and support unit:

> I'm always getting sent out of my lessons and having to go to the support unit. It just means that you end up sitting in there and not doing much or just answering questions out of a text book. Sometimes, I prefer being there. At least you don't get any hassle but I often can't do the work because you are not allowed to talk or ask for help.   (Kaleem Malik)

Such findings were consistent across this half of the sample. For instance, only one child from the five vulnerable families that were tracked was not excluded at some point during the year. This meant that students were not allowed to enter school grounds for a period of days determined by the school as a punishment.

The main factor which seemed to underlie the division in educational experiences was the pressure on the school to raise attainment levels. As Gillborn and Youdell (2000) argue, the emphasis on attainment means that schools direct resources towards students who are likely to achieve. Students are, using a medical analogy, put into 'educational triage' and are divided between those considered as 'safe' and likely to achieve, suitable for treatment—that is, capable of achieving the expected levels but needing intervention to do so—or 'hopeless cases' who are unlikely to achieve that level and so are thus 'left to die' (ibid., p. 134). In this sense, students' educational experiences are rationed in different ways. In the case of Weston Academy, those who were deemed capable of achieving tended to be offered a fairly narrow curriculum but received extensive training to achieve high grades. In contrast, less academic students were separated from the mainstream classroom and were more likely to be excluded but had access to different types of vocational courses.

Such findings also gave rise to concerns over inclusion. Students who were low attaining and had behaviour problems spent significant periods of time in a specialist unit away from the mainstream classroom. Teachers spoke of how the pressure to raise attainment meant that they did not have the time to focus on students with additional learning or behavioural needs. As one teacher who taught Stacey Baldock, a vulnerable student in the sample, explained:

> I don't have time to give her the extra help she needs so she ends up struggling with her work and when she gets frustrated and can't do it she acts up. It's very stressful because now the school is an academy we

have to make sure those who can are getting their target grades so I don't have time to pander to her needs. (Stacey Baldock)

Thus, rather than adapting the classroom environment to cater for the diverse needs of students, mainstream school processes seemed to become standardised, narrow and restrictive. This meant that students who did not 'fit in' had to be catered for elsewhere.

As Golby and Gulliver's (1985, p. 14) seminal piece on 'remedial education' long ago argued, such practices leave the curriculum largely unchanged and although the system is 'accident prone,' special education acts as the 'ambulance service' which compensates for an otherwise 'functioning' system. In the case of Weston Academy, the behaviour and support unit became increasingly important and valued resource, and whilst students no doubt benefited from this extra layer of support, they became separated from the mainstream school and had less contact time with qualified classroom teachers.

The second theme that was significant in terms of the impact of efforts to improve attainment was how the school adopted some practices which seemed contrary to what some students and their families seemed to value in terms of the purposes of education. There were a number of students in the sample who reported that they found it difficult to 'fit in' to the school. For some, as we saw in the previous quotes, this seemed to be because they struggled to meet the demands of the curriculum and the expectations of the classroom. For others, the 'sixth form' (post sixteen learning provision) with its academic focus and expectation that students would go on to study at university was at odds with young people's understandings of themselves and what they wanted to do. For example, Katie Harrison's mother explained how:

Weston sixth form isn't really for people like us. We want her to stay local. Katie needs to be able to get a job after college and doing a childcare course will mean she can get a job in a local nursery and carry on looking after neighbours' kids for cash in hand money. (Mrs. Harrison)

Similarly, Luke Grove, one of the two sample members who decided to continue his education at Weston sixth form said that he felt the school was trying to 'mould me into something I'm not.' This seemed in response to their efforts to encourage him to attend university. Luke expressed how the expense put him off because 'from living round here I know what debt does to people.'

Interestingly, both Luke and Katie's responses are tied to their experiences of their local community and thus their identities as learners seem shaped by 'place'. Scholars working on these issues of place, space and identity have suggested that 'what it means' to be disadvantaged or poor is 'constructed in and through space' (Raffo, 2011, p. 4). Using Massey (1994) Raffo (op. cit.) sees 'space and place as theoretically intertwined so that place is seen as an articulated moment in spatial relations'. He thus suggests that places and identities in disadvantaged neighbourhoods are 'similar yet different' to others. This implies that young people living in these neighbourhoods have identities and agency, which are 'place-based' and are reflective of 'particular manifestations of spatial social relations' (Raffo 2011, p. 5). Different processes operating at the school and policy level value or recognise these student's 'place-specific identities' to differing degrees. Thus in this sense, Luke and Katie's experiences symbolise a particular manifestation of how macro-level policy processes such as efforts to encourage higher attainment and improve aspirations seem to contribute to how students at a local level experience misrecognition.

In summary, evidence from the family case studies showed that Weston Academy's attempts to raise standards had mixed or limited impacts on students. Although it is true to say that some students in the sample seemed to be positively affected by the school's efforts to raise attainment, it seemed that these students were already likely to achieve. In contrast, students who were more vulnerable and of a lower ability seemed to be further adversely affected by the narrow focus on attainment since within this framework these students found it difficult to 'fit in.' Findings from the case studies also suggested that because of the narrow and restrictive processes operating within the school, there was limited space for students to be recognised on their own terms. This seemed to create a mismatch between what students and families expected from the school and placed value upon and what the school provided in practice.

Two themes in relation to the impact of Weston Academy's efforts to improve broader educational outcomes and community engagement will now be discussed. First, from the families in the sample who were more vulnerable, there was evidence to show significant positive impact from the increased multi-agency support they received. Due to the partnership between the school and Weston Housing Trust, together with closer relationships with other service providers, families benefited from the collaboration of professionals with different specialisms. Such arrangements proved particularly successful in terms of providing multi-agency responses to particularly vulnerable families.

For example, during the tracking process the Houghton family experienced safeguarding issues and their son was placed in care. Mrs Houghton reported that she 'wouldn't have coped' had it not been for the multi-agency support, whilst having access to a range of professionals had meant that the school-based support workers had been able to make use of the 'pluses and minuses' of their jobs to overcome professional boundaries and provide a quick and effective response. As in Edwards et al.'s (2010, p. 28) work on inter-professional collaboration, a 'new space of action' thus seemed to be developing at the boundaries of Weston Academy. This enabled staff to provide a 'sensitive and responsive' approach whilst the new multi-agency collaboration meant that expertise outside the usual world of education was being shared (loc. cit.).

It is important not to under-estimate the impact that such advances in practice had on vulnerable families. Although, their efforts were often not transformational simply because of the level of challenges such families faced, they mattered to the individuals involved. Indeed, the lives of students and their parents may have been quite different without this additional layer of support. Such arrangements seemed to be particularly significant in terms of linking home and school and providing families with a central access point to a variety of services. However, mainstream classroom teachers were not involved in these developments of practice, and there was limited sharing of expertise or information between them and support staff. As one Humanities teacher explained:

> I used to enjoy the pastoral side of this job but now we just have to pass stuff like that on. I never really get to hear what's happening because they work really flexibly and are not constrained by targets and timetables like us.

Thus, these advances in meeting the needs of such students were not extended into the mainstream classroom. Instead, teachers increasingly operated within narrow and restrictive structures and practices that were designed to improve attainment rather than engage with pastoral issues. Therefore, national policy imperatives in terms of the pressure placed on schools to improve standards again seemed to curtail the extent of any impact Weston Academy was able to achieve.

The second theme in relation to the impact of Weston Academy's efforts is concerned with the extent to which the school was able to engage the community. As previously mentioned, Weston Academy offered a wide variety of extended services, out-of-hours opportunities and support by collaborating with a range of community service providers. Weston Housing Trust were also keen not only to ensure the academy acted as a 'community hub' but also that their regeneration work was extended by empowering students and their families to become more involved in decision-making about how to transform their community.

In respect of engagement with services, the most significant impacts seem to have been on families in receipt of targeted support. However, there was limited evidence of impact of the out-of-hours activities and community events on the families in my sample, as their participation was rare. There seemed to be a variety of reasons for this, including issues in communication and reluctance on the part of some students to engage in anything offered by the school that was not a formal requirement. In contrast, I found evidence of higher levels of engagement with activities that were offered in the community itself. For example, 'family liaison officers' were found to act in a variety of capacities in order to provide the role of 'cultural broker' (Howland et al., 2006, p. 52) enabling families to seek support not just from the school but a range of service providers. As Farooq Habeeb, the family liaison officer for Asian heritage students explained:

> I am not just their support worker, I am their friend, their religious advisor, their legal representative, their career advisor or even their immigration officer. (Farooq Habeeb)

However, there was also limited evidence to show that members from the family case studies were involved in opportunities that were designed to elicit their views. For example, although the school formed a school council, none of the students from the sample was involved. Instead, the school seemed to rely on professionals to design and run the services and means of support. Although this approach seemed to work fairly well for targeted interventions, the evidence was that this approach worked less well for activities that were offered on a more voluntary basis.

Some local factors seemed to contribute to this lack of engagement, such as a long history of failed community engagement attempts together with poor existing structures to facilitate such efforts. However, in light of the exclusionary practices that the school seemed to practice together with the difference between what the school and community seemed to value, it perhaps is unsurprising that families were difficult to engage on a voluntary basis. Thus, the school's efforts to offer a variety of inclusionary measures and services to engage families were at odds with more exclusionary practices, which had been adopted as part of their efforts to improve attainment. The school also seemed reluctant to go beyond the 'four-wall mentality' and use its connections to engage families from within the community. Furthermore, the school adopted a somewhat deficit-oriented approach. As one support worker put it:

> We are providing the things they need, filling in the gaps ... It would be great if the impetus came from them but in practice this rarely happens because most of them are experiencing multiple issues and in some cases are just used to the support. (Support Worker)

In keeping with the national policy context, education is often positioned as an 'escape route' whilst the problems experienced by disadvantaged communities are highlighted rather than their ability to cope. Therefore, professionals tend to rely on 'their own best judgement' rather than attempt to look to community members for solutions (Cummings et al., 2007, p. 198).

Summary—why Weston Academy only achieved limited impacts

It becomes clear from this discussion that, despite the promising initial signs, Weston Academy achieved limited impacts overall. The sponsorship of the school by the local social housing provider was innovative whilst the executive board's vision was in keeping with the policy context at the time and thus aimed for transformative change. However, in practice the school that materialised was largely synonymous with standard school improvement approaches. Although local factors contributed to this state of affairs it seemed that national policy imperatives, which put pressure on the school to improve narrow standards of attainment, dictated the course of direction to a much greater extent. This meant that efforts to increase standards dominated at the cost of those which were concerned with broader educational outcomes, with the result that the impact of those associated with each type was limited.

Conclusion: What can be learnt from the case of Weston Academy?

These findings may come as little surprise to many critics and those working at the ground level in deprived contexts. Despite the hopes and expectations of national and local policy actors that such attempts would achieve transformative change, Weston Academy joins the long line of regeneration initiatives that have tended to ameliorate the effects of socio-economic disadvantage rather than dramatically impact whole communities. However, when we consider the nature of disadvantage, the odds seem stacked against those working at a local level. As Rees et al. (2007, p. 271) argue, such policy responses fail because they treat such communities as 'remaining 'pockets' of disadvantage in a wider context of increasing affluence' rather than recognising that the social and economic issues that deprived areas face are local manifestations of structural inequalities at play in wider society. Therefore, it is not surprising that efforts directed solely at how these processes play out in particular communities at a local level do not have the capacity to tackle the endemic inequalities that are a part of British society at large. As Cummings et al. (2011, p. 111) argue, 'a smattering of full service and extended schools will change little in societies where social and economic inequalities are rampant, and poverty is allowed to grow.' Thus, attempts made by the Labour governments to tackle inequality were merely presenting the image of an '*active government*, but within the highly restricted policy repertoire which in reality is available' (Rees et al., 2007, p. 272) and thus act as a substitute rather than being a serious-minded attempt to transform the lives of those living in disadvantage (Dyson et al., 2009).

This explanation of why Weston Academy only achieved limited impacts is helpful if not a little predictable. We know from the literature from other similar attempts (Anyon, 1997; Dyson, Jones and Kerr, 2011; Dyson, Gallannaugh and Kerr, 2011; Hasley, 1972; Rees et al., 2007; Smith, 1987) that such outcomes were likely and that without macro-structural level policies and serious attempts to redistribute wealth, local actors have little to no chance of achieving transformative change. Such conclusions could in some ways, have been reached without under-taking such in-depth research. Furthermore, in terms of what can be learnt from Weston Academy, it leaves us with a somewhat limited picture since one is forced simply to argue for a radical new approach, which in the present neoliberal context seems unlikely (Dyson et al., 2010).

This chapter has aimed to recognise such realities but also explain some of the reasons as to how and why Weston Academy achieved limited impacts and in particular identify how national and local factors seemed to impede what they were able to do. The research team had unique access to Weston Academy whilst family case studies have rarely, if at all, been conducted to this level of depth in the literature on extending the role of schools. Thus, this research study was conducted in particularly favourable conditions, which enables new insights into what happens when actors seek to engage in such efforts at a local level.

In terms of what can be learnt from Weston Academy for efforts which seek to ameliorate the effects of inequality more effectively in future, but which envisage doing so without a radical transformation of social and political conditions, two points seem particularly noteworthy. Throughout this discussion it has been clear that, whilst some local factors seemed to limit the impact Weston Academy was able to have, national policy imperatives to raise attainment seemed to impede their efforts to extend the boundaries of the school to a much greater degree. Such findings show that in an attempt to build more favourable conditions for schools, the balance between the purposes of education in national policy needs to be readdressed. Thus, schools should not simply be places where a students' ability to acquire knowledge and skills for employment is measured by standardised tests, but should also be places where they learn civic duties and come to understand the wider functions of society. As James Callaghan, then Labour Prime Minister, asserted some forty years ago, education is a balance between 'equip[ping] children to the best of their ability for a lively, constructive, place in society' and fitt[ing] them to do a job of work' (Callaghan, 1976). As the case of Weston Academy shows, the emphasis placed on attainment was destructive not only in terms of the effects on individual learners but also to the extent that the school could address socio-economic issues experienced by community members. As Cummings et al. (2011, p. 131) argue, 'schools can ignore what lies beyond the school gates, but they cannot escape it'. If they are going to have a chance at improving educational attainment, which seems clearly related to socio-economic disadvantage, national policy needs to create suitable conditions to enable actors to meaningfully tackle these issues at a local level.

The second point is the need for national policy to create conditions that enable greater local control and less centralised government intervention. As I suggested earlier, one of the most interesting elements of Weston Academy is that it indicates how new forms of school governance are possible that are not necessarily inimical to equity concerns. Furthermore, organisations that are outside the world of education can provide complementary ways of working and increased potential for impact. To some extent, these realities have increasingly been recognised by governments in the UK. However, what has not been recognised, perhaps, is that such partnerships need to be given the freedom and space to try out new approaches that are locally driven and contextually sensitive without the fear that they will face penalties for not achieving quick results. Such conditions also need to foster greater community voice and involvement since the continuation of deficit-oriented, professionally-led approaches will otherwise continue to struggle to engage disadvantaged communities. As Craig et al. (2004, p. 35) observe; 'simply dictating undifferentiated, unresponsive services will miss the point entirely.'

There are no doubt other conditions which would favourably impact on the success schools could have when intervening in non-educational issues. However the case study of Weston Academy suggests that the two points that have been identified are particularly fundamental and pressing. Although the present neoliberal policy trajectory makes such hopes seem unlikely, this chapter shows that studies of schools which attempt to take a greater role in their communities are important, as much can be learnt from their efforts. Furthermore, the very fact that innovative attempts to engage with issues of equity and broaden the role of schools in tackling the effects of deprivation are in existence, despite these challenging times, is a reason for optimism. However, as Cummings et al. (2007, p. 198) recognise, 'we must hope for more'.

Chapter 11

Independent state-funded schools and system change: Addressing educational equity?

Maija Salokangas, Christopher Chapman, Dennis Beach

The two education systems under examination in this volume have been subject to somewhat similar education reforms during recent decades. Of these reforms, this chapter focuses specifically on the emergence and development of independent state-funded schools: *friskolor* (free schools) in Sweden, and academies in England. These schools may be located in the wider international independent state-funded school movement, which also exists in other systems including the United States and Canada (LaRocqua, 2008; Meyland-Smith and Evans, 2009).

What is distinctive about academies and *friskolor* is that they are state-funded, but may be privately managed. They also enjoy increased autonomy in comparison to maintained sector schools, including autonomy from teaching pay and conditions and they may be run by sponsors. Academies were first introduced to urban areas with a history of low educational attainment in an attempt to raise performance. However, since the introduction of early academies, the programme has undergone significant changes and the focus has shifted from raising educational attainment in schools in difficulty to a large-scale systemic change. The academies, as well as *friskolor* have raised controversy throughout their existence, and the debate regarding their efficacy and desirability has remained fierce in media, as well as in academic discourses. Lundahl et al.(2013) describes the development of *friskolor* and academies as more than just a technical change in the delivery of education. Ball and Youdell (2008) argue, that these schools and the concepts developed around them, about them and through them contribute to 'a new language, a new set of incentives and disciplines and a new set of roles, positions and identities within which what it means to be a teacher, student/learner, parent etc. are all changed' (Ball and Youdell, 2008:11). This chapter presents an account of the emergence of independent state-funded schools in Sweden and England and offers some observations regarding the extent to which these reforms have addressed educational equity. It outlines the evolution of the Swedish *friskolor* and English academies, and draws some parallels between the two systems. The key parallels discussed include:

> An increase of school-level autonomy and diminishing role of local authorities (LA) in England and municipalities in Sweden,
> Cross-party politics driving the independent state-funded school agenda in both countries,
> A growing importance of sponsor and private entity involvement in the provision of these schools,
> A diversified local school market that the emergence and growth of these systems has created.

Drawing from these brief historical accounts, the chapter then argues that the Swedish *friskola* movement has influenced the English academy debate, and problematises such comparative approaches in policy. Finally the chapter discusses the extent to which these reforms have addressed issues in educational equality in both national contexts. As the Swedish *friskolor* were introduced almost a decade earlier than English academies, we begin the historical account from Sweden.

Swedish *Friskolor*

Friskolor were introduced in Sweden in the early 1990s, where they were described in terms of an effort to modernise education and to reduce public sector costs in school funding. The introduction was made possible by the introduction of student vouchers to enable, according to the government, a free choice between private and public education (Govt. Bill, 2008/09:171 in Erixon Arreman and Holm, 2011). The voucher reform, as well as a reduction of regulations inhibiting the entry of new schools into the education market, was a necessary condition for the *friskola* to emerge (Böhlmark and Lindahl, 2008). It was part of several parallel processes of neoliberal conversion that occurred in the Scandinavian countries at the time (Antikainen, 2010). These changes, that were initiated in earnest in education through reforms in the eighties and nineties, occurred in very concentrated forms, with negative consequences for many groups: particularly lower-class fractions of recipient-consumers (Beach, 2010) and immigrant groups and the economically disadvantaged from territorially stigmatised regions on the outskirts of our major cities (Bunar, 2010).

The development of the *friskolor* has thus not been a politically neutral one. It has affected many people and has contributed to educational developments in a period that has seen a significant fall in the level of general educational performances in Sweden as well as a very significant growth in the level of class differences in these performances. Moreover, the *friskolproject* is primarily actively driven from the political right (Beach, 2010), as an example of policy that is not merely the output of a political system, but also as a process that has brought certain principles or ideas into practice as a means to both codify and publicise the particular values that the government desires to inform future practice (Olssen, Codd, and O'Neill, 2004). It is a course of action relating to 'the selection of goals, the definition of values or the allocation of resources (and) the exercise of political power and the language [discourse] to legitimate that process' (Olssen Codd and O'Neill, 2004:72).

The introduction of independent schools in Sweden and the wider neoliberal conversion in welfare state education policy, according to Lundahl et al.(2013), can be described as a process in two steps. These are firstly Municipalisation and decentralisation and then secondly Marketisation and the introduction of free school choice. *Friskolor* are thus part of the second wave of conversion as they are also associated with increased *school level autonomy from municipality control*.

Decentralisation developed successively from the end of the seventies and culminated in the municipal education act in 1989 (Prop. 1989/90:41). It was politically motivated by investigations and propositions in relation to an expressed need for democratisation and increased citizen participation in public affairs, and this kind of decentralisation and increased layperson influence has been part of the Swedish school political agenda since the 1940s (SOU 1948;27). At this point decentralisation was primarily driven by the Social Democrats. It was later that it was taken over by the political right. Decentralisation, or municipalisation as it became known in education as it was the municipalities that took over responsibility for the direct administration and management of schools, was expected to expand the local scope for action and to, in this sense, become more responsive to local needs and conditions. Talk centered at this point on a free space for professional action (Swedish: *frirum*) from the decentralisation policy (e.g. Berg, 1995). It came to work differently, in ways conducive to neoliberal conversion later on, but this was not the expressed aim from the outset. The shift occurred when government control moved to the right and as public opinion became swayed through the employment of a new economic discourse (Lundahl et al., 2013). As such it could be argued that the *political right and left have had overlapping projects driving the friskol agenda* but there have been some distinctions in their causes.

Another development in relation to, or following on from decentralisation, was that the number of school leadership posts increased markedly and the terminology changed equally markedly. Originally called *rektor* (basically headteacher in the English system), a title reserved for a male grammar school lecturers, the title (*rektor*) first became applied at both the preschool, elementary and secondary school levels for male and female school leaders, and also for leaders at various levels of management with different responsibilities: i.e. not only pedagogical management ones. This meant that a school with students from preschool to grade nine may have three or more head teachers (heads) and that, unlike previous situations, these leaders could be professionals with diverse educational backgrounds, and who may not necessarily have any kind of teaching experience or exam. They operated accordingly through the adoption of other values than those that are mediated in a professional teacher education. As the market emerged so too did new posts and positions within the educational field. In 1988 the number of headmasters was 2900. Twenty years later they were nearly double, 5200, sixty-five per cent of them females (SCB, Statical Yearbook 1990 and Occupational Statistics 2011).

Decentralisation through the Municipal School Act based on Government Bill 1991/92:95 gave rise to school policy changes that thus both opened the way for private suppliers to begin to take their place in the field of education and to begin to manage these schools using leaders who did not necessarily hold to (or even were aware of) deeper professional pedagogical values and value systems. The expansion of the independent school sector was expressed as intended to strengthen the rights of parents and students to choose an education that best suits their own needs, but policy developments suggest that an economic (investment) logic has always been important (Beach, 2008, 2009, 2010). The school policy documents of the nineteen-nineties were imbued with markers of the neoliberal credo: improved quality, cost efficiency through free school choice and competition between different schools and forms of school ownership adjusted to conditions on a free school market.

Thus, whilst at the surface level *friskolor* are publicly funded but privately managed schools and associated with increased autonomy in comparison to other publicly funded schools, the *friskola reform opened school provision for non-public entities*, such as for-profit companies, charities, religious communities as well as parent groups, individuals and different interest groups. This has been most predominant in the post 16, upper secondary school sector, as in 2011-2012 already 49.7 per cent of the upper secondary schools operated as *friskola* educating 26 per cent of all students of the age group (Friskolornas Riksförbund, 2013; Ekonomifakta, 2013). Although steady, the increase has not been quite as accelerated in the primary and secondary sectors, in which recent data suggests that 16.5 per cent of all schools are *friskola*, educating 13.3 per cent of the age group (Ekonomifakta, 2013). Many of these schools now operate on a for-profit basis and are organised by international finance capital in operational chains. Thus, as Lundahl et al. (2013) point out, from having, prior to the nineties reforms, been organisations that were kept relatively separate from the economy in order to serve the needs of the individual and society, in the neoliberal policy paradigm, far greater importance is placed on the economic functions of schools education as direct factors of economic investment and calculation and crucial instruments for fostering economic growth and competitiveness at multiple levels. Schools are now sites and targets for investment, marketisation and commercialisation.

Chains of schools dominate the provision of *friskola* in Sweden and there are several nation wide chains as well as examples of chains reaching abroad in operation. The majority of Swedish *friskolor* are run by for-profit organisations and as Erixon Arreman and Holm (2011) found, seventy-nine per cent of them were sponsored by commercial companies in the academic year 2007-2008. This comprises education in all levels from pre-primary to upper secondary level. They also point out that the provision of *friskola* on the upper secondary level, is heavily dominated by commercial companies; out of ten largest sponsoring organisations one is a non-profit organisation and nine are for-profit organisations (Erixon Arreman and Holm, 2011). According to their calculations this means that altogether forty-nine per cent of all upper secondary level students are educated by the nine biggest ISS group sponsors, which are all commercial companies.

A highly *diversified market* has emerged (Erixon Arreman and Holm, 2011). According to the Swedish National Agency for Education (2012) the Swedish school landscape is best described as ninety-four school markets with different conditions: metropolitan, regional centers, community centers. In some of these markets the supply of schools has increased, such as in the urban and regional transport network centers, whilst it has decreased in others, such as the so-called commuting municipalities and countryside regions. Antikainen has shown similar tendencies in the Finnish market (Antikainen, 2010). Moreover, the broadening and increased economic instability of schools as a competitive venture along with the increasing incidence of choice under opaque conditions has led to more problems of choice (Puaca, 2013), increasing the numbers of school closures and, as a consequence, more students changing education suppliers, which results in extended training time and thus higher total education costs per pupil.

As also Lundström and Holm (2011) have suggested, the development and expansion of market solutions is one of the most important changes in Swedish education in the last thirty years. Amongst the main features of market competition and orientations and the extension of teachers' tasks have been the intensification of teachers' work and the change in professional values and identities. A new type of service-minded and flexible teacher has been discursively created and practices have shifted in accordance with this discourse. This has happened, Lundström and Holm add, along with a devaluation of traditional assumptions about the profession's societal role and position. As Lundahl et al.(2013:499) wrote: 'Even if the emergence of large free-school companies is the most eye-catching aspect of the marketisation of Swedish education, it is far from the only one. Competition has been established between all schools at municipal, and in the case of upper secondary education, even national level. Further, the work of schools is now orchestrated by new managerialism, and school curricula and educational assessment have been reformed in order to enhance employability, raise academic performance and increase effectiveness.'

All this considered, the *friskola* movement, since their introduction in the early 1990s have contributed significantly to the change of education landscape in Sweden in which much of the publicly funded education is managed by public entities with varying missions and visions, which has undoubtedly contributed to the diversification of local school markets especially in urban areas. In what follows, we will outline some of the key developments of the English academies, and notify some of the key parallels between these two systems.

English academies

The academies programme in England was launched under the New Labour Government in year 2000, a decade later than the Swedish *friskolor*. However, the foundations for academies were laid much before the programme was launched and can be traced back to the period of the Conservative governments initially led by Margaret Thatcher who came to power in 1979. Some of the key policy changes of this era that had long-term consequences include: the introduction of a free market approach to education by increasing parental choice and school diversity; the introduction of public league tables changing funding allocations to a per-pupil basis; and the introduction of the national curriculum (West and Bailey, 2013). The two key policies of Conservative Governments that were introduced in the late 1980s and which paved the way for the English independent state-funded school movement were the introduction of city technology colleges (CTCs) in 1986 and the launch of grant-maintained (GM) schools in 1988. GM schools were publicly funded, but able to opt out from local authority (LA) governance and receive their funding directly from the central government (Walford, 1997), a feature which has been seen as an important step in government policy towards the introduction of independent state-funded schools. However, of the two initiatives, CTCs have been labelled more frequently as the forerunner of academies, as they were sponsored by businesses and aimed at secondary schools associated with poor educational attainment and operating in industrial areas (DfE, 2010; Curtis, 2009; Caldwell, 2011). Although the CTC programme never grew large in numbers, the following Labour Government referred to CTCs as a successful example in justifying their independent state-funded school policy (Whitty et al., 1993; Adonis, 2012).

Like *friskolor* in Sweden, English academies have also enjoyed *cross-party support*, as both the political left and right have driven academisation. The first academies were launched in year 2000 under the New Labour government. These early academies were closely related to the idea of CTCs, as they were also introduced to cut the cycle of under-performance in urban areas. What was distinctive about early academies was that, although they were state-funded, they were set free from constraints maintained sector schools were subject to such as local authority control and union agreements on teachers' pay and conditions, and as such *enjoyed significant increased autonomy in comparison to other state-funded schools*. Also distinctive was that, instead of LA governance, these schools were in sponsorship agreements. These radical reforms were seen as a 'remedy' to tackle under-performance (West and Bailey, 2013), and the fundamental idea was that providing these schools with autonomy leading to educational and managerial innovation and change in areas of low educational attainment.

The first three academy schools opened in the year 2002 under the New Labour government, followed by a steady annual increase. By 2005 there were twenty-eight academies up and running and after five years of the launch of the first new schools, eight-seven academies were operating across the country (DfE, 2014a). Since the launch of the programme the debate over academies has been polarised, and the programme has faced substantial criticism. During the early days of academies a major area of debate focussed on raising student attainment. Academies under New Labour were criticised for not fulfilling the promises of improved student outcomes when compared to maintained schools (Gorard, 2009; Curtis et al., 2008). Although some individual academies were reported to show rapid progress, the programme as a whole had not proved to be as successful as its early advocates had predicted considering that diversity on outcomes was rather significant and as such no distinct 'academy effect' was be seen (Machin and Wilson, 2009; PricewaterhouseCoopers, 2008). However, quantitative analysis of school federations including academies has demonstrated that federations of academies outperform a matched sample of their non-federated counterparts (Chapman and Muijs, 2013). The early academies were also criticised for their admission policies, in particular for high exclusion rates (Beckett, 2004; Quinn, 2008). Indeed, PricewaterhouseCoopers reported in 2007, that academy exclusion rates were three times higher than their neighbouring schools (Asthana, 2007).

The changes in New Labour academies have been mapped and debated in greater detail elsewhere (i.e. Gunter, 2011; Woods and Woods, 2009; Ball, 2007) and as the debate is rich and nuanced, it is beyond the scope of this chapter to review. Although this is a relatively limited overview of the development and the implications of New Labour academies, it is clear the programme raised significant controversy during its early years, as various aspects of the policy and practice were debated.

Eight years after the opening of the first academies the Conservative-Liberal Democrat Coalition government was elected in spring 2010. Under the Coalition government, the pace of change has been fierce, as significant policy changes regarding academies have been introduced and new forms of independent state-funded schools have emerged (Chapman and Salokangas, 2012). The future direction of travel for the independent state-funded school movement was set out in the Academies Act 2010, the first piece of legislation enacted by the new government. The Act (2010) changed significantly the criteria regarding schools that could apply for the programme, inviting all English secondary and primary schools to become academies. Also a fast track lane was provided for the schools rated outstanding by Ofsted, and schools that were in difficulty were forced to convert. These changes in policy have brought academies from the margins to the mainstream. In spring 2010, as the new government stepped in, there were 203 academies up and running. Fast forwarding four years to the time of writing (May 2014), altogether 3879 academies are listed as open on the DfE website (DfE, 2014).

The expansion of the academies programme has also increased the number of sponsors and further increased the spread of multi-academy sponsors. The expansion of chains is one of the distinctive features of the sponsored academy movement, and a development the advocates of the movement have cherished (O'Shaughnaessy, 2012; Gilbert et al., 2013). The supporters of the academies movement have consistently supported the development and expansion of chains, as they believe they benefit from economies of scale, tested effective quality assurance as well as the possibilities to pool resources (Adonis, 2012; Hill et al., 2012). The largest academy sponsor at the time of writing (May 2014) is Academies Enterprise Trust (AET) associated with 78 academies. Other sponsors managing chains of 30 or more academies include: School Partnership Academies Trust, E-Act, The Kemnal Academy Trust, Oasis Community Learning and United Learning (DfE, 2014).

Some of the chains listed have been involved in academy sponsorship since the city academies programme, e.g. AET opened their first academy in 2002 and United Learning in 2003. Some of the large multi-academy sponsors are much later additions in the academy provision as for example, The Kemnal Academy Trust began their operations under the present Coalition government. As such, the expansion of many of the largest multi-academy sponsors has been rapid. In addition to these big sponsors, there are several smaller chains running nine or less academies.

The evidence regarding the implications of chains of academies remains limited to date. The major research focusing on chains conducted so far, by Hill et al. (2012) for the National College for School Leadership, has examined the expansion of chains and their implications on school leadership. Some of the emerging findings suggest that multi-academy sponsors have adopted a variety of governance models (Hill, 2010; Hill et al., 2012), resulting in differing levels and interpretations of local, school-level autonomy (Kauko and Salokangas, 2015; Muijs, Chapman and Reynolds, 2014; Salokangas and Chapman, 2014; Gilbert et al., 2013; Chapman, 2013). Altogether, independent research on the local implications of academy chains remains rather limited and considering the rapid growth of these enterprises, their implications at local level should be on the focus of more rigorous academic attention. Concerns over the lack of transparency on academy sponsors, remains a topic of heated public debate at the time of writing (Adams, 2014; Downs, 2014).

In addition to expanding academies, the Coalition Government has also introduced other types of independent state-funded schools: free schools, studio schools and university technical colleges. Free schools, were tied into the government idea of Big Society (Higham, 2013), emphasising the empowerment of local communities and actors. These schools were set up under the Academies Act 2010 and operate on a similar legal basis as academies, being entitled to greater autonomy, and may be set up and run by religious and business sponsors as well as by parent or community groups (Hatcher, 2011). The distinctive feature of free schools distinguishing them from academies is the emphasis policy rhetoric puts on parental and local community group involvement and empowerment (Hodgson, 2012; Higham, 2013). All these new school systems are in their infancy, and their impact is yet to be seen. However this expansion of the independent state-funded school movement have been claimed to be a further step in the government agenda to extend individual choice in public sector education (Hodgson, 2012) as well as in *diversification of the publicly funded education provision* (Hatcher, 2011).

We have outlined here briefly the evolution of both Swedish *friskola* and English Academies and in doing so we have drawn parallels between the two systems. Some similarities we have discussed include first, that in both countries the independent state-funded school movement has enjoyed cross-party support, as in both countries the political right and left have taken turns in riding the independent state-funded school agenda. Second, it has become apparent that in both England and Sweden the independent state-funded schools emerged after gradual steps were taken in increasing school level autonomy. Third, we have discussed the growing importance of sponsors running both English academies and Swedish *friskolor*, as in both countries significant number of schools are run by independent sponsors, many of which are organised in chains or federations. Finally we have cast some light on the ways in which the independent state-funded school movement has diversified education markets in both countries.

In what follows we will continue to draw parallels between these two systems, by firstly focussing on the ways in which the Swedish *friskolor* have been used as policy examples to justify English academies. We will problematise and critique such policy borrowing and extend our discussion to the implications *friskolor* and academies have had on educational equity.

Policy borrowing and amalgamations of the two systems

The change in Sweden as a social democratic welfare state with one of the most centrally planned and uniform school systems in the OECD area to one of the most decentralised market systems with greater scope for economic exploitation than in any other developed economy has been faster and more radical than it has in any other nation state (Beach, 2009). This development (or transformation) has also attracted significant international interest on Swedish *friskolor*, of which English policy rhetoric provides an example:

> Over the past 15 years, Sweden has introduced a new system that has allowed the creation of many new high quality state schools that are independent from political control. All parents have the power to take their child out of a state school and apply to a new independent state school. ... The results? Hundreds of new schools have been started. Thousands of children have been saved from failing schools and given a chance in life. In particular, thousands of children from the poorest areas have been able to escape failing state schools.
> (The Conservative Party, 2007:16)

Over the course of the English academies programme, Swedish *friskola* have been held as an example of successful educational reform. The statement above is an illustrative example of how in the English policy rhetoric *friskolor* have been articulated to offer increased and better choices for Swedish parents—especially in disadvantaged areas—as well as offering a solution to wider systemic improvement. However, we will argue here, that such comparisons between English and Swedish systems are problematic for a variety of reasons.

First of all, the conditions from which Swedish *friskola* emerged were of social democratic welfare state tradition, of a rather homogeneous education system, in which equity and equal access and opportunities to education, as well as economic and social justice were considered fundamental principals guiding education policy (Sainsbury, 1996). Considering the long and strong traditions of English private education, which have influenced also the academies movement (Glatter, 2012), the basis on which these systems differ are considerable. Regardless of these contextual differences in which the Swedish voucher reform, and English independent state-funded schools emerged, English policy makers have consistently made comparisons between the two and used Swedish *friskola* as a policy example for English academies and free schools (Conservative party, 2007, 2010; Shepherd, 2010; Wiborg, 2010). However, the English policy rhetoric referencing to the Swedish *friskola* movement has been rather selective, simplistic, and has focussed on certain aspects and implications of the reform, whilst ignoring others. For example, this is how Michael Gove, prior to becoming a Secretary of State for Education explained the role of *friskola* in raising attainment in Sweden:

> We believe schools should be engines of social mobility—where talent and hard work can help individuals overcome accidents of background and the barriers thrown up by prejudice and disadvantage. And we are concerned that the [English] education system isn't delivering social mobility at the moment. As they go through school, the most disadvantaged pupils fall behind their peers. It's because we wanted to overturn that injustice that we looked to social democratic Sweden for reform. Fifteen years ago the Swedes decided to challenge declining standards by breaking the bureaucratic stranglehold over educational provision and welcome private providers into the state system ... Those new providers have not only created schools with higher standards than before, the virtuous dynamic created by the need to respond to competition from new providers has forced existing schools to raise their game. There is a direct correlation between more choice and higher standards—with the biggest improvements in educational outcomes being generated in those areas with the most new schools.(Gove, 2008)

Of this rather conflicting quote, we would like draw attention to three points: the notion of improved student performance, exhilarated social mobility, and the notion of social democratic Sweden. Focussing first on the latter, Gove's notion of social democratic Sweden is somewhat problematic, considering that, as Lundahl et al.(2013) have put it, a 'Swedish model' is of quite another kind than its predecessor has emerged. The former model referred to consensual relations in the labour market and a commitment to the goals of full employment and social equality, whereas the new model exploits the old as a market strategy but represents a very different value set more in line with the current global economic hegemony. There is now an emphasis on instrumentality of education as compared to the social and cultural functions of education and although schools are still expected to make a crucial contribution to social inclusion and democratic citizenship, the definition and characteristics of this democracy and citizenship have changed as has their modes of reproduction in school policies and practices. Beach and Dovemark (2011) have described a new policy hegemony in which education is primarily regarded and acted towards as a private good and performance in which competition and individualism are core values.

Secondly, we would like to draw attention to the implications of *friskolor* on student outcomes as the evidence available conflicts Gove's statement and suggests that there actually is no real '*friskola* effect'. For example, Böhlmark and Lindahl (2008) found indications of moderately improved short-term student outcomes, but no evidence of improved long-term outcomes. Available evidence also suggests that students with short-term improvements come mainly from families with highly educated parents, as opposed to students from disadvantaged backgrounds (Allen, 2010). These findings directly contradict much of the English policy rhetoric, which raise Swedish *friskola* on a pedestal, using them as an example of successful reform promoting rising educational attainment on the areas of low educational attainment.

This brings us to the third point in Gove's argument: the implications *friskolor* have had on social segregation. Evidence available suggests quite the opposite to what Gove proposes, as it has been reported that social segregation has increased in Swedish schools since the choice reforms (Skolverket, 2009). However, to what extent this is a result of the school reforms and to what extent of wider societal changes remains debated. Indeed, developments in the education provision are closely entwined with wider societal issues such as housing, and as Bunar contributes to the debate: '*the most worrying segregation process is occurring within public education, due to a poorly organised education market in combination with housing segregation*' (2008: 435). Altogether, there is clear evidence regarding the increase in segregation in the Swedish education system since the introduction of the voucher reform and *friskola*, which has not received much attention in the English policy rhetoric advocating these schools.

There are also other implications of *friskolor* that have not been sufficiently scrutinised in light of English policy rhetoric. An interesting implication of *friskola* autonomy is that the expansion of these schools has fragmented the teacher labour market. In particular, the number of unqualified teaching staff is relatively higher in *friskolor* than in the municipal sector. According to the National Agency for Education (Skolverket, 2010), in 2008/2009 the ratio of qualified teaching staff in the municipal sector upper secondary schools was 78.1 per cent whereas in *friskola* sector only 54.6 per cent of the teaching staff were formally qualified. There is stark contrast between these figures and the English policy rhetoric, on one hand celebrating Swedish *friskolor* and on the other highlighting the importance of 'the quality of teachers and teaching' (DfE,

2010). This is particularly interesting considering that academy sponsors also enjoy considerable autonomy over teaching pay and conditions. Little is yet known about the current practice and the implications such autonomy has at local levels, but the emerging findings (Salokangas, 2013), and revelations in the national media (Paton, 2013) indicate that sponsors have embraced their increased autonomy, resulting varying pay and conditions and type and nature of qualifications required to become a teacher. These developments have been coupled with policies that have increased the diversity of provision of initial teacher education, which for the most part has moved from more traditional university-based programmes with some school placements, to programmes such as Teach First, School Centred Initial Teacher Training (SCITT) and School Direct programmes where work-based preparation and training provided by experienced, practising teachers in schools.

Critical voices of the Swedish *friskola* movement have also raised concerns in relation to the financial management of chains of schools. Erixon Arreman and Holm (2011), for example, investigated the governance and management of the largest upper secondary providers running chains of schools, and raised concerns regarding the unstable nature of these enterprises. Two years later, in June 2013, one of the chains at the centre of their study announced it had gone bankrupt (JB Education, 2013), making international media headlines concerning who would take over the schools the organisation is running during the summer holiday months. A number of providers expressed interest in buying former JB Education schools, many of them other chains of *friskola*, such as Karl-Oskarskolan and AcadeMedia, of which the latter was also included in the Erixon Arreman and Holm (2011) study concerned of the stability of the sector. Although the education secretary Michael Gove has celebrated the Swedish *friskola* system previously (Shepherd, 2010), he did not comment on the bankruptcy of JB Education and the possible consequences it has on students, teachers, and or the local communities in which these schools operate. Considering that at the time of writing, the debate regarding sponsor accountability in England remains heated (Adams, 2014; Downs, 2014) the Swedish *friskola* financial management scandals could provide alarming examples of poor practice and financial management.

Related to this, although so far academy sponsorship has only been available for non-profit organisations, speculation on the current government's interest in allowing for-profit companies to enter the market have been fierce. Recently, a leak was published concerning Michael Gove's interests to expand the independent state-funded school provision to for-profit businesses (Cusick, 2013). This sparked up a debate in the media, and a series of articles were published suggesting that English 'edubusinesses' are currently preparing for the opening market (Exley, 2011; Vasagar, 2012).

The relationship between the two school reform movements have not solely been articulated in policy rhetoric, but have also materialised in practice. Swedish *friskola* providers have already entered the English education market, for example Kunsakpskola, which runs thirty-six *friskola* in Sweden (Kunskapskola, 2014) sponsors four academies in England under a charitable organisation called Learning Schools Trust (Learning Schools Trust, 2013). The company has operations also in America where they sponsor Innovative Manhattan Charter School, and in private school sponsorship in India (Kunskaspkola, 2014). Also, other major sponsors in the Swedish *friskola* business either already have international branches and operations, or have expressed their interest in doing so in their company strategies (Erixon Arreman and Holm, 2011). In addition to Swedish *friskola* providers, also American charter school providers have entered academies management. For example ARK (Absolute Return for Kids) and Edison Learning have expanded from the United States to the United Kingdom, with the former sponsoring twenty-four academies and the latter involved in various education services, providing school management services and consultancy for academies (DfE, 2014; Edison Learning, 2011). The global developments of these enterprises are interesting, and remain to date an under-researched area.

Conclusions

In this chapter, we have discussed some of the key developments of English academies and Swedish *friskolor*. In so doing we have illustrated how English education policy makers have looked upon the Swedish *friskola* movement as an example of successful independent state-funded school reform. We have also problematised such comparisons. This has led us to conclude that the evidence used in English policy rhetoric is selective, and has focussed on individual cases of success, and selected evidence, rather than attempting to paint a comprehensive picture of the implications the *friskola* have had on the Swedish education.

We have also argued that, rather than addressing educational equity, the emergence and spread of independent state-funded schools in both national contexts have contributed to the diversification of publicly funded education. The landscape of schooling has become increasingly challenging for local actors to navigate as the number of school providers, as well as specifically in England the number of new types of schools has diversified the local school markets especially in urban contexts. How parents and students exercise their right to choose in these diverse environments is beyond the scope of this chapter, and should become a focus of rigorous academic attention.

In addition to students and parents, also other local stakeholders such as members of school staff navigate in this diverse landscape of schooling. Teachers and school leaders may work under varying employment contracts depending on the type of school, and the provider in charge. What implications varying teaching pay and conditions have on student populations, remains to be seen.

Finally, independent state-funded school reform has diminished significantly the role of local public administration, local authorities in England and municipalities in Sweden, as the new actors have entered school provision. Lack of transparent decision-making of these relatively new actors has raised substantial controversy in both national contexts, and remains a key focus of independent state-funded school debate as these actors expand operations nationally and internationally.

Conclusions

Equity and education in England and Sweden, tentative conclusions

Dennis Beach and Alan Dyson

The picture of equity and education which emerges from this book is complex and even contradictory. The authors have delved into different aspects of the education systems of two countries that have many similarities. Both are affluent, by global standards. Both are relatively stable liberal democracies with long-established social democratic strands in their political lives, and with enduring concerns for issues of disadvantage, equality and equity which mainstream politics of all kinds have at least to acknowledge and which have often led to concerted action. In educational terms, both have long since achieved the goal of education for all which continues to challenge the global education community, and both have well-resourced, sophisticated education systems which set out—to some extent at least—to maximise opportunities for all learners, regardless of their backgrounds. As a tangible expression of this, we have seen throughout this book how both countries invest heavily in their special education systems and in supporting the academic work of schools with a range of human services for those learners experiencing personal and social difficulties.

At the same time, both countries have had to navigate the consequences of what is often seen as a process of economic globalisation (Stiglitz, 2002)—the relative decline of heavy industry, an increasing focus on the high-tech manufacturing and service sectors and a consequent bifurcation of the labour market between those with higher and lower levels of skills and credentials. These processes in turn have been complicated latterly by the consequences of the 2008 financial crisis in Europe and the USA, and by relatively large-scale inward migration from economically-poorer countries. Amongst the many consequences of these macro-level economic changes has been the reinforcement of segregation by socio-economic status and by place. In relation to many other affluent countries, social mobility in Britain as a whole—and therefore in England—is low, and although mobility in Sweden is usually held to be higher than in Britain, it too is low in comparison to other Nordic countries (Blanden,

Gregg, and Machin, 2005; Blanden and Machin, 2007). Indeed, some recent work suggests that rates of social mobility in Sweden may in fact be similar to those in the UK and USA (Clark, 2013). Moreover, there is some evidence that, in Britain at least, mobility may be declining (Blanden et al., 2005; Blanden and Machin, 2007; Blanden and Macmillan, 2014). As an official assessment of the 'state of the nation' recently put it:

> Britain remains a deeply divided country. Disadvantage still strongly shapes life chances. A balanced economic recovery, between different parts of Britain, is not currently within reach. If, as seems likely, the recovery sees the trend of the last decade continuing, where the top part of society prospers and the bottom part stagnates, inequalities will grow and the rungs of the social ladder will grow further apart ... Incremental improvements and promising reforms in schools and welfare do not counterbalance a series of present-day problems—most notably high youth unemployment and falling living standards—that are storing up trouble for the future. We see a danger that social mobility—having risen in the middle of the last century then flat lined towards the end—could go into reverse in the first part of this century.
> (Social Mobility and Child Poverty Commission, 2013, pp. 4-5)

This ossification of social mobility is reflected in the perpetuation of poor areas. In both countries, areas grew up—or, indeed, were specially constructed—to house industrial workers, most of whom had limited educational opportunities and qualifications, and consequently had relatively low skills. The decline of heavy industry removed the economic base of such areas and the economic purpose of residents' lives—a process which, in many places, has been allied to complex patterns of immigration and internal migration. This has created what Wacquant (2008), reviewing parallel developments in French cities, has characterised as 'anti-ghettos', incapable of generating collective pride or shared cultural identity. Certainly, in both Sweden and England there are extensive urban areas where, despite repeated policy interventions, significant numbers of people experience poverty and a range of associated social problems, and where these factors limit both educational attainments and wider opportunities for progression (Dorling and Pritchard, 2010; Dorling et al., 2007; Lupton, Fenton, and Fitzgerald, 2013).

Not surprisingly, the processes of economic globalisation and the social tensions that are associated with it have changed the meaning of politics-as-usual.

The social democratic traditions of both countries have ensured a continuing concern with issues of inequality and disadvantage. In the UK, for instance, the 'New Labour' governments between 1997 and 2010 undertook a wide range of policy initiatives aimed at tackling child poverty, unemployment, area disadvantage and educational inequality (Lupton, Hills, Stewart, and Vizard, 2013), and even the right-of-centre Conservative government installed in 2015 has its own Equalities minister and commitments on poverty and social justice. Yet those traditions, however strong, have always been engaged in struggles with other strands of political thinking, and have by no means always been triumphant. In recent decades, not only have parties of the right enjoyed a share of electoral success, but neoliberal thought has embedded itself across large parts of the political spectrum in the form of a commitment to market solutions, a distrust of public sector professionals and a celebration of individual economic success as much as or more than social solidarity. At best, this has created a 'third way' (Giddens, 1998) that has helped revitalise social democratic thinking. At worst, however, the dominance of neoliberal thought has simply weakened both countries' commitment to progressive social change.

These trends are, of course, evident in the two countries' education systems. The commitment to maximising opportunities for all and supporting the most vulnerable stands in tension with an imperative to produce well-qualified and highly-skilled entrants to an increasingly demanding labour market. Confidence in education as a publicly-managed service dependent for its effectiveness on professional expertise has been eroded. Market forces have been introduced and the role of public management—particularly at the local level—has been reduced. Professionals have become held to account increasingly for the outcomes they produce, and those outcomes have progressively been reduced to narrowly-defined measures of performance. As this has happened, the inequalities in both education systems, and the problems posed by educational disadvantage have become increasingly apparent. Although the complex mix of social democratic and neoliberal approaches is often presented by policy makers as the solution to these problems, the reality is that the evidence for success is mixed, to say the least (Björklund et al., 2005; Lupton and Obolenskaya, 2013).

Assessing educational equity in Sweden and England

With this in mind, it is to the question of how successful England and Sweden have been from an equity perspective in navigating these developments that we now turn. Is it possible to produce a score card for each country, and if so, can we say which country has done best and what might be learned from that country's approach? Certainly, some analyses have been undertaken which suggest this is possible. OECD's Programme for International Student Assessment (PISA), for instance, seeks to compare the performance of education systems by testing samples of learners in those systems (OECD, no date). By analysing differences in the test performance of learners in different countries, and relating these to some basic demographic information about which groups of learners do more and less well, PISA claims to reach conclusions about equity of outcomes in different systems (OECD, 2013).

On this basis, both Sweden and England appear to be moderately equitable. In terms of gaps between median performance on the PISA assessments and low attainers, the two countries are fairly close to one another and somewhere in the middle of the pack of affluent western countries. If anything the UK (the results are not disaggregated for England) does a little better than Sweden in this respect; on the other hand, the relationship between learners' socio-economic backgrounds and their performance is stronger in the UK than in Sweden (OECD, 2010). PISA offers a range of similar analyses, in terms, for instance, of the impacts of gender and immigrant status on performance.

Moreover, by relating assessments of this kind to information on the characteristics of participating education systems, PISA seeks to offer some explanations as to the factors which drive equity and inequity in those systems (OECD, 2008, 2012). Early tracking, untrammelled school choice, grade repetition, and a failure to respond appropriately to minority groups are all associated with higher levels of inequity. In all, PISA identifies ten system-level factors that need to be addressed to promote educational equity and, as one might expect, Sweden and England appear to do reasonably well on most of these, but with some obvious areas for improvement.

Similar types of analyses are available from other sources. For instance, the European Agency for Special Needs and Inclusive Education offers analyses of the levels of segregation and inclusion of learners identified as having special needs in participating countries (European Agency for Development in Special Needs Education, 2012). These tend to show Sweden as making relative less use of special school settings than England, but more use of segregated settings within mainstream schools. Similar, UNICEF produces 'report cards' on child well-being—and by implication, therefore, how successful countries are in enabling their children to do well (UNICEF Office of Research, 2013). In terms of overall child well-being, Sweden outperforms the UK (again, results for England are not disaggregated) and, indeed, comes out well in comparison to most other affluent countries. In terms of education indicators, however (defined broadly as participation in pre- and post-school education and levels of achievement), Sweden does less well, whilst still significantly out-performing England.

Examples such as these could be multiplied many times over. Taken together, they paint a picture of two education systems which are highly equitable compared to those of many countries (notably, those countries that are also marked by very high levels of economic inequality), but which it would be hard to describe as world-leading. In broad terms, Sweden and England perform in a similar manner—though, as we have seen, their relative performance on particular indicators can differ. Whether this offers a complete account of the state of equity in these two systems is a moot point, however. For one thing, there are, of course, formidable technical challenges in undertaking international comparisons of this kind, in terms of finding good measures that can function across different education systems, drawing representative samples of students, identifying appropriate demographic and system indicators, and making statistically robust comparisons between systems. Moreover, performances and rankings change over time—sometimes quite rapidly. Sweden, for instance, appears in recent years to have been in rapid decline in terms of overall school performance and system equity, at least as measured by PISA (OECD, 2014). England also appears to have been in decline, though it is less clear in this case whether this reflects real change in performance or simply the inadequacies and inconsistencies of different performance measurement systems (Smithers, 2013).

Perhaps more important, statistically-based international comparisons tend to involve reducing educational outcomes—and therefore the assessment of equity in those outcomes—to a limited range of quantifiable indicators. What learners know and can do becomes reduced to how they perform on a small number of tests at a particular point in time. Differences between learners are reduced to differences in test scores. Their daily experiences in the education system become reduced to data on what form of provision they attend—and so on. Such information, understood and used appropriately, is, of course, useful for alerting policy makers and practitioners to the potential achievements and failures of their systems. From an equity point of view, it matters, for instance, that the association of measures and socio-economic background in the UK is stronger than in Sweden. If it causes policy makers to ask why this should be the case and whether there is anything to learn from the Swedish experience, this is all to the good. However, in many cases policy makers appear not to take into account the reductionist nature of these assessments and they are taken to be authoritative characterisations of what is the case in different countries rather than as distinctly problematic indicators. As a result, nuanced reflection on differences between countries is replaced by superficial comparisons, simplistic policy borrowing, and the pursuit of higher positions in international 'league tables' to the exclusion of other educational considerations. The serious nature of these impacts has led many researchers to conclude that PISA in particular does more harm than good in the task of securing better and more equitable educational outcomes internationally (see, for instance, Meyer and Zahedi, 2014).

An alternative assessment

In this situation, it is useful to return to the equity framework which Kerr and Raffo offered in chapter one. There are two aspects of that framework that are of particular significance. The first is that it explicitly sees equity as multi- rather than uni-dimensional. There is, they imply, no such thing as 'the equity of an education system'. Instead there are different forms of equity, or different lenses through which the issue of equity can be viewed. Following Fraser, for instance, they draw a distinction between equity as achieved through a redistribution of education goods—outcomes and resources to support the achievement of those outcomes—and equity as achieved through the recognition of cultural and personal differences between learners. The second is that they see equities and inequities as arising in different 'educational spaces'. In other words, education systems are neither homogeneous wholes, nor perfectly nested systems in which lower levels accurately reflect the characteristics of higher levels. Put simply, what happens in one school or classroom may be quite different from what happens in another, and equitable or inequitable policies may not necessarily produce equally equitable or inequitable practices.

For these reasons, Kerr and Raffo encourage us not to carry out uni-dimensional assessments of equity, but to ask multiple questions in and of multiple 'spaces'. The implication, of course, is that we might need to give somewhat different answers to the questions we ask. Assessing the state of equity in an education system, therefore, is about producing a rich and complex picture of that system—a picture that will be full of variation and, indeed of contradiction. Comparing two such pictures may not be impossible, but it will involve a much more nuanced process than simply reading off the scores of each system from a scale.

In many ways, it is precisely this kind of nuanced depiction that the authors of this book have attempted. Given the complexity of education systems, it is impossible to offer a comprehensive assessment of equity in Sweden and England. It has, however, been possible to take a series of Kerr and Raffo's lenses to look at each and to draw comparisons where this has been appropriate. Moreover, a number of the chapters make clear the kinds of methodologies that are necessary to form these lenses, and that constitute an alternative to the narrowly focused methodologies used in the kinds of quantitative assessments outlined above. So, for instance, we have Berndtsson's reminder of the importance of eliciting and listening to the voices of marginalised people rather than simply viewing them statistically. Likewise, Rowley demonstrates the importance of patient ethnographic case study work in understanding the complexities of equity and the processes which underlie or subvert it, while Goldrick shows what can and cannot be achieved through teacher research. And where analyses in this volume are statistical—as in the case of Giota and Emanuelsson's study of special needs education in Sweden—the aim is to ask searching questions about forms of equity and inequity which might otherwise remain hidden. This methodological diversity is not accidental, but follows directly from the complex, multi-dimensional view of equity adopted here. Where equity and inequity take many forms in many spaces, many methodological approaches are needed to explore them.

Not surprisingly, what the chapters reveal is precisely the sort of complex, contradictory picture which Kerr and Raffo's framework might lead us to expect. We can see this, for instance, in Alves et al.'s chapter on the construction of special educational needs in the two countries. In line with their broadly equitable policy orientations, both Sweden and England invest heavily in their special needs systems and dedicate considerable resource and staff expertise to supporting their most vulnerable learners. This has led both countries to develop systems of assessment and categorisation in order to be able to target their investments at the learners who are most likely to benefit. Yet the outcomes of these policies, Alves et al. argue, have by no means been unequivocally equitable. Whatever benefits students may experience, they are also labelled and, to some extent, marginalised, whilst a focus on the 'needs' of the student leaves unchallenged the normative practices of the school and system. Moreover, we might add, the fact that this phenomenon occurs in two separate systems suggest that the causes of the problem are deep-rooted, and that they cannot be tackled simply by modifying this or that surface feature of practice and procedures.

We can see something similar in the chapters by Salokangas et al. and by Rowley. The former traces the spread of 'independent' schools, outside of local democratic control, in the two countries. The loss of local control, and the challenges facing many families in exercising school 'choice' has, the authors argue, created threats to equity. Again, the appearance of similar phenomena in different education systems suggest that there are some underlying processes— the authors implicate a pan-national 'neoliberal conversion'—that lie beyond the surface features of those systems. Rowley, by contrast, looks inside one of these new 'independent' schools in England. Much of what she reports fits neatly with the analysis by Salokangas et al.—a school removed from local democratic control but tightly controlled by central government, and constrained to pursue nationally-mandated targets rather than to respond to the perceived needs of the local population. However, the different lens she brings to bear also reveals different kinds of equity issue. The school does indeed lie outside local democratic control, but is instead in the hands of a not-for-profit organisation with a major responsibility to the local community. This organisation—a housing trust—brings a new perspective from beyond education to bear on the running of the school, and seeks to turn it into a community-oriented institution aimed at tackling disadvantage in the area as a whole as well as improving the life chances of its students. What her account reports is not, by any means, the straightforward driving out of equity concerns by policy shifts at national and, indeed, supra-national level, but rather an ongoing struggle between forces which push the school in different directions and which result in a complex pattern of more and less equitable outcomes.

The dynamics of equity

Reviewing these chapters helps shift our focus from how equity can be assessed to why the state of equity is as it is in different countries, and, more important, what might countries learn from each other about how to become more equitable. Kerr and Raffo's framework powerfully illuminates the complex and contradictory nature of equity when viewed through multiple lenses. However, his notion of equity as multidimensional and as manifesting itself in different educational spaces also implies that there are unlimited possibilities for different forms of equity and inequity to be developed side by side, and for them to be developed differently in different spaces. Helpfully, policy scholars in recent years have traced many examples of these processes at work, moving from a concept of policy 'implementation'—in which coherent decisions taken at the centre are more or less well implemented at the periphery—to a more nuanced notion of policy 'formation' (Ozga, 2000), in which policy decisions are not necessarily coherent and are constantly formed and reformed in what Kerr and Raffo would call the different spaces within education systems. They have also drawn on notions of power to understand how different actors within (and sometimes beyond) education systems seek to compel, enlist and resist one another. It is for these reasons that Ozga (2000) characterises policy as a 'contested terrain'. From our perspective, it is not simply that equity is complex and potentially contradictory, but that struggles take place around equity issues between actors with different views of the educational world and responding to different external imperatives.

One way to conceptualise the different 'educational spaces' in which struggles around equity take place is to think in terms of a broad distinction between a 'macro' level, defined by national and supra-national spaces, a 'meso' level, defined by education institutions and local networks of such institutions, and a 'micro' level, defined by the immediate contexts within which learning takes place—most notably, the classroom (Raffo et al., 2010). To some extent, these levels form a hierarchy in which lower levels are shaped by higher levels. So, the 'neoliberal conversion' to which Salokangas et al. allude, or the broad historical changes which Kerr in this volume describes, constrain the ways in which schools organise and practice, and the ways in which teachers set about their educational tasks. However, the notion of contests around policy alerts us to the interactive nature of the relationship between levels, in which lower levels can 're-form' the imperatives from higher levels and in which, to some extent at least, what happens at lower levels creates possibilities and constraints for what happens at higher levels. Moreover, as Bronfenbrenner (1979), in seeking to understand the processes shaping child development, reminds us, if we look at all of this from the perspective of what happens to the learner, the most powerful factors may be those that are closest to the learner, and, indeed, the learner her/himself is an actor helping to shape both immediate experiences and the wider system.

The implication of all of this is that educational equity is not only complex, but is also dynamic. Bald statements, such as 'Sweden and England have (or do not have) equitable education systems' need to be modified. We need to say 'Sweden and England have education systems that are equitable in these ways and in these educational spaces', and we need to add 'at this time'. Better still, we need to give an account of the contending forces in the struggle for equity in particular spaces and at particular times in order to understand how these impact on learners, what the likely outcome of the struggle will be, and what new struggles that outcome will give rise to.

Moving to action

The dynamic nature of educational equity is important in understanding what might be done to enhance equity and what different education systems might learn from each other. It is certainly the case that dynamic processes are capable of increasing inequities in education systems. We have seen throughout this book how global economic and political changes have impact on the education systems of both countries. There is, perhaps, a particular sense of loss in Sweden, where what appeared to be a strongly-entrenched social democratic consensus around equitable values has been destabilised by neoliberal ideologies and policies. Yet this is not simply a matter of a sudden shift from one state of affairs to another. We can see this in Assarson et al.'s chapter in this volume on the policy efforts to formulate a set of fundamental values which Swedish schools might seek to develop in their students. Whilst Assarson et al. are critical of some aspects of those efforts, it is striking (to an English reader, at least) how the social democratic traditions of Sweden persist, not as historical relics, but as active forces in the education system. Indeed, to English visitors to Swedish schools, the continuing sense of education as being more than about academic attainment, and the enactment of democratic values in the relationship between teachers and students is striking.

Similarly, Kerr's chapter in this volume, whilst commenting on the increasingly narrow focus of the English education system on attainment, also concedes that there have been improvements in the system from an equity perspective—the ongoing view of education as a means of tackling inequality, the opening up of educational opportunities through the 1944 Education Act and the later move to comprehensivisation, and, latterly, New Labour's efforts to eliminate the poor performance of schools serving disadvantaged populations and to link the work of schools to a wider strategy for tackling disadvantage. The point here is that things change in dynamic systems, and, despite the undoubted impacts of economic globalisation and neoliberal ideologies, they do not necessarily always change for the worse.

Particularly significant in this respect is Goldrick's chapter in this volume reporting the efforts by teams of teachers to explore equity issues in their schools and to take action to reduce inequities. Again, we see the impact of the pressures teachers face in their schools and from national policy, and the ways in which these shape and constrain their efforts. However, we also see these teachers learning to think and act differently. They may not be able to escape the pressures to which they are subject, but neither are their actions entirely determined by them. Above all, they are able to think seriously about equity and to take practical action to make their schools more equitable educational places.

In other words, within dynamic systems, action to tackle inequities and enhance equity is possible, even in what at first glance appear to be the most unpromising of circumstances. Teachers can and do take actions that are not simply determined by policy, and policy makers themselves, even when substantially in thrall to neoliberal approaches, can and do formulate policies which embody other ways of thinking. The implication of all of this is that the enhancement of equity in education systems need not wait for ideal conditions at the macro level to be in place. The development of equitable systems is not a matter of a once-for-all transformation of the system as a whole, but of multiple actions that need to be taken in a wide range of educational spaces. And whilst those spaces and actions necessarily interact, they do so by providing constraints and possibilities rather than by straightforwardly determining one another.

This gives us a somewhat different way of assessing the state of equity in Swedish and English education, and of asking what they might learn from one another. Undoubtedly, Sweden and England are countries in which the forces of economic globalisation and neoliberalism have been strongly felt, and in which social democratic traditions have been under threat. However, those traditions have not disappeared. They remain active forces in education policy and practice. In both countries, therefore, policy makers and practitioners—even as they follow mantras of 'choice' or 'excellence'—feel compelled to pay attention to those learners who do worst or face the greatest challenges, and to tackle disparities in outcomes and experiences between different groups of learners. In both countries too, there is a degree of autonomy of action at local and school level which enables—and to differing extents—encourages schools and teachers to find their own solutions to educational problems. Whilst formal accountability for those solutions may rely heavily on test scores, teachers have a degree of freedom—and in some ways are required—to pay attention to broader educational concerns. Given that, by international standards, the educational workforce in both countries is highly qualified and professionalised, the education systems of Sweden and England are relatively healthy, from an equity perspective, in that they have considerable capacity and opportunity for equity issues to be addressed.

The obvious question, then, is where and how efforts to enhance equity might best begin in the current context. There are, of course, political struggles to be undertaken, both through 'normal politics' and through more direct action. It may be that, paradoxically, the relatively stable and liberal nature of normal politics in both countries has made it more difficult for more direct, activist approaches to emerge. Perhaps this is the time for something like a community organising movement of the kind seen in the US (Warren and Mapp. 2011) to emerge. Certainly, in England the vacuum created by the fragmentation of the school system and the erosion of local democratic control is beginning to draw in not just concerned middle class parents but also community groups keen to shape schools according to their wishes. Whilst such moves have been hugely controversial (Clarke, 2014), they indicate that not all communities are content to influence the education system through the ballot box alone.

Beyond direct political action, there are key issues around which struggles for equity can form, even in systems that are dominated by neoliberal policy approaches. These are issues to do with low attainment and social cohesion. The former is a problem even in systems predicated on social democratic values, where education aims to enable every learner to make the most of themselves. However, when the emphasis shifts to the economic role of education, and particularly when economic well-being is seen to depend on the availability of a highly-skilled workforce, low attainment becomes a threat to national prosperity. As Kerr in this volume shows, concerns with tackling low attainment have led to vigorous education reforms where policy makers have felt compelled to pay attention to those learners who do worst in the education system. Moreover, those concerns are reflected in a range of educational spaces. Whilst the pressures on teachers and schools undoubtedly constrain them to focus their attention on a narrow range of performance, they also encourage them to focus on those students who are not doing well under current arrangements, and whose limited attainments threaten the overall performance of the school. Likewise, social cohesion, understood broadly as the capacity of a society or social group to live and work together amicably (Bertelsmann Stiftung and Eurofound, 2014) becomes a particular issue in societies with growing inequalities, particularly where those societies begin to accumulate significant migrant populations. Neither societies nor education systems nor educational institutions can afford to have situations in which tensions between social groups arise and where people work against rather than with each other, let alone where open conflict breaks out.

The initial responses to these threats may indeed be quite narrowly conceived—a tightening of accountability procedures, the introduction of some time-limited interventions for low attainers, or a flurry of 'social cohesion' projects. However, they do not need to stay like this. Writing about the problematic nature of special needs education, Skrtic (1991) characterises such threats as 'anomalies'. Learners who do not quite 'fit' the practices and priorities of their schools and education systems provoke a response, and while that response might typically be to find some way of dealing with the threat without changing established practices and structures, it need not be. Teachers and policy makers can—and sometimes do—think more deeply about what these anomalies tell them about the inadequacies of current practices and the way in which those practices might need to change. It is precisely this process, at a school and teacher level, which we can see happening in the cases described by Goldrick in this volume.

The struggle for equity, therefore, may, at least in part, be about bringing different perspectives to bear on the presenting problems of the education system. Consistent with our equity framework, we see these perspectives as arising and engaging with each other in multiple educational spaces. At school level, much depends on enabling teachers to engage with each other both within their own schools and across schools so that they are encouraged to see familiar problems in a different light (Ainscow et al., 2012). For both teachers and policy makers, however, there is much to be gained by looking at different education systems, seeing how things are done differently, and thinking what the implications might be 'back home'.

It is in this context that comparisons between Sweden and England are particularly valuable. The two education systems are, as we have seen, sufficiently similar to each other for direct comparisons to be made, yet sufficiently different for them to offer divergent perspectives on apparently similar problems. If we simply take the issues that this volume has touched upon (and there are, of course, more), there are many questions that can be asked. What, for instance, can be learned from an equity perspective about the ways in which each country has set about fragmenting (or, some might argue, diversifying) its school system? What has been lost and (Rowley's chapter suggests) gained by the introduction of non-educational providers into the system—and if there have been gains, how might they be maximised? What role in safeguarding equity remains for intermediary bodies such as municipalities and local authorities? Similarly, what can be learned from the special needs systems of the two countries? How can it be that systems set up to resource and support the most vulnerable have in both cases become so heavily bureaucratised and so incapable of challenging inequities in schools and the wider education system? Are these matters that can be tackled by changing the regulatory frameworks governing special needs education, or do they demand a more fundamental rethink of how mainstream education operates? What, finally, are the values that should be embedded within schools and education systems? What can be learned from Sweden's attempts to make those values explicit as opposed to England's traditionally more implicit approach? How do such values hold up in the context of the divergent value base in wider society, not least in areas with substantial migrant and/or ethnic minority populations?

Asking questions of this kind is not a first step in a process of 'policy borrowing' (Phillips, 2005), if by that we mean cherry-picking attractive ideas without understanding either the context in which they have originated or the context in which they are to be implemented. As Salokangas et al. point out in this volume, the borrowing of the free school idea by England in recent times has not been an entirely happy experience, at least from an equity perspective. By contrast, the kind of questioning we are advocating is very much about understanding. It takes into account the complexity of equity itself, and the complexity of the dynamic processes out of which equities and inequities arise. The answers which result from such questioning are rarely in the form of 'do this', much less of 'do here what works there'. Rather, they are means of problematising what is taken for granted in one's own situation and thinking how things might be otherwise. On this basis, Sweden and England have much to teach—but also much to learn.

References

Academies Act (2010) c.32. Available at:, www.legislation.gov.uk/ukpga/2010/32/contents/data.htm, [Accessed 2 July 2013]

Academies Commission (2013) *Unleashing greatness: Getting the best from an academised system. The report of the Academies Commission*, London: RSA/Pearson.

Adams, R. (2014) UK council leaders call for more power over academies and free schools, *The Guardian*, 16 June.

Adonis, A. (2012) *Education, education, education, reforming England's schools*, London: Biteback Publishing.

Aghion, P., Besley, T., Browne, J., Caselli, F., Lambert, R., Lomax, R., Pissarides, C., Stern, N., Van Reenen, J. (2013) *LSE Growth Commission report—investing for prosperity. Skills, infrastructure and innovation. Report of the LSE Growth Commission in partnership with the Institute for Government*, www2.lse.ac.uk/growthcommission [Accessed 1 August 2014].

Ainscow, M. (1999) *Understanding the development of inclusive schools*, London: Falmer Press.

Ainscow, M., (2002) Using research to encourage the development of inclusive practices, in Farrell, P. and Ainscow, M. (Eds.) *Making special education inclusive*, London: Fulton.

Ainscow, M., Booth, T. and Dyson, A. (2004) Understanding and developing inclusive practices in schools: a collaborative action research network, *International Journal of Inclusive Education*, 8(2): 125-139.

Ainscow, M., Booth, T. and Dyson, A. (2006a) Inclusion and the standards agenda: negotiating policy pressures in England, *International Journal of Inclusive Education*, 10(4-5): 295-308.

Ainscow, M., Booth, T. and Dyson, A. with Farrell P., Frankham, J., Gallannaugh, F., Howes, A. and Smith, R. (2006b) *Improving Schools, Developing Inclusion*, London: Routledge.

Ainscow, M., Conteh, J., Dyson, A., and Gallannaugh, F. (2007) *Children in primary education: demography, culture, diversity and inclusion (Primary Review research survey 5/1)*. Cambridge: University of Cambridge Faculty of Education.

Ainscow, M., Dyson, A., Goldrick, S., and Kerr, K. (2009) Using research to further inclusion and equity within the context of New Labour education reforms, in Chapman, C. and Gunter, H.M. (Eds.), *Radical reforms: Perspectives on an era of educational change*, London: Routledge.

Ainscow, M., Dyson, A., Goldrick, S., Kerr, K. and Miles, S., (2008) *Equity in education: Responding to context*, Manchester: Centre for Equity in Education, University of Manchester.

Ainscow, M., Dyson, A., Goldrick, S., and West, M. (2012) *Developing equitable education systems*, London: Routledge.

Allen, R. (2010) Replicating Swedish free school reforms in England, *Research in Public Policy*, 10 (CMPO Bulletin), pp. 4-7.

Alves, I. (2015) *Responding to diversity, constructing difference: A comparative case-study of individual planning in schools in England and Portugal*, PhD thesis, University of Manchester.

Andersson, B., (2002) Samhällets demokratiska värdegrund är skolans. Problematisering i åtta delar för debatt [Society's democratic fundamental values are the school's fundamental values. Problematisation in eight parts for debate], in Andersson, B. (ed.) *Lärande dialoger: Ämnes-didaktiska perspektiv*. [Learning Dialogues: Subjects' Didactic Perspective], Göteborg: Göteborgs universitet.

Andersson, S., (2004) What is the essence? 'Kristen etik' och 'västerländsk humanism': Ett omaka par? [What is the Essence? 'Christian Ethics' and 'Western Humanism': An Ill-Matched Pair?] *Religionsvetenskaplig internettidskrift RIT* [Religion Study Internet Magazine RIT]., www.teol.lu.se/rit/7.html

Andreasson, I. (2007). *Elevplanen som text—om identitet, genus, makt och styrning i skolans elevdokumentation* [The individual education plan as text. About identity, gender, power and governing in pupils' documentation at school]. PhD thesis, University of Gothenburg.

Andreasson, I. Asp-Onsjö, L. and Isaksson, J. (2013) Lessons learned from research on individual educational plans in Sweden: Obstacles, opportunities and future challenges, *European Journal of Special Needs Education* 28(4): 413-426.

Antikainen, A., (2010) The Capitalist State and Education: The Case of Restructuring the Nordic Model, *Current Sociology* 58(4): 530-550.

Anyon, J., (1997) *Ghetto schooling—A political economy of urban educational reform*, New York: Teachers College Press.

Arnesen, A., and Lundahl, L. (2006) Still social and democratic? Inclusive education policies in the Nordic welfare states, *Scandinavian Journal of Educational Research*, *50*(3): 285-300.

Arnesen, A. and Lundahl, L. (2006) Still social and democratic? Inclusive education policies in the Nordic welfare states, *Scandinavian Journal of Educational Research* 50 (3): 285-300.

Artiles, A. J. (2003) Special education's changing identity: Paradoxes and dilemmas in views of culture and space, *Harvard Educational Review*, *73*(2): 164-202.

Artiles, A., Kozleski, E., Dorn, S., and Christensen, C. A. (2006) Learning in inclusive education research: Re-mediating theory and methods with a transformative agenda, *Review of Research in Education*, *30*: 65-108.

Asp-Onsjö, L.(2006). Åtgärdsprogram—dokument eller verktyg? *En fallstudie i en kommun* [Individual education plan—document or tool?], PhD thesis, University of Gothenburg.

Assarson, I., (2007) *Talet om en skola för alla: pedagogers meningskonstruktion i ett politiskt uppdrag* [The Subject of a School for Everyone: Teachers' Construction of Meaning in Political Office]. *PHD diss.*, Malmo: Teacher Education, Malmö University.

Assarson, I., (2009a) *Utmaningar i en skola för alla. Några filosofiska trådar* [Challenges in Education for Everyone. Some Philosophical Threads], Stockholm: Liber

Assarson, I., (2009b) Specialpedagogik I spänningsfältet mellan mångfald och normalisering [Special needs education in the field of tension between diversity and normalisation] *Krut 2009:4*

Asthana, A. (2007) Academy exclusion 'is selection by the backdoor', *The Observer*, 12 August.

Baker, E. T., Wang, M. C., and Walberg, H. J. (1995) The effects of inclusion on learning, *Educational Leadership*. *52*(4): 33-35.

Beach, D., and Dovemark, M. (2007) *Education and the commodity problem: Ethnographic investigations of creativity and performativity in Swedish schools*. London: the Tufnell Press.

Ball, S. (2007) *Education PLC: Understanding private sector participation in public sector education*. London: Routledge.
Ball, S.J. and Youdell, D., (2008) Hidden Privatisation, Education International Report, Brussels, Education International.
Barber, M. (1994) Power and control in education 1944-2004, *British Journal of Educational Studies*, 42(4): 348-362
Barnes, E (2013) David Cameron revives 'classless society' promise, *The Scotsman*, 2 October, www.scotsman.com/news/uk/david-cameron-revives-classless-society-promise-1-3121297 [Accessed 28 July 14].
Bartley, M., (2006) *Capability and resilience: Beating the odds*, London: Capability and resilience network.
Bartley, M., Power, C., Blane, D., Smith, G. D. and Shipley, M., (1994) Birth weight and later socioeconomic disadvantage: evidence from the 1958 British cohort study, *British Medical Journal*, 309(6967): 1475
Bauman, Z. (1992). *Intimations of post modernity*. London: Routledge.
Bauman, Z. (2004). *Wasted lives*. Cambridge: Polity Press.
BBC News (2005) Poor pupils 'go to worst schools' 24 February, news.bbc.co.uk/1/hi/education/4290279.stm [Accessed 7 September 2014].
BBC News (2014) Practical education 'needs more focus', *BBC News*, 4 June, www.bbc.co.uk/news/education-27678842 [Accessed 7 September 2014].
Beach, D., (2008) The changing the relations between education professionals, the state and citizen consumers in Europe: Rethinking restructuring as capitalisation, *European Educational Research Journal*, 7(2): 195-207.
Beach, D., (2009) Omstrukturering av utbildning och vård i Norden från ett socialt användbart till ett kommersialiserat och ekonomiskt produktivt arbete: I vems intressen?, *Nordisk Pedagogik*, 29(3): 294-302.
Beach, D., (2010) Identifying Scandinavian ethnography: comparisons and influences, *Ethnography and Education*, 5(1): 1-19.
Beach, D., and Dovemark, M. (2007) *Education and the commodity problem: Ethnographic investigations of creativity and performativity in Swedish Schools*. London: the Tufnell Press.
Beach, D. and Dovemark, M., (2011) Twelve years of upper-secondary education in Sweden: The beginnings of a neoliberal policy hegemony? *Educational Review*, 64(4): 313-327.
Beach, D., and Sernhede, O. (2011) From learning to labour to learning for marginality: School segregation and marginalisation in Swedish suburbs, *British Journal of Sociology of Education*, 32: 257-274.
Beckett, F. (2004) How car dealers can run state schools, *New Statesman*, 20 September, pp. 30-31.
Beckett, F., (2011) Foreword, in Gunter, H. M. (Ed.) (2011) *The state and education policy: The Academies Programme*, London: Continuum Books.
Behtoui, A. and Neergaard, A. (2015) Social capital and the educational achievement of young people in Sweden, *British Journal of Sociology of Education*. DOI: 10.1080/01425692.2015.1013086
Bel Habib, I. (2001) *Elever med invandrarbakgrund i särskolan: specialpedagogik eller disciplinär makt* [*Pupils with immigrant background in education for intellectually disabled*], Kristianstad: Högskolan i Kristianstad. Enheten för kompetensutveckling.
Bell, C., (2007) Space and place: urban parents' geographical preferences for schools, *Urban Review*, 39(4): 375-404.

Bengtsson, J., (1991) *Den fenomenologiska rörelsen i Sverige. Mottagande och inflytande 1900-1968 [The phenomenological movement in Sweden]*, Göteborg, Sweden: Daidalos.

Bengtsson, J., (2005) En livsvärldsansats för pedagogisk forskning [A lifeworld approach for research in education], in Bengtsson, J., (Ed.) *Med livsvärlden som grund [With the lifeworld as ground]*, second ed., Lund, Sweden: Studentlitteratur.

Bengtsson, J., (2013a) With the lifeworld as ground. A research approach for empirical reserarch in education: The Gothenburg tradition, *Indo-Pacific Journal of Phenomenology*, 13, Special Edition, September: 1-18.

Bengtsson, J., (2013b) With the lifeworld as ground: Introduction to the special issue. An outline of the Gothenburg tradition of the lifeworld approach, *Indo-Pacific Journal of Phenomenology*, 13, Special Edition, September: 1-9.

Berndtsson, I., (2001) *Förskjutna horisonter. Livsförändring och lärande i samband med synnedsättning eller blindhet [Shifting horizons. Life changes and learning in relation to visual impairment or blindness]*, Thesis (Phd), Göteborg Studies in Educational Sciences, University of Gothenburg, Sweden.

Berndtsson, I. C., (2015) *Teoretiska grunder till livsvärldsbaserad rehabilitering vid synnedsättning och blindhet [Theoretical foundations for lifeworld based rehabilitation]*. (Manuscript, work in progress)

Berndtsson, I., Claesson, S., Friberg, F. and Öhlén, J., (2007) Issues about thinking phenomenologically while doing phenomenology. *Journal of Phenomenological Psychology*, 38(2): 256-277.

Berhanu, G. (2006) *Framgångsfaktorer för delaktighet och jämlikhet.* [Favorable factors to enhance participation and equality], Specialpedagogiska institutet.

Berhanu, G. (2008) Ethnic minority pupils in Swedish schools: Some trends in overrepresentation of minority pupils in special educational programs, *International Journal of Special Education*, 23(3): 17-29.

Berhanu, G. (2009, February) *Challenges and responses to inclusive education in Sweden: Mapping issues of equity, participation and democratic values.* Presented at a research forum on a comparative analysis of equity in inclusive education. Center for Advanced Study in the Behavioral Sciences (CASBS), Stanford University, Palo Alto, California, U.S.A., February 1-5, 2009.

Berhanu, G. (2010) Even in Sweden excluding the included: Some reflections on the consequences of new policies on educational processes and outcomes, and equity in education. *International Journal of Special Education*, 25(3): 148-159.

Berhanu, G. (2011) Challenges and responses to inclusive education in Sweden: Mapping issues of equity, participation and democratic values, in Artiles, A.J., Kozleski, E.B. and Waitoller, F.R. (eds.), *Inclusive education: Examining equity on five continents* (pp. 101-119). Cambridge, Massachusetts: Harvard Education Press.

Berhanu, G. (2012) Challenges and responses to inclusive education in Sweden. Mapping issues of equity, participation, and democratic values, in Artiles, A.J., Kozleski, E.B. and Waitoller, F.R. *Inclusive education. Examining equity on five continents*, Cambridge, Massachusetts: Harvard Education Press.

Berhanu, G. (in press) Special education in Sweden: Mapping out issues of inclusion, equity and social justice, in A. F. Rotatori, J. P. Bakken, S. Burkhardt, F. Obiakor, and U. Sharma (eds.), *Special Education International Perspectives: Practices Across the Globe.* Bingley, UK: Emerald Group Publishing Limited.

Berhanu, G., and Dyson, A. (2012) Special education in Europe: Overrepresentation of minority students, in J. Banks (ed.), *Encyclopedia of diversity in education* (pp. 2070-2073). Thousand Oaks, CA: SAGE Publications.

Berhanu, G., Dyson, A. and Luciak, M. (2013). Disproportionality in special education in Europe: A comparative study. International Association of Special Education, July 7-11, 2013 (Conference Proceedings, pp. 149-150).

Bertelsmann Stiftung and Eurofound (2014) *Social cohesion and well-being in the EU*, Guttersloh and Dublin: Bertelsmann Stiftung and Eurofound.

Beveridge, W. (1942) *Social insurance and allied services*, London: HMSO CMND 6404.

Biesta, G., (2002) *Bildung and Modernity: The future of bildung in a world and difference*, Exeter, GB: University of Exeter. School of Education and Lifelong Learning Big Lottery Fund, (2006) *Program for young people: What we have learned*, London: Big Lottery Fund

Björklund, A., Clark, M. A., Edin, P.-A., Fredriksson, P., and Krueger, A. B. (2005) *The market comes to education in Sweden: An evaluation of Sweden's surprising school reforms*, New York: Russell Sage Foundation.

Blanden, J., Gregg, P., and Machin, S. (2005) *Intergenerational mobility in Europe and North America*, London: Centre for Economic Performance, London School of Economics for The Sutton Trust.

Blanden, J., and Machin, S. (2007) *Recent changes in intergenerational mobility in Britain*, London: Sutton Trust.

Blanden, J., and Macmillan, L. (2014) *Education and intergenerational mobility: Help or hindrance?*, London: Institute of Education, University of London, Department of Quantitative Social Science.

Block, D., (2003) *The social turn in second language acquisition*, Edinburgh: Edinburgh University Press.

Blunkett, D., (2000) *Raising aspirations for the 21st Century. Speech to the North of England education conference, Wigan, 6 January 2000* [online], www.dfes.gov.uk/speeches/search_detail.cfm?ID=34 [Accessed 5 December, 2004].

Blunkett, D. (2000) Blunkett sets out radical new agenda for inner city school diversity and improvement'. Press notice, 15 March, London: DCSF, Available at:, www.dcsf.gov.uk/pns/DisplayPN.cgi?pn_id=2000_0106, [Accessed 2 October 2009].

Booth. T., and Ainscow, M., (1998) *From them to us: An international study of inclusion in education,* London: Routledge.

Braveman, P., (2003) Monitoring equity in health and healthcare: A conceptual framework. *Journal of Health Population and Nutrition.* 21(3): 181-192.

Braveman, P. and Gruskin, S., (2003) Defining equity in health, *Journal of Epidemiology and Community Health*, 57: 254-258.

Broadfoot, P. (2001) Empowerment or performativity? Assessment policy in the late twentieth century, in: R. Phillips and J. Furlong (Eds.) *Education, reform and the state: Twenty-five years of politics, policy and practice.* London: Routledge Falmer

Bunar, N. (2008) The free schools 'riddle': between traditional social democratic, neoliberal and multicultural tenets, *Scandinavian Journal of Educational Research*, 52(4), pp. 423-438.

Bunar, N., (2010). Choosing for quality or inequality—current perspectives on the implementation of school choice policy in Sweden, *Journal of Education Policy*, 25(1): 1-18.

Bronfenbrenner, U. (1979) *The ecology of human development: Experiments by nature and design*, Cambridge, Massachusetts: Harvard University Press.

Böhlmark, A., and Lindahl, M. (2008) Does school privatisation improve educational achievement? Evidence from Sweden's voucher reform, IZA discussion paper 3691. Available at: ftp.iza.org/dp. 691.pdf, [Accessed 30 September 2014].

Börjesson, M. and Palmblad, E. (2003). *Problembarnets århundrade—normalitet, expertis och visionen om framsteg* [The century of the troublesome child—normality, expertise and the vision of progress], Lund: Studentlitteratur.

Caldwell, B. (2011) The new enterprise logic of the academy programme, in Gunter, H. (ed.) *The state and education policy: the academies programme*. London: Continuum, pp. 171-186.

Callaghan, J. (1976) *A rational debate based on the facts*, Ruskin College Oxford, 18 October 1976, www.educationengland.org.uk/documents/speeches/1976ruskin.html [Accessed 1 August 2014].

Cameron, D. (2011) *Welcome to the free schools conference*, speech delivered at free schools conference, Available at:, www.education.gov.uk/schools/leadership/typesofschools/ freeschools/conference/b0074146/speeches, [Accessed 14 July 2013]

Cameron, D. L., Nilholm, C. and Persson, B. (2012) School district administrators' perspectives on special education policy and practice in Norway and Sweden, *Scandinavian Journal of Disability Research*, 14(2): 213-221.

Carlsson, N., (2011) *I kamp med skriftspråket: Vuxenstuderande med läs—och skrivsvårigheter i ett livsvärldsperspektiv [Fighting the written language]*, Thesis (Phd), Göteborg Studies in Educational Sciences, University of Gothenburg, Sweden.

Carpenter, H., Papps, I., Bragg, J., Dyson, A., Harris, D., Kerr, K., Todd, L. and Laing, K. (2013) *Evaluation of pupil premium: Research report*, London: DfE

Cassen, R. and Kingdon, G., (2007) *Tackling low educational achievement*, York: Joseph Rowntree Foundation.

Castells, M., (2000) *The rise of the network society*, Cambridge MA: Blackwell.

Central Advisory Council for Education (England), (1963) *Half our future,* London: HMSO

Chapman, C. (2014) From one school to many: reflections on the impact and nature of school federations and chains in England. *Educational Management Administration and Leadership*. ISSN 1741-1432 (doi:10.1177/1741143213494883)

Chapman, C. (2013) Academy federations, chains and teaching schools in England: reflections on leadership, policy and practice. *Journal of School Choice: International Research and Reform,* 7(3). pp. 334-352.

Chitty, C., (2008) The academy fiasco: special issue, *Forum*, 50, (1), 3-102.

Clark, G. (2013) *What is the true rate of social mobility in Sweden? A surname analysis 1700-2012* [online], www.econ.ucdavis.edu/faculty/gclark/The%20Son%20Also%20 Rises/Sweden%202014.pdf [Accessed 17 August 2015].

Clarke, P. (2014) *Report into allegations concerning Birmingham schools arising from the 'Trojan Horse' letter* [online], London: Her Majesty's Stationery Office, dera.ioe. ac.uk/20549/1/Report_into_allegations_concerning_Birmingham_schools_arising_ from_the_Trojan_Horse_letter-web.pdf [Accessed 17 August 2015].

Cole, M. (2003) Might it be in the practice that it fails to succeed? A marxist critique of claims for postmodernism and poststructuralism as forces for social change and social justice, *British Journal of Sociology of Education*, 24(4): 487-500.

Confederation of British Industry (2012a) *Learning to grow. What employers needs from education and skills. Education and skills survey 2012*, www.cbi.org.uk/media/1514978/cbi_education_and_skills_survey_2012.pdf [Accessed 31 July 2014].

Confederation of British Industry (2012b) First steps: A new approach for our schools, CBI, www.cbi.org.uk/campaigns/education-campaign-ambition-for-all/ [Accessed 1 August 2014].

Conservative Party (2007) *Raising the bar, closing the gap*, London: The Conservative Party. (Cited in Hatcher, R. 2011).

Conservative Party (2010) *The Conservative manifesto 2010*, London: The Conservative Party.

Coughlan, S. (2014a) Shanghai teachers flown in for maths, *BBC News*, 12 March, www.bbc.co.uk/news/education-26533428

Coughlan, S. (2014b) A-level grades edge down, as university places rise, *BBC News*, 14 August, www.bbc.co.uk/news/education-28772974

Cox, C. and Boyson, R. (1975) *Black paper 1975: The fight for education*, London: Dent.

Cox, C. and Boyson, R. (1977) *Black paper 1977*, London: Maurice Temple Smith.

Craig, J., Huber, J. and Lowensworth, H., (2004) *Schools out: Can teachers, social workers and health staff learn to live together?* Demos/Hay Group: London.

Corbett, J., and Slee, R. (2000) An international conversation on inclusive education, in F. Armstrong, D. Armstrong, and L. Barton (eds.), *Inclusive education: Policy, contexts and comparative perspectives* (pp. 133-146). London: David Fulton.

Cribb, J., Jesson, D., Sibieta, L., Skipp, A., Vignoles, A. (2013) *Poor grammar: Entry into grammar schools for disadvantaged pupils in England,* London: The Sutton Trust

Cummings, C., Dyson, A. and Todd, L., (2007) Towards extended schools? How education and other professionals understand community-orientated schooling, *Children and Society*, 21: 189-200.

Cummings, C., Dyson, A. and Todd, L., (2011) *Beyond the school gates. Can full service and extended schools overcome disadvantage?* London: Routledge.

Curtis, A. (2009) Academies and school diversity, *Management in Education*, 23(3), pp. 113-117.

Curtis, A., Exley, S., Sasia, A., Tough, S., and Whitty, G. (2008), *The Academies Programme : Progress, Problems And Possibilities*, A report for the Sutton Trust, London: Institute of Education.

Cusick, J. (2013) Cash for classrooms: Michael Gove plans to let firms run schools for profit, *The Independent*, 1 July.

DCSF, (2008) *Sponsorship guide: Establishing an academy: An overview for sponsors* [online], webarchive.nationalarchives.gov.uk/20081029161713/standards.dfes.gov.uk/academies/publications/?version=1 [Accessed 7 August 2011].

DfE (2010) *The importance of teaching—the Schools White Paper 2010*. Available at:, www.education.gov.uk/publications/standard/publicationdetail/Page1/CM%20 7980#downloadableparts, [Accessed 12 March 2011]

DfES, (2005) *Extended schools: Access to opportunities and services for all. A prospectus,* London: DfES.

DfE (2014) *Open academies and academy projects in development.* Available at:www.education.gov.uk/schools/leadership/typesofschools/academies/open/b00208569/open-academies [Accessed 17 May 2014].

Dahlstedt, M. (2007) 'I val(o)frihetens spår: Segregation, differentiering och två decennier av skolreformer' [*In the direction of choice and freedom: Segregation, differentiating and two decades of school reforms*], *Pedagogisk Forskning i Sverige*, 12(1): 20-38.

Dean, C., Dyson, A., Gallannaugh, F., Howes, A. and Raffo, C., (2007) *Schools, governors and disadvantage*, York: Joseph Rowntree Foundation.

Demeuse, M., Crahay, M., and Monseur, C. (2001) Efficiency and equity, in W. Hutmacher, D. Cochrane, and N. Bottani (eds.), *In pursuit of equity in education—Using international indicators to compare equity policies*, Kluwer: Dordrecht.

Department for Education. (2011). *Support and aspiration: A new approach to special educational needs and disability. A consultation. Cm 8027*, London: The Stationery Office.

Department for Education (2014a) *Impact indicator 8: Attainment gap at age 16 between free school meal pupils and the rest*, https://www.gov.uk/government/uploads/system/uploads/attachment_data/file/293662/KS4_Impact_indicator_8_v2.pdf [Accessed 1 August 2014].

Department for Education (2014b) *Raising the achievement of disadvantaged children. Supporting detail: Pupil premium*, https://www.gov.uk/government/policies/raising-the-achievement-of-disadvantaged-children/supporting-pages/pupil-premium [Accessed 1 August 2014].

Department for Education and Department for Health (2014). *Special educational needs and disability code of practice: 0 to 25 years*, London: DfE.

Department for Education and Employment. (1997). *Excellence for all children: Meeting special educational needs*, London: The Stationery Office.

Department for Education and Science (1965) *Circular 10/65. The organisation of secondary education*, London: Department of Education and Science.

Department for Education and Science. (1978). *Special educational needs: Report of the committee of enquiry into the education of handicapped children and young people (The Warnock Report)*, London: Her Majesty's Stationery Office.Daniels, H., Hey, V., Leonard, D. and Smith, M. (1999) Issues of equtiy in special needs education from a gender perspective. *British Journal of Special Education*, 26(4): 189-195.

Department for Education and Skills. (2001a). *Special educational needs code of practice*, London: DfES.

Department for Education and Skills. (2001b). *Inclusive schooling: Children with special educational needs*, London: DfES.

Department for Education and Skills (2004) *Removing barriers to achievement: The government's strategy for SEN*, London: DfES.

Department for Work and Pensions and Department for Education (2014) *Helping to reduce poverty and improve social justice*, www.gov.uk/government/policies/helping-to-reduce-poverty-and-improve-social-justice [Accessed 30 July 2014].

Derrida, J., (2003) *Marx spöken: skuldstaten, sorgearbetet och den nya internationalen* [Specters of Marx: The state of the debt, the work of mourning and the New International], Gothenburg: Daidalos. Dorling, D., and Pritchard, J. (2010) The geography of poverty, inequality and wealth in the UK and abroad: Because enough is never enough. *Applied Spatial Analysis*, 3: 81-106.

Desforges, C. and Abouchaar, A. (2003) *The impact of parental involvement, parental support and family education on pupil achievement and adjustment: A literature review. Research report 433*, London: DfES.

Dir. 1991:9, *Mål och riktlinjer inom barnomsorgen och det offentliga skolväsendet* [Targets and guidelines within child care and the public educational system], Stockholm: Ministry of Education.

Dir 1991:117, *Nya direktiv till läroplanskommittén* [New directives to the curriculum committee], Stockholm: Ministry of Education

Ds 1997:57, *En värdegrundad skola—idéer om samverkan och möjligheter* [A value-based school—ideas about collaboration and opportunities], Stockholm: Ministry of Education.

Dorling, D. & Pritchard, J. (2010) The geography of poverty, inequality and wealth in the UK and abroad: Because enough is never enough, *Applied Spatial Analysis*, 3: 81-106.

Dorling, D., Rigby, J., Wheeler, B., Ballas, D., Thomas, B., Fahmy, E., Lupton, R. (2007) *Poverty, wealth and place in Britain, 1968 to 2005*, Bristol: The Policy Press for the Joseph Rowntree Foundation.

Douglas, J. W. B., (1964) *The home and the school: A study of ability and attainment in the primary school*, London: MacGibbon and Kee.

Downs, C. (2014) Birmingham 'Trojan Horse plot' raises questions about school accountability, *The Guardian*, 24 April.

Duncan, G. J. and Brooks-Gunn, J., (Eds) (1997) *Consequences of growing up poor* (New York, Russell Sage).

Dyson, A. (1999). Inclusion and inclusions: theories and discourses in inclusive education, in Daniels, H. and Garner, P. (Eds.), *World yearbook of education 1999: Inclusive Education*. London: Kogan Page.

Dyson, A. (2001). Special needs in the twenty-first century: where we've been and where we're going, *British Journal of Special Education*, 28(1), 24-29.

Dyson, A., (2005) Philosophy, politics and economics? The story of inclusive education in England, in D. Michel, (Ed) *Contextualising inclusive education, evaluating old and new international perspectives* (pp. 63-84), Oxfordshire and New York: Routledge.

Dyson, A., Gallannaugh, F. and Kerr, K., (2011) *Conceptualising school community relations in disadvantaged areas* [online], www.ahrc.ac.uk/Funding-Opportunities/Research-funding/Connected-Communities/Scoping-studies-and reviews/Documents/Conceptualising%20school-community%20relations%20in%20disadvantaged%20 areas.pdf [Accessed 16 October 2012].

Dyson, A., Gunter, H., Hall, D., Raffo, C., Jones, L. and Kalambouka, A. (2011) What is to be done? in *Education and poverty in affluent countries*, ed. Raffo, C., Dyson, A., Gunter, H., Hall, D., Lisa, J. and Kalambouka, A, 195-215. London: Routledge, 2011.

Dyson, A., Jones, L., and Kerr, K., (2011). Inclusion, place, and disadvantage in the English education system, in Artiles, A.J., Kozleski and Waitoller, F.R. (Eds.), *Inclusive education: Examining equity on five continents*, Cambridge, Massachusetts: Harvard Education Press.

Dyson, A., Kerr, K., Raffo, C., Wigelsworth, M., with Wellings, C. (2012) *Developing children's zones for England*, London: Save the Children.

Dyson, A. and Millward, A. (2000) *Schools and special needs: Issues of innovation and inclusion*, London, Paul Chapman.

Dyson, A., and Millward, A. (2002) Looking them in the eyes: is rational provision for students 'with special educational needs' really possible? In Farrell, P. and Ainscow, M. (Eds.), *Making special education inclusive*, London: David Fulton Publishers.

Dyson, A. and Raffo, C. (2007) Education and disadvantage: The role of community-oriented schools, *Oxford Review of Education*, 33:3, 297-314

Dyson, A., Raffo, C., Gunter, H., Hall, D., Jones, L. and Kamalbouka, A., (2010) What is to be done? Implications for policy makers, in Raffo, C., Gunter, H., Hall, D., Dyson, A., Jones, L., and Kalambouka, A., *Education and poverty in affluent countries*, London: Routledge.
Edison Learning (2011), *Home*, Available at: www.edisonlearning.net/ [Accessed 8th February 2011]
Edwards, A., Lunt, I. and Stamou, E., (2010) Inter-professional work and expertise: New roles at the boundaries of schools, *British Educational Research Journal*, 36(1): 27-45.
Egelund, N., Haug, P. and Persson, B. (2006) *Inkluderande pedagogik i skandinaviskt perspektiv* [Inclusive education in a Scandinavian perspective], Stockholm: Liber AB.
Ekonomifakta (2013) Available at:, www.ekonomifakta.se/sv/Fakta/Valfarden-i-privat-regi/ Skolan-i-privat-regi/Elever-i-friskola/ [Accessed July 22 2013]
Emanuelsson, I., (1974) *Utbildningshandikapp i långtidsperspektiv [Handicape in education seen from a long term perspective]*, Stockholm: Lärarhögskolan, Pedagogiska institutionen.
Emanuelsson, I., (1979) *Utvärdering genom uppföljning av elever. Ett nytt individualstatistikprojekt [Evaluation through follow up of students. A new individual statistics project]*, Rapporter från institutionen för pedagogik (nr 11), Stockholm: Högskolan för lärarutbildningen.
Emanuelsson, I., (1997) Special education research in Sweden 1956-1996, *Scandinavian Journal of Educational Research*, 41(3-4): 461-474.
Emanuelsson, I. (2001) Reactive versus proactive support coordinator roles: An international comparison, *European Journal of Special Needs Education*, 16(2): 133-142.
Emanuelsson, I. (2003) Differentiation, special education and equality: A longitudinal study of self-concepts and school careers of students in difficulties and with or without special education support experiences, *European Educational Research Journal*, 2(2): 245-261.
Emanuelsson, I., Haug, P., and Persson, B. (2005) Inclusive education in some Western European countries: Different policy rhetorics and school realities, in D. Mitchell (ed.), *Contextualising inclusive education: Evaluating old and new international perspectives* (pp. 114-138). London: Routledge/Falmer.
Emanuelsson, I., and Persson, B., (2002) Differentiering, specialpedagogik och likvärdighet. En longitudinell studie av skolkarriär bland elever i svårigheter *[Differentiation, special education and equity. A longitudinal study on educational career among students in difficulties]*, *Pedagogisk forskning i Sverige*, 7(3): 193-199.
Emanuelsson, I., Persson, B., and Rosenqvist, J., (2001) *Forskning inom det specialpedagogiska området: En kunskapsöversikt [Research in the field of special education: A knowledge review]*, Stockholm: Skolverket.
Englund, T. (2004): Inledning [Introduction], in Englund, T. (Ed.) (2004) *Skillnad och konsekvens. Mötet lärare—studerande och undervisning som meningserbjudande* [Difference and consequences. The encounter between teachers and students and education as an offer of meaning], Lund: Studentlitteratur.
Englund, T. (2005) The discourse on equivalence in Swedish education policy, *Journal of Education Policy*, 20(1): 39-57.
Equality and Human Rights Commission (2011) *How fair is Britain? The first triennial review*, www.equalityhumanrights.com/key-projects/how-fair-is-britain/full-report-and-evidence-downloads/#How_fair_is_Britain_Equality_Human_Rights_and_Good_Relations_in_2010_The_First_Triennial_Review [Accessed 6 April 2014].

Erixon Arreman, I. and Holm, A. (2011) Schools as 'Edu-business': four 'serious players' in the Swedish upper secondary school market. *Education Inquiry*, 2(4), pp. 637-657.
European Agency for Development in Special Needs Education (2012) *Special needs education country data 2012*, Odense and Brussels: European Agency for Development in Special Needs Education.
Evaldsson, A-C. and Karlsson, Y. (2012) Shaping marginalized identities and indexing deviant behaviours in a special educational needs group, in Hjörne, E. van der Aalsvoort, G. and de Abreu, G. (Eds.), *Learning, social interaction and diversity. Exploring school practices*, Rotterdam/Boston: Sense Publisher.
Exley, S. (2011) Profiting from schools—Who cares, says former Ofsted chair, *Times Educational Supplement*, 20 May, p. 13.
Florian, L., and McLaughlin, M. J. (Eds.) (2008). *Disability classification in education: Issues and perspectives*, Thousand Oaks: Corwin Press.
Florian, L., and Rouse, M. (2001) Inclusive practice in English secondary schools: Lessons learned, *Cambridge Journal of Education*, 31(3): 399-412.
Fraser, N., (1996) *Social justice in the age of identity politics: Redistribution, recognition and participation, The Tanner lecturers on human values*, Stanford University, May 1996.
Fraser, N. (1997) *Justice interruptus: Critical reflections on the 'postsocialist' condition*. London: Routledge.
Fredelius, C. (1977) *Det socialdemokratiska försöket: om arbetarkontroll och företagsdemokrati i svensk arbetarrörelse*. (1. uppl.) Göteborg: Barrikaden.
Fridlund, L. (2011) *Interkulturell undervisning—ett pedagogiskt dilemma. Talet om undervisning i svenska som andraspråk och i förberedelseklasser* [*Intercultural education -A Pedagogical dilemma. Professional talk about the teaching of Swedish as a second language and in preparatory classes*] (Doctoral thesis, Gothenburg Studies in Educational Sciences 310). Göteborg: Acta Universitatis Gothoburgensis.
Friskolornas Riksförbund (2013) *Friskolorna I siffror*. Available at, www.friskola.se/Om_friskolor_Friskolorna_i_siffror_DXNI-25907_.aspx [Accessed 13 July 2013]
Gadamer, H-G., (1960/1995) *Truth and method*, second ed., New York: Continuum.
Gans, Herbert J. (1973) *More equality*. New York: Pantheon Books.
Gewirtz, S. (1998) Conceptualising social justice in education: mapping the territory, *Journal of Education Policy*, 13(4): 469-484.
Gewirtz, S. (2004) Equity in education—What counts as success? In L. Moreno Herrera and G. Francia (Eds.), *Educational Policies: Implications for equity, equality and equivalence* (pp. 25-40). Orebro: Orebro University Department of Education.
Giddens, A. (1990) *The contradictions of modernity*. Cambridge: Polity Press.
Giddens, A. (1998) *The third way: The renewal of social democracy*, Cambridge: Polity Press.
Gilbert, C., Husbands, C., Wigdortz, B. and Francis, B. (2013) *Unleashing greatness, getting the best from an academised system*, The report of Academies Commission, RSA.
Gillborn, D. and Youdell, D., (2000) *Rationing education: Policy, practice, reform, and equity*, Buckingham: Open University Press.
Giota, J., (2013) *Individualiserad undervisning i skolan—En Forskningsöversikt* [*Individualisation in school—A research review*], Vetenskapsrådets rapportserie 3:2013, Stockholm: Vetenskapsrådet.

Giota, J., Berhanu, G., and Emanuelsson, I., (2013) Pedagogisk och organisatorisk differentiering—konsekvenser för elevers delaktighet och lärande *[Pedagogical and organisational differentiation—consequences for students'participation and learning]*, i I. Wernersson and I. Gerrbo, (Red) *Differentieringens janusansikte. En antologi från Institutionen för pedagogik och specialpedagogik vid Göteborgs universitet.* Göteborg: Göteborg studies in educational sciences 347, Acta Universitatis Gothoburgensis.

Giota, J., and Emanuelsson, I., (2011a) *Specialpedagogiskt stöd, till vem och hur? Rektorers hantering av policyfrågor kring stödet i kommunala och fristående skolor [Special education support, for whom and how? Headteachers' ways of dealing with policy issues in special education support in regular and independent schools]*, (RIPS nr 2011:1), Göteborg: Göteborgs universitet, Institutionen för pedagogik och specialpedagogik.

Giota, J., and Emanuelsson, I., (2011b) Policies in special education support issues in Swedish compulsory school: a national representative study of head teachers' judgements, *London Review of Education,* 9(1): 95-108.

Giota, J., Lundborg, O., and Emanuelsson, I., (2009) Special education in comprehensive school: extent, forms and effects, *Scandinavian Journal of Educational research,* 53(6): 557-578.

Giota, J. and Lundborg, O. (2007). *Specialpedagogiskt stöd i grundskolan. Omfattning, former och konsekvenser.* [Special need support. Extent, form and consequenses] IDP-rapport 2007:03.

Glatter, R. (2012) Persistant preoccupations: the rise and rise of school autonomy and accountability in England, *Educational Management Administration and Leadership*, 40(5): 559-575.

Golby, M. and Gulliver, J. (1985) Whose remedies, whose ills? A critical review of remedial education, in C. Smith, *New directions in remedial education*, London: The Falmer Press.

Goodman, A. and Gregg, P. (eds.) (2010) *Poorer children's educational attainment: How important are attitudes and behaviour?*, York: Joseph Rowntree Foundation.

Gorard, S. (2009) What are academies the answer to? *Journal of Education Policy*, 24(1): 101-113

Gove, M. (2008) We need a Swedish education system, *Independent*, 3 December.

Gove, M. (2011) *Speech to the Policy Exchange on free schools, 20 June 2011,* https://www.gov.uk/government/speeches/michael-goves-speech-to-the-policy-exchange-on-free-schools [Accessed 15 December 2013].

Gove, M., (2013) *Michael Gove's speech to the Conservative conference* [online], www.politicshome.com/uk/article/85798/michael_goves_speech_to_the_conservative_conference.html [Accessed 3 January 2014].

Govt bill. (2008/09:171) *Offentliga bidrag på lika villkor.* Stockholm: Ministry of Education.

Green, A. E. and White, R. J. (2007) *Attachment to place: Social networks, mobility and prospects of young people*, York: Joseph Rowntree Foundation.

Gregory, J. (2009) *In the mix: Narrowing the gap between public and private housing*, London: Fabian Society.

Grenholm, C. H., (2003) *Bortom humanismen. En studie i kristen etik* [Beyond humanism. A Study in Christian Ethics]*,* Stockholm: Verbum

Grundén, I., (2005) *Att återerövra kroppen. En studie av livet efter en ryggmärgsskada [Reclaiming the body. A study of life after a spinal cord injury],* Thesis (Phd), Göteborg Studies in Educational Sciences, University of Gothenburg, Sweden.

Gunter, H. M. (Ed.), (2011) *The state and education policy: The Academies Programme*, London: Continuum Books.
Gunter, H. (2011) Introduction: contested education reform, in Gunter, H (ed.) *The state and education policy: the academies programme.* London: Continuum, pp. 1-18.
Gustavsson, A., (2001) Studying personal experiences of disability. What happened to Verstehen when Einfühlung disappeared, *Scandinavian Journal of Disability Research,* 3(2): 29-40.
Gustavsson, A., (2004) The role of theory in disability research—springboard or straitjacket?, *Scandinavian Journal of Disability Research,* 6(1): 55-70.
Gustavsson, A. and Tøssebro, J., (2005) Introduction: approaches and perspectives in Nordic disability research, in Gustavsson, A., Sandvins, J., Traustadóttir, R. and Tøssebro, J., (Eds.) *Resistance, reflection and change. Nordic disability research,* Lund, Sweden: Studentlitteratur.
Gustavsson, B., (2001) Bildning och kunskap i det moderna samhället. [*Bildung* and Knowledge in Modern Society], in Östborn, A., (ed.) *Folkbildning: en hållbar idé— framtida förväntningar.* [Adult Education: Sustainable Idea—Future Expectations], Mora: Mora stift.
Gustafsson, J.-E. (2006) *Barns utbildningssituation. Bidrag till ett kommunalt barnindex* [Children's educational situation. Contribution to a local child index; in Swedish]. Stockholm, Sweden: Rädda Barnen.
Göransson, K., Nilholm. C. and Karlsson, K. (2011). Inclusive education in Sweden? A critical analysis, *International Journal of Inclusive Education,* 15(5): 541-555.
Hahne Lundström, K. (2001) *Intagningskriterier till gymnasiesärskolan i Göteborg.* [Admission criteria to upper high school for educationally disabled in Gothenburg] Projektarbete vid Arbetslivsinstitutets Företagsläkarutbildning 2000/2001.
Hallam, S., and Toutounji, I., (1996) *What do we know about the grouping of pupils by ability? A research review,* University of London: Institute of Education.
Halsey, A. H. (Ed.), (1972) *Educational priority: EPA problems and practices,* London: HMSO.
Hargreaves, A., (1998) *Läraren i det postmoderna samhället* [The Teacher in the Postmodern Society], Lund: Studentlitteratur.
Hargreaves, D. (2013) Inequality is tearing apart our society, *Huffington Post,* 8 October, www.huffingtonpost.co.uk/deborah-hargreaves/ [Accessed 30 July 2014].
Harling, M. (2014) *A Fair (Af)fair? On Subjectivation and differentiation in educational capitalism,* University of Gothenburg: Gothenburg *(licentiate dissertation).* (Department of Education and Special Education).
Hatcher, R. (2011) The Conservative-Liberal Democrat coalition government's 'free schools' in England, *Educational Review,* 63(4), pp. 485-503
Haug, P., (1998) *Pedagogiskt dilemma: Specialundervisning [A pedagogical dilemma. Special education],* Stockholm: Skolverket.
Haug, P., (1999) Formulation and realisation of social justice: the compulsory school for all in Sweden and Norway, *European Journal of Special Needs Education,* 14(3): 231-239.
Haug, P., (2010) Approaches to empirical research on inclusive education, *Scandinavian Journal of Disability Research,* 12(3): 199-209.
Hautaniemi, B., (2004) *Känslornas betydelse i funktionshindrade barns livsvärld [The meaning of feelings in the world of disabled children],* Thesis (Phd), University of Stockholm, Department of Education.
Heater, D., (1999) *What is citizenship?* Oxford: Polity Press.

Heidegger, M., (1927/1993) *Varat och tiden [Being and time],* Göteborg, Sweden: Daidalos.
Heimdahl Mattsson, E. (2006) *Mot en inkluderande skola* [*Towards a school for all*], Stockholm: HLS Förlag.
Helgoy, Ingrid and Homme, Anne (2006) Policy tools and institutional change: comparing education policies in Norway, Sweden and England, *Journal of Public Policy* 26(1): 141-165.
Hellspong, L. and Brumark, Å., (2003) The role of the teacher in deliberative discussions. A sketch of a rhetorical-didactic, in *Didaktikens mångfald: artiklar presenterade vid 2002 års Rikskonferens i didaktik vid Högskolan i Gävle* [Didactic's Diversity: Articles Presented at 2002's National Conference in Didactics at the University of Gävle], Gävle: University of Gävle.
Higham, R. (2014) Free schools in the big society: The motivations, aims and demography of free school proposers. *Journal of Education Policy,* 29(1): 122-139.
Hill, R. Dunford, J., Parish, N., Rea, S., and Sandals, L. (2012) *The growth of academy chains: implications for leaders and leadership*, Nottingham: National College for School Leadership. Available at, www.thegovernor.org.uk/freedownloads/acadamies/the-growth-of-academy-chains.pdf [Accessed 20 June 2013]
Hills, J. C., Brewer, M., Jenkins, S., Lister, R., Lupton, R., Machin, S., Mills, C., Modood, T., Rees, T. and Riddell, S., (2010) *An anatomy of economic inequality in the UK: Report of the National Equality Panel.* London: Government Equalities Office and Centre for Analysis of Social Exclusion.
Hirdman, Y. (1990) *Vi bygger landet: den svenska arbetarrörelsens historia från Per Götrek till Olof Palme.* ([2., rev. uppl.]). Stockholm: Tiden.
Hjörne, E. (2004). *Excluding for inclusion? Negotiating school careers and identities in pupil welfare settings in the Swedish school.* Göteborg: Acta Universitatis Gothoburgensis.
HM Government (1944) 1944 Education act. 7 and 8 Geo. 6. Ch. 31.
HM Government (1988) Education Reform Act 1988. 1988 Chapter 40.
HM Government, (2007). *Extended schools: Building on experience* [online], www.dcsf.gov.uk/everychildmatters/resources-and-practice/IG00046/ [Accessed 17 August 2010].
Hodgson, N. (2012) The only answer is innovation +...' Europe, policy and the big society, *Journal of Philosophy of Education,* 46(4): 537-545.
Hopkins, D., West, M. and Ainscow, M. (1996), *Improving the quality of education for all: progress and challenge,* London: David Fulton Publishers.
Howes, A., Booth, T., Dyson, A., and Frankham, J. (2005) Teacher learning and the development of inclusive practices and policies: framing and context, *Research Papers in Education,* 20(2): 133-148.
Howes, A., Frankham J., Ainscow, M. and Farrell, P. (2004) The action in action research: mediating and developing inclusive intentions, *Educational Action Research,* 12(2): 239-257.
Howland, A., Anderson, J. A,. Smiley, A. D. and Abbott, D.J., (2006) School liaisons: bridging the gap between home and school, *The School Community Journal,* 16(2): 47-68.
Hughes, B. and Paterson, K., (1997) The social model of disability and the disappearing body: towards a sociology of impairment, *Disability and Society,* 12(3): 325-340.
Humphrey, N., Bartolo, P., Alec, P., Callejab, C., Hofsaessd, T., Janikovae, V., et al. (2006). Understanding and responding to diversity in the primary classroom: an international study. *European Journal of Teacher Education,* 29(3): 305-318.

Husserl, E., (1948/1973) *Experience and judgment*, Evanston, Illinois: Northwestern University Press.
Hutmacher, W., Cochrane, D., and Bottani, N. (Eds.) (2001) *In Pursuit of equity in education*. Dordrecht, Kluwer, Dordrecht: Kluwer Academic Publishers.
Härnqvist, K., (2000) Evaluation through follow-up. A longitudinal program for studying education and career development, in C.-G., Janson, (Ed) *Seven Swedish longitudinal studies in behavioural science*. Stockholm: Forskningsrådsnämnden.
Ireson, J., (2004) Private tutoring: how prevalent and effective is it? *London Review of Education*, 2(2): 109-122.
Isaksson, J., Lindqvist, R., and Bergström, E., (2007) School problems or individual shortcomings? A study of individual educational plans in Sweden, *European Journal of Special Needs Education*, 22(1): 75-91.
Isaksson, J., Lindqvist, R., and Bergström, E. (2010) 'Pupils with special educational needs': a study of assessments and categorising processes regarding pupils' school difficulties in Sweden. *International Journal of Inclusive Education*, 14(2): 133-151.
Jackson, B. (2007) *Equality and the British left: A study in progressive political thought 1900-1964*, Manchester University Press: Manchester.
JB Education (2013) *JB Education går ur all utbildningsverksamhet*, Available at: www.jbeducation.se/om-jb-education. [Accessed 15 July 2013]
Johansson, K-Å., (1974) *När doktorn gjort sitt. En studie av livsvillkoren för vuxna som blivit synskadade [A study of the living conditions of adults turned blind]*, Stockholm, Sweden: PAN/Norstedts.
Jonsson, J. O. (1993) Persisting inequalities in Sweden, in Y. Shavit and H. P. Blossfeld (eds.), *Persistent Inequality. Changing Educational Attainment in Thirteen Countries* (pp. 101-132). Boulder: Westview Press.
Karlsson, G., (1995) *Psychological qualitative research from a phenomenological perspective*, second ed., Stockholm, Sweden: Almqvist and Wiksell International.
Karlsson, Y. (2007). *Att inte vilja vara problem. Social organisering och utvärdering av elever i en särskild undervisningsgrupp*. [Resisting problem talk. Social organisation and evaluation practices in a special teaching group, Linköping: Univeristy of Linköping.
Karlsson, Y. (2012). Barns aktörskap och identitetsarbete i en särskild undervisningsgrupp. Children's agency and identity work in a special teaching group, *Utbildning och Demokrati*, 21(3): 35-52.
Kauko, J., and Salokangas, M. (2015) The evaluation and steering of English academy schools through inspection and examinations: national visions and local practices, *British Educational Research Journal*, ahead of print, available at: onlinelibrary.wiley.com/doi/10.1002/berj.3184/full
Kerr, K., Dyson, A., and Raffo, C., (2014) *Education, disadvantage and place: Making the local matter*. Bristol: Policy Press
Kerr, K. and West, M., (Eds.) (2010) *Insight 2: Social inequality: Can schools narrow the gap?* Macclesfield: British Educational Research Association.
Kintrea, K., Bannister, J., Pickering, J., Reid, M. and Suzuki, N. (2008) *Young people and territoriality in British cities*, York: Joseph Rowntree Foundation.
Kjellgren, H., (2007) Skolan som värdeförmedlare. [School as a Mediator of Values], in Pierre J., (ed.) *Skolan som politisk organisation* [School as a Political Organisation], Malmo: Gleerups Utbildning AB.

Korp, H. (2006) *Lika chanser i gymnasiet? En studie om betyg, nationella prov och social reproduktion [Equal chances in upper secondary schools: A study of grades, national administered tests and social reproduction]*, Malmö högskola, Lärarutbildningen: Malmö Studies in Educational Sciences. 24.

Korp, H. (2011) What counts as being smart around here? The performance of smartness and masculinity in vocational upper secondary education, *Education, Citizenship and Social Justice*, 6(1): 21-37.

Kulik, J. A., and Kulik, C. C., (1982) Effects of ability grouping on secondary school students: A meta analysis of evaluation findings, *American Educational Research Journal*, 19(3): 415-428.

Kunskapskola (2014) *USA*, Available at:, www.kunskapsskolan.com/sitescontact/ usa.4.52155b18128a87c7cfd80009919.html [Accessed 05 May 2014]

Kymlicka, W., (1995) *Multicultural citizenship: A liberal theory of minority rights* Oxford: Clarendon Press

Lgr 11 (2011) *Läroplan för grundskolan, förskoleklassen och fritidshemmet 2011 [Curriculum for compulsory school, preschool class and leasure time activity]*, Stockholm: Skolverket.

Lgr 62 (1962) *Läroplan för grundskolan, allmän del [Curriculum for compulsory school, general part]*, Stockholm: SÖ-förlaget.

Lgr 69 (1969) *Läroplan för grundskolan, allmän del [Curriculum for compulsory school, general part]*, Stockholm: SÖ-förlaget.

Lgr 80 (1980) *Läroplan för grundskolan, allmän del [Curriculum for compulsory school, general part]*, Stockholm: Liber Utbildningsförlaget.

Lp. 94 (1998) *Läroplan för det obligatoriska skolväsendet, förskoleklassen och fritidshemmet [Curriculum for compulsory school, preschool class and leasure time activity]*, Stockholm: Skolverket and Fritzes.

La Caze, M., (2007) Kant, Derrida, and the relation between ethics and politics. *Political Theory* 35(6): 781-805.

Laclau, E. (1993) Power and representation, in: M. Poster (Ed.). *Politics, theory and contemporary culture*. New York, NY: Columbia University Press.

Laclau, E., (1996) The death and resurrection of the theory of ideology. *Journal of Political Ideologies*, 1(3): 297-321,

Laclau, E. (2004) Ontology and rhetoric: Politics and doxa, *theory@buffalo*, 9: 5□10. Buffalo, NY: theory@buffalo

Laclau, E. and Mouffe, C., (1985) *Hegemony and Socialist strategy. Towards a Radical Democratic Politics*, London: Verso

Lahdenperä, P. (1997): Invandrarbakgrund eller skolsvårigheter? En textanalytisk studie av åtgärdsprogram för elever med invandrarbakgrund, *Studies in Educational Sciences* 7, Stockholm: HLS Förlag.

Landrum, T., Tankersley, M. and Kauffman, J. (2003). What is special about special education for students with emotional or behavioural disorders? *The Journal of Special Education*, 37(3): 148-156.

Langeveld, M. J., (1984) How does the child experience the world of things?, *Phenomenology + Pedagogy*, 2(3): 215-223.

LaRocqua (2009) The practice of public-private partnerships pp. 71-87 in Chakrabarti, R. and Peterson P. (eds.) *School choice international: exploring public-private partnerships* Cambridge, Massachusetts: MIT Press

Lauesen, H.P., (2001) *Magt over sproget—om sproglig bevisthed i andet sprogtilegnelsen.* [The power of language: Linguistic consciousness in second language acquisition], Copenhagen: Akademisk Forlag.
Learning Schools Trust (2013) *Home,* Available at: www.learningschoolstrust.org.uk/home.106.e754c9812af37de0768000643.html [Accessed 5 May 2013]
Leijon, S., and Omanovic, V. *(*2001) *Mångfaldens mångfald-olika sätt at se på och leda olikheter.* ['Manifoldness manifold'—Different ways of seeing and handling diversity]. FE-rapprt 2001-381.
Lindblad, S. and Lundahl, L. (eds.) (2014) *Utbildning—makt och politik (Education -power and politics.* Lund: Studentlitteratur.
Lipsett, A. (2008) National curriculum constrains teachers and pupils, *The Guardian,* 11.06.2008, www.theguardian.com/education/2008/jun/11/schools.uk4 [Accessed 06.09.2014]
Lipsky, D. K., and Gartner, A. (1996) Inclusion, school restructuring and the remaking of American society, *Harvard Educational Review*, 66(44): 762-796.
Losen, D. J., and Orfield, G. (2002) *Racial inequity in special education.* Cambridge, MA: Harvard Education Press.
Lundahl, L., Erixon Arreman, I., Holm, A-S., and Lundström, U. (2013) Educational marketisation the Swedish way *Education Inquiry,* 3(3): 497-517.
Lundström, U., and Holm, A-S.,(2011) Market competition in upper secondary education: Perceived effects on teachers' work, *Policy Futures in Education*, 9(2): 193-205.
Lupton, R. (2005) Social justice and school improvement: Improving the quality of schooling in the poorest neighbourhoods. *British Educational Research Journal,* 31(5): 589-604.
Lupton, R., Fenton, A., and Fitzgerald, A. (2013) Labour's record on neighbourhood renewal in England: Policy, spending and outcomes 1997-2010*. Social Policy in a Cold Climate working paper 6,* London: Centre for Analysis of Social Exclusion, London School of Economics.
Lupton, R., and Obolenskaya, P. (2013) Labour's record on education: Policy, spending and outcomes 1997-2010, *Social Policy in a Cold Climate WP03.* London: Centre for Analysis of Social Exclusion, London School of Economics.
Luyten, Hans (1994) School size effects on achievement in secondary education: Evidence from the Netherlands, Sweden and the USA, *School Effectiveness and School Improvement,* 5(1): 75-99, DOI: 10.1080/0924345940050105
Machin, S. and Wilson, J., (2009) Academy schools and pupil performance, *Centre Piece*, pp. 6-8. Available at: cep.lse.ac.uk/pubs/download/cp. 80.pdf [Accessed 12 July 2013]
Massey, D. (1994) Double articulation: a place in the world, in Bammer, A. (Ed.) *Displacements: Cultural identities in question.* Bloomington: Indiana University Press.
McLaughlin, M. J., Dyson, A., Nagle, K., Thurlow, M., Rouse, M., Hardman, M., et al. (2006). Cross-cultural perspectives on the classification of children with disabilities: Part II. Implementing classification systems in schools, *The Journal of Special Education,* 40(1): 46-58.
Mehan, H. (1993) Beneath the skin and between the ears: A case study in the politics of representation, in S. Chaiklin, and J. Lave (eds.), *Understanding practice: Perspectives on activity and context* (pp. 241-268). Cambridge: Cambridge University Press.
Merleau-Ponty, M., (1945/2012) *Phenomenology of perception*, London: Routledge.
Meyer, H.-D., and Zahedi, K. (2014) Open letter to Andreas Schleicher, OECD, Paris. *Policy Futures in Education,* 12(7), 872-877.

Meyland-Smith, D., and Evans, N. (2009) *A guide to school choice reforms*, London: Policy Exchange

Mitchell, D. (2005) Introduction: Sixteen propositions on the contexts of inclusive education, in D. Mitchell (ed.), *Contextualising inclusive education: Evaluating old and new international perspectives* (pp. 1-21). London: Routledge/Falmer.

Mitchell, D. (2010) *Education that fits: Review of international trends in the education of students with special educational needs.* Wellington: New Zealand Ministry of Education.

Moreno Herrera, L., Jones, G. and Rantala, J. (eds.) (2006) *Enacting equity in education: Towards a comparison of equitable practices in different European local contexts*, Research Report 8. Research Centre for Social Studies Education, University of Helsinki.

Mortimore, P. and Whitty, G. (2000) *Can school improvement overcome the effects of disadvantage?*, (Revised edition), London: Institute of Education.

Mouffe, C., (2008) *Om det politiska* [About the Political], Hägersten: Tankekraft Muijs, D. Chapman, C. And Reynolds, D. (2014) *Towards franchising in education? An empirical investigation of chains of academies in England.* Paper presented at International Congress of School Effectiveness and School Improvement January 2-7, Yogyakarta

Muijs, D., and Dunne, M. (2010). Setting by ability—or is it? A quantitative study of determinants of set placement in English secondary schools, *Educational Research and Evaluation*, 52(4): 391-407.

Murphy, R. F., (1990) *The body silent*. New York: W. W. Norton.

Neighbourhood Renewal Unit (2003) *Factsheet 17. Education and skills and neighbourhood renewal*, Nottingham: ODPM.

Nilholm, C. (2006a) *Including av elever 'I behov av särskilt stöd'—vad betyder det och vad vet vi?' [Including children with special needs: what does it mean? what do we know?]*, Myndigheten för Skolutveckling: Forskning i fokus nr. 28.

Nilholm, C. (2006b) Special education, inclusion and democracy, *European Journal of Special Needs Education*, 21(4): 431-445.

Nilholm, C. (2007) *Perspektiv på specialpedagogik*, Lund: Studentlitteratur.

Nilholm, C., Persson, B., Hjerm, M., and Runesson, S., (2007) *Kommuners arbete med elever i behov av särskilt stöd—En enkätundersökning [Municipalities work with students in need of special support—A survey study]*, Stockholm. INSIKT 2007:2. Vetenskapliga rapporter från Högskolan för lärande och kommunikation, Högskolan i Jönköping

Nirje, B. (1992) *The normalisation principle papers*, Uppsala: University, Sweden, Centre for Handicap Research.

Norberg☐Schönfeldt, M. (2008) Children's school achievement and parental work: An analysis for Sweden', *Journal of Education Economics*, 6(1): 1-17, DOI:10.1080/09645290701273525

Norwich, B. (2002). Education, inclusion and individual differences: recognising and resolving dilemmas, *British Journal of Educational Studies*, 50(4): 482-502.

Norwich, B. (2007). Dilemmas of inclusion and the future of education, in Cigman, R. (Ed.), *Included or excluded? The challenge of mainstream for some SEN children*, Oxford: Routledge.

Norwich, B. (2010). Dilemmas of difference, curriculum and disability: international perspectives, *Comparative Education*, 46(2): 113-135.

NUT (2016) *What are free schools?* [online], www.teachers.org.uk/freeschools [Accessed 11 February 2016].

OECD (1999a). *Inclusive education at work, students with disabilities in mainstream schools*. Paris: OECD.
OECD (1999b) *early childhood education and care policy in Sweden*, Country Note, revised December 1999. Paris: OECD.
OECD (2000a) *Special needs education—statistics and indicators*. Paris: OECD.
OECD (2000b) *Education at a glance*, 2000 Edition. Paris: OECD.
OECD (2001) *Education at a glance:* OECD Indicators 2001. (Paris, OECD).
OECD (2005a). *Students with disabilities, learning difficulties and disadvantages—Statistics and indicators*, Paris: Organisation for Economic Co-operation and Development.
OECD (2005b). *Equity in education: Thematic Review*, Sweden, Country note. Paris: OECD (Organisation for Economic Cooperation and Development).
OECD (2007) Executive summary: No more failures: ten steps to equity in education [online], www.oecd.org/education/school/39676364.pdf [Accessed 17 August 2015].
OECD (2008) *Ten steps to equity in education*, Paris: OECD Publishing.
OECD (2010) *PISA 2009 results: Overcoming social background. Equity in learning opportunities and outcomes. Volume II*, Paris: OECD Publishing.
OECD (2012) *Equity and quality in education: Supporting disadvantaged students and schools*, Paris: OECD Publishing.
OECD (2013) *Are countries moving towards more equitable education systems? Pisa in focus 25* [online], www.oecd.org/pisa/pisaproducts/pisainfocus/pisa%20in%20focus%20n25%20(eng)—FINAL.pdf [Accessed 1 August 2013].
OECD (2014) *Improving schools in Sweden: An OECD perspective*, Paris: OECD.
OECD (no date). *Programme for international student assessment (PISA)* [online], www.oecd.org/pisa/aboutpisa/PISA-trifold-brochure-2014.pdf [Accessed 18 February 2015].
Oakes, J., (1990) *Multiplying inequalities: the effects or race, social class and trackning on opportunities to learn mathematics and science,* Santa Monica; CA: The Rabd Corporation.
Office for Standards in Education (2000) *Improving city schools,* London: Ofsted.
Ofsted (2000) *Evaluating educational inclusion*, London: Ofsted
Ofsted (2010). *The special educational needs and disability review: A statement is not enough*, Manchester: Ofsted.
O'Hara, M (2010) Why Britain's battle to bring down social inequality has failed, *The Guardian,* 21 April.
Olssen, M., Codd, J. and O'Neill, A-M., (2004) *Education policy: Globalisation, citizenship, democracy*, London: Sage.
O'Shaughnaessy, J. (2012) *Competition meets collaboration helping: school chains address England's long tail of educational failure*. London: Policy Exchange.
Overseas Development Institute, (2001) *Economic theory, freedom and human rights: The work of Amartya Sen*, [online] ODI Briefing Paper, www.odi.org/sites/odi.org.uk/files/odi-assets/publications-opinion-files/2321.pdf [Accessed 2 June 2015].
Ozga, J. (2000) *Policy research in educational settings: Contested terrain*, Buckingham: Open University Press.
Palmer, R. E., (1969) *Hermeneutics. Interpretation theory in Schleiermacher, Dilthey, Heidegger, and Gadamer*, Evanston: Northwestern University.
Paton, G. (2013) More state school head teachers paid £100,000 salaries, *The Telegraph*, 30 April.
Peetsma, T.,Vergeer, M., and Karsten, S.(2001) Inclusion in education: Comparing pupils' development in special and regular education, *Educational Review*, *53*(2): 125-135.

Perry, E. and Francis, B. (2010) *The social class gap for educational achievement: a review of the literature*, London: RSA.
Persson, B., (1998a) *Specialundervisning och differentiering. En studie av grundskolans användning av specialpedagogiska resurser [Special education and differentiation. A study of how compulsory school uses special education resources]*, Specialpedagogiska rapporter nr 10, Göteborgs universitet: Institutionen för specialpedagogik.
Persson, B., (1998b) *Den motsägelsefulla specialpedagogiken—Motiveringar, genomföranden och konsekvenser [The contradictory special education—motivations, uses and consequences]*, Specialpedagogiska rapporter nr 11, Göteborgs universitet: Institutionen för specialpedagogik.
Persson, B., (2001) Special education, academic self-concept and achievement: profile differences between six groups of students, *Journal of Research in Special Educational Needs*, 1(2): 289-330.
Persson, B. (2003) Exclusive and inclusive discourses in special education research and policy in Sweden. *International Journal of Inclusive Education* 7(3): 271-80.
Persson, B., (2008) On other people's terms: schools encounters with disabled pupils, *European Journal of Special Needs Education*, 23(4): 337-347.
Persson, B., and Berhanu, G. (2005) *Politics of difference: The emergence of special needs in a school for all*. (Research Programme) Project Document, Göteborg University.
Persson, B. and Persson, E. (2012) Inkludering och måluppfyllelse -att nå framgång med alla elever [*Inclusion and goal attainment to achieve success too all pupils*], Stockholm: Liber.
Peters, S.J. (2003) *Inclusive education: Achieving education for all by including those with disabilities and special educational needs*. Washington DC: Disability Group, The World Bank. URL. (Access date Oct. 18, 2008).
Phillips, D. (2005) Policy borrowing in education: frameworks for analysis, in J. Zajda (Ed.), *International handbook on globalisation, education and policy research*, Dordrecht, The Netherlands: Springer.
Philpott, J (2012) *Britain at work in the reign of Queen Elizabeth II*, London: Chartered Institute of Personnel and Development.
PricewaterhouseCoopers (2008) *Academies Evaluation Fifth Annual Report*, Annesley: DCSF Publication.
Prop., (1989/90:41) Regeringens proposition 1989/90:41 om kommunalt huvudmannaskap för lärare, skolledare, biträdande skolledare och syofunktionärer. Stockholm: Regeringen.
Prop. 1992/93: 220, *En ny läroplan för grundskolan och ett nytt betygssystem för grundskolan, sameskolan, specialskolan och den obligatoriska särskolan* [A new curriculum for primary and lower-secondary schools and a new grading system for primary and lower-secondary schools, lapp schools, special schools and the compulsory schools for handicapped children], Stockholm: Ministry of Education.
Puaca, G., (2013) *Educational choices of the future. A sociological inquiry into micro-politics in education.* (Academic Thesis), Gothenburg: Dept of Sociology, University of Gothenburg.
Pijl, S. J., Meijer, C. J. W., and Hegarty, S. (Eds.) (1997) *Inclusive education: A global agenda*. London: Routledge.
Power, S., Edwards, T., Whitty, G. and Wigfall, V., (2003) *Education and the middle classes*, Buckingham: Open University Press.

Quinn, B. (2008) 40 pupils excluded in academy discipline crackdown, *Sunday Times*, 18 September.
Raffo, C. (2011) Educational equity in poor urban contexts—exploring issues of place/space and young people's identity and agency, *British Journal of Educational Studies* 59(1) 1-19.
Raffo, C. (2014) *Improving educational equity in urban contexts*, London: Routledge.
Raffo, C. and Dyson, A. (2007) Full service extended schools and educational inequality in urban contexts—new opportunities for progress? *Journal of Education Policy*, 22(2), 263-282.
Raffo, C., Dyson, A., Gunter, H., Hall, D., Jones, L., and Kalambouka, A. (2010) Education and poverty in affluent countries: An introduction to the book and the mapping framework, in Raffo, C., Dyson, A., Gunter, H., Hall, D., Jones, L., and Kalambouka, A. (Eds.), *Education and poverty in affluent countries*, Abingdon: Routledge.
Rawls, J., (1971 (revised edition 1999)) *A theory of justice*, Cambridge, Massachusetts: Belknap Press of Harvard University Press.
Rees, G., Power, S. and Taylor, C., (2007) The governance of educational inequalities: The limits of area-based initiatives, *Journal of Comparative Policy Analysis*, 9(3): 261-74.
Reay, D. (2006) The zombie stalking English schools: Social class and educational inequalities. *British Journal of Educational Studies*, 54(3): 288 -307
Ricoeur, P., (1993) *Från text till handling [From text to interpretation]*, Stockholm, Sweden: Symposion.
Riddell, R., (2007) Urban learning and the need for varied urban curricula and pedagogies, in W. Pink and G. Noblit, (Eds) *International handbook of urban education*, Dordrecht: Springer.
Roldão, M. d. C. (2003) Diferenciação curricular e inclusão, in D. Rodrigues (Ed.), *Perspectivas sobre a Inclusão—Da Educação à Sociedade*, vol. 14, Porto: Porto Editora.
Rosenqvist, J. (2007) *Specialpedagogik i mångfaldens Sverige: Om elever med annan etnisk bakgrund än svensk i särskolan [Special education in multicultural Sweden: Ethnic minority pupils in education for intellectually disabled]* (Ett samarbetsprojekt mellan Specialpedagogiska institutet och Högskolan Kristianstad (HKr), Specialpedagogiska institutet.
SFS 1979:717 *Skolförordning* (1979:717) om ändring i skolförordningen (1971:235) *[The school regulation]*, Stockholm: Allmänna Förlaget.
SFS 1985:1100 *Skollagen [The Education Act].* Ändrad 1997:1212, Stockholm: Allmänna förlaget.
SFS 1994:1194 *Grundskoleförordningen [The compulsory school regulation]*, Stockholm: Allmänna Förlaget.
SFS (2008:132) *Förordning om ändring i högskoleförordningen [Ordinance amending the Higher Education* (1993:100)], Stockholm: Utbildningsdepartmentet.
SFS 2010:800 *Skollag [The education act]*, Stockholm: Utbildningsdepartementet.
SFS 2011:185 *Skolförordning [The school regulation]*, Stockholm: Utbildningsdepartementet.
SOU (1948:27) 1946 års skolkommissions betänkande med förslag till riktlinjer för det svenska skolväsendets utveckling. Stockholm: regeringen.
SOU 1992:94, *Skola för bildning: Huvudbetänkande med förslag till riktlinjer för det svenska skolväsendets utveckling* [School for *Bildung*: main report with guideline proposals for the development of the Swedish school system], Stockholm: Allmänna Förlaget.
SOU 1996:22 *Inflytande på riktigt [Influence for real]*, Stockholm: Fritzes.

Sainsbury, D. (1996) *Gender, equality and welfare states*. Cambridge: Cambridge University Press.
Salokangas, M. (2013) *Autonomy and innovation in English academy schools: a case study*, Thesis (PhD) University of Manchester.
Salokangas, M., and Chapman, C. (2014) Exploring governance in two chains of academy schools A comparative case study, *Educational Management Administration and Leadership*, 42(3): 372-386.
Savage (2013) *The British class system is becoming more polarised between a prosperous elite and a poor 'precariat'*, blogs.lse.ac.uk/politicsandpolicy/archives/32264 [Accessed 7 April 2014].
Sawyer, L. and Kamali, M., (2006) *Utbildningens dilemma. Demokratiska ideal och andrafierande praxis* [Dilemma of Education. Democratic Ideals and Otherisation Practice], Stockholm:Fritzes.
Schüllerqvist, U., (1996) Förskjutning i svensk skolpolitisk debatt under det senaste decenniet [Shift in Swedish School Policy Debate over the Past Decade], *in Englund, T. (ed.) Utbildningspolitiskt systemskifte?* [System Change in Educational Policy?], Stockholm: HLS Förlag.
Schutz, A., (1962) *Collected papers I. The problem of social reality*, The Hague: Martinus Nijhoff.
Schutz, A., (1932/1967) *The phenomenology of the social world*, Evanston, Illinois: Northwestern University.
Schutz, A. and Luckmann, T., (1973) *The structures of the life-world*, Evanston, Illinois: Northwestern University.
Scollon, R., (1998) *Mediated Discourse as Social Interaction: A Study of News Discourse*, London: Addison Wesley Longman.
Seddon, T. (2003) Framing justice: challenges for research, *Journal of Education Policy*, 18(3): 229-252.
Sen, A., (2002) Why health equity? *Health Economics*, 11: 659-666
Shepherd, J. (2010) Swedish-style 'free schools won't improve standards', *The Guardian*, 9 February.
Shepherd, J. (2011) Academies pay £200k salaries, *The Guardian*, 14 November.
Sigurdson, O., (2002) *Den goda skolan: om etik, läroplaner och skolans värdegrund* [The good school: About ethics, curricula and the school's fundamental values], Lund: Studentlitteratur
Simon, B. (1991) *Education and the social order 1940—1990*, London: Lawrence and Wishart.
Skidmore, D. (2004) *Inclusion: The dynamic of school development*. Buckingham: Open University Press.
Skolverket (2000) [The Swedish National Agency for Education]. *Hur särskild får man vara? En analys av elevökningen i särskolan. [How different one has to be? A study of the increase of pupils in education for intellectually disabled]* Uppföljning/Utvärdering Dnr 2000:2037 2000-09-29. Stockholm: Skolverket.
Skolverket (2002a) [The Swedish National Agency for Education] *Barnomsorg, skola och vuxenutbildning i siffror 2002 del 2.* [Childcare, school and adult education in numbers 2002 part 2], *Rapport 214*. Stockholm: Skolverket.
Skolverket (2002b), (Gustafsson, J-E. and Myrberg, E.) *Ekonomiska resursers betydelse för pedagogiska resultat—en kunskapsöversikt [The importance of economical resources for educational results—a knowledge review]*, Stockholm: Skolverket.

Skolverket (2003) (Persson, B. and Andreasson, I.) *Kartläggning av åtgärdsprogram och särskilt stöd i grundskolan [A survey of action programme and special education support in compulsory school]*, Stockholm: Skolverket.

Skolverket (2004) Nationella utvärderingen av grundskolan 2003: sammanfattande huvudrapport *[National evaluation of compulsory school 2003: a summary of the main report]*, Stockholm: Skolverket.

Skolverket (2006a) *Schools like any other?* Stockholm: Skolverket

Skolverket (2006b) *Individ—och klassvariation i grundskolan åk 9. Studier av individ och klassvariationen i NU-materialet 2003 [Individual and class variation in grade 9 of compulsory school. Studies of individual and class variation in the national evaluation study in 2003]*, Stockholm: Fritzes.

Skolverket (2008). *Särskilt stöd i grundskolan. En sammanställning av senare års forskning och utvärdering [Special education support in compulsory school. A review of the latest research and evaluation studies]*, Stockholm: Skolverket.

Skolverket (2009) *Vad påverkar resultaten i svensk grundskola? Kunskapsöversikt om betydelsen av olika faktorer [What influece the achievement results in the Swedish compulsroy school?]*, Stockholm, Skolverket: Fritzes.

Skolverket (2010) Gymnasieskolan-Personal-Riksnivå. Table 4 A. Available at: www.skolverket.se/sb/d/1719/a/15474 [Accessed 12 January 2012]

Skolverket (2005) *Handikapp i skolan. Det offentliga skolväsendets möte med funktionshinder från folkskolan till nutid [Disability in the school context: The public school system's approach/services for the disabled- from Folk School to the present]*, Rapport 270. Stockholm: Fritzes. (www.skolverket.se).

Skolverket (2011) [The Swedish National Agency for Education]. *Läroplan för grundskolan, förskoleklassen och fritidshemmet.* Stockholm: Fritzes kundservice.

Skolverket (2013) *PISA 2012. 15-åringars kunskaper i matematik, läsförståelse och Naturvetenskap [PISA 2012. 15-year-old students' knowledge in mathematics, reading comprehension and natural science]*, Rapport 398, Stockholm: Skolverket.

Skrtic, T. M. (1991) *Behind special education: A critical analysis of professional culture and school organisation*, Denver: Love.

Slavin, R. E., (1987) Ability grouping and student achievement in elementary schools: A best evidence synthesis, *Review of Educational Research*, 57(3): 293-336.

Slavin, R. E., (1990) Class size and student achievement: Is smaller better? *Contemporary Education*, 62(1): 6-12.

Smith, A., (1818) *An inquiry into the nature and causes of the wealth of nations* [online], www.gutenberg.org/files/3300/3300-h/3300-h.htm [Accessed 2 June 2015].

Smith, G., (1987) Whatever happened to Educational Priority Areas?, *Oxford Review of Education*, 13(1): 23-38.

Smithers, A. (2013) *Confusion in the ranks: How good are England's schools?* London: Sutton Trust.

Social Mobility and Child Poverty Commission (2013) *State of the nation 2013: Social mobility and child poverty in Great Britain* [online], London: Her Majesty's Stationery Office, https://www.gov.uk/government/uploads/system/uploads/attachment_data/file/292231/State_of_the_Nation_2013.pdf [Accessed 13 May 2015]..

Sonnander, K., Emanuelsson, I., and Kebbon, L., (1993) Pupils with mild mental retardation in regular Swedish schools: Prevalence, objective characteristics and subjective evaluations, *American Journal on Mental Retardation*, 97(6): 692-701.

Spjuth, R.,(2006) *Kristen moralhistoria: sökandet efter det goda livet* [Christian History of Morality: The search for the good life], Örebro: Libris.
Stangvik, G., (1979) *Self-concept and school segregation*, Doctoral thesis, Acta Universitatis Gothoburgensis, 28, Gothenburg: University of Gothenburg.
Statistics Sweden (2009) *Education in Sweden 2009*. Statistics Sweden. Örebro: Sweden.
Stiglitz, J. (2002), *Globalisation and its discontents*, London: Penguin.
Strand, S. and Demie, F., (2006) Pupil mobility, attainment and progress in primary school, *British Educational Research Journal*, 32(4), 551-568.
Svenska Unescorådets skriftserie 1 (2001:43) *Salamancadeklarationen [The Salamanca declaration]*, Stockholm: Svenska Unescorådet.
Svensson, A., (red.) (2011) *Utvärdering genom uppföljning. Longitudinell individforskning under ett halvsekel [Evaluation through follow up. Longitudinal individual research during a half century]*, Göteborgs universitet, 305, Göteborg: Acta Universitatis Gothoburgensis.
Söder, M., (2009) Tensions, perspectives and themes in disability studies, *Scandinavian Journal of Disability Research*, 11(2): 67-81.
Söder, M. (2013). Swedish social disability research: a short version of a long story, *Scandinavian Journal of Disability Research*, 15(Supplement): 90-107.
Taylor, S. J. and Bogdan, R., (1998) *Introduction to qualitative research methods*, third ed., New York: John Wiley and Sons.
Teese, R. and Polesel, J. (2003) *Undemocratic schooling: Equity and quality in mass secondary education in Australia*, Carlton, Victoria: Melbourne University Press.
Thrupp, M., and Lupton, R. (2006) Taking school contexts seriously: the social justice challenge, *British Journal of Educational Studies*, 54: 398-328.
Tideman, M., (2000) *Normalisering och kategorisering—Om handikappideologi och välfärdspolitik i teori och praktik för personer med utvecklingsstörning [Normalisation and categorisation—About handicape ideology and welfare policy in theory and practice for individuals with disability]*, Lund: Studentlitteratur.
Tideman, E. (2007) Special education in Sweden, in *Encyclopedia of special education: A reference for the education of children, adolescents, and adults with disabilities and other exceptional and other exceptional individuals* (pp. 1944-47) John Wiley and Sons, New York, NY: Wiley.
UNESCO. (1994) *The Salamanca statement and framework for action on special needs education*. Adopted by the World Conference on Special Needs Education: Access and Quality. Salamanca, Spain, June 7-10.
Thomas, G. and Vaughan, M., (2004) *Inclusive education: Readings and reflections*, Maidenhead: Open University Press.
Tomlinson, J. (1991) Comprehensive education in England and Wales, 1944-1991, *European Journal of Education*, 26(2): 103-117.
Townson, L., Macauley, S., Harkness, E., Chapman, R., Docherty, A., Dias, J., Eardley, M. and McNulty, N., (2004) We are all in the same boat: doing 'people-led research', *British Journal of Learning Disabilities*, 32(2): 72-76.
Trankell, A., (1973) *Kvarteret flisan [The block Flisan]*, Stockholm, Sweden: P. A. Norstedt and Söner.
United Nations (1989) *Convention on the rights of the child*, New York: United Nations
United Nations (2006) *Convention on the rights of persons with disabilities*, New York: United Nations.

UNICEF Office of Research (2013) *Child well-being in rich countries: A comparative overview*. Innocenti report card 11, Florence: UNICEF Office of Research.
van Manen, M., (1990) *Researching lived experience. Human science for an action sensitive pedagogy*, Ontario, Canada: The State University of New York Press.
van Peursen, C. A., (1977) The horizon, in Elliston, F. A. and Mc Cormick, P., (Eds.) *Husserl: Expositions and appraisals*, London: University of Notre Dame.
Polkinghorne, D. E., (1995) Narrative configuration in qualitative analysis, *Qualitative Studies in Education*, 8(1): 5-23.
Vasagar, J. (2012) Academy Schools federation hopes to run college for profit, *The Guardian*, 25 March.
Vislie, L. (2003) From integration to inclusion: focusing global trends and changes in the Western European societies. *European journal of special needs education*, 18(1):17-35.
Vinterek, M., (2006) *Individualisering i ett skolsammanhang [Individualisation in a school context]*, Myndigheten för skolutveckling, Stockholm: Liber.
Vygotskij, L.S., (1978), *Mind in society: The Development of Higher Psychological Processes*, Cambridge, Mass, Harvard U.P.
Walford, G. (1997) 'Sponsored Grant-maintained Schools: extending the franchise?' *Oxford Review of Education*, 23(1): 31-44.
Wacquant, L. (2008) *Urban outcasts: A comparative sociology of advanced marginality*, Cambridge: Polity Press.
Walker, M., (2006) Towards a capability based theory of social justice for education policy making, *Journal of Education Policy*, 21(2): 163-85.
Warren, M. R., and Mapp, K. L. (2011) *A match on dry grass: Community organising as a catalyst for school reform*, Oxford: Oxford University Press.
Wernersson, I., and Gerrbo, I. (2013) *Differentieringens janusansikte [The double face of differentiation]*: En antologi från Institutionen för pedagogik och specialpedagogik vid Göteborgs universitet *[Anthology from the Department of Education and Special Education]*. Göteborg: University of Gothenburg.
Westling Allodi, M. (2000) Self-concept in children receiving special support at school, *European Journal of Special Needs Education*, 15: 69-78.
Westling Allodi, M. (2002) *Support and a resistance. Ambivalence in special education*. Stockholm: HLS Förlag.
Wiborg, S. (2010) Swedish Free-schools do they work? *LLakes Research Paper 18*. Available at http:, www.llakes.org/wp-content/uploads/2010/09/Wiborg-online.pdf [Accessed 10 February 2011]
Wildt-Persson, A., and Rosengren, P. G. (2001) Equity and equivalence in the Swedish school system, in W. Hutmacher (ed.), *In pursuit of equity in education. Using international indicators to compare equity policies* (pp. 288-321). Hingham, MA: Kluwer Academic Publishers.
Whitty, G., (2002) *Making sense of education policy*, London: Paul Chapman.
Whitty, G., Edwards, T., and Gewirtz, S. (1993) *Specialisation and choice in urban education: the city technology college experiment*. London: Routledge.
West, A., and Bailey, W. (2013) The development of the Academies Programme: 'privatising' school-based education in England 1986-2013, *British Journal of Educational Studies*, 61(2): 137-159.
Wolfensberger, W. (1972) *The principle of normalisation in human services*. Toronto: NIMR.
Woods, G.J. and Woods, P.A. (2009) Editorial, *Management in Education*, 23(3), pp. 94-95.

Working Group on 14-19 Reform (2004) *14-19 curriculum and qualifications reform. Final report of the working group on 14-19 reform*, Nottingham: DfES.

Young, I. M. (1990) *Justice and politics of difference*. Princeton: Princeton University Press.

Zackari, G. and Modigh, F., (2002) *Värdegrundsboken* [The Book of Values], Stockholm: Skolverket.

Ödman, P-J., (1995) *Kontrasternas spel I [A history of education]*, Stockholm, Sweden: Norstedts.

Ödman, P-J., (2007) *Tolkning, förståelse, vetande [Interpretation, understanding and knowledge]*, Stockholm, Sweden: Norstedts Akademiska.

Österling, O., (1967) *The efficacy of special education. A comparison of classes for slow learners*, Studia Scientiae Pedagogicae Upsaliensia, VII, Stockholm: Svenska bokförlaget/Nordstedts.

www.ingramcontent.com/pod-product-compliance
Lightning Source LLC
Chambersburg PA
CBHW060339170426
43202CB00014B/2822